ART, CULTURE AND INTERNATIONAL DEVELOPMENT

T0341290

Culture is not simply an explanation of last resort, but is itself a rich, multifaceted and contested concept and set of practices that needs to be expanded, appreciated and applied in fresh ways if it is to be both valued in itself and to be of use in practical development. This innovative book places culture, specifically in the form of the arts, back at the centre of debates in development studies by introducing new ways of conceptualizing art in relation to development.

The book shows how the arts and development are related in very practical ways – as means to achieve development goals through visual, dramatic, filmic and craft-inspired ways. It advocates not so much culture *and* development, but rather for the development *of* culture. Without a cultural content to economic and social transformation the problems found in much development – up-rooting of cultures, loss of art forms, languages and modes of expression and performance – may only accelerate. Paying attention to the development of the arts as the content of development helps to amend this culturally destructive process. Finally, the book argues for the value of the arts in attaining sustainable cultures, promoting poverty alleviation, encouraging self-empowerment, stimulating creativity and the social imagination, which in turn flow back into wider processes of social transformation. Discussion questions at the end of each chapter make this book ideal to help foster further thinking and debate.

This book is an inspiring read for postgraduate students and researchers in the fields of development studies, cultural studies and sociology of development.

John Clammer is visiting professor of development sociology at the United Nations University, Tokyo where he also runs the film and art programmes, and is adjunct professor of art and society at Kanda University of International Studies and the International University of Japan.

Rethinking Development

Rethinking Development offers accessible and thought-provoking overviews of contemporary topics in international development and aid. Providing original empirical and analytical insights, the books in this series push thinking in new directions by challenging current conceptualizations and developing new ones.

This is a dynamic and inspiring series for all those engaged with today's debates surrounding development issues, whether they be students, scholars, policy makers and practitioners internationally. These interdisciplinary books provide an invaluable resource for discussion in advanced undergraduate and postgraduate courses in development studies as well as in anthropology, economics, politics, geography, media studies and sociology.

Popular Representations of Development
Insights from novels, films, television and social media
Edited by David Lewis, Dennis Rodgers and Michael Woolcock

Celebrity Advocacy and International Development
Daniel Brockington

International Aid and the Making of a Better World
Reflexive practice
Rosalind Eyben

New Media and International Development
Representation and affect in microfinance
Anke Schwittay

Art, Culture and International Development
Humanizing social transformation
John Clammer

ART, CULTURE AND INTERNATIONAL DEVELOPMENT

Humanizing social transformation

John Clammer

Routledge
Taylor & Francis Group

LONDON AND NEW YORK

First published 2015
by Routledge
2 Park Square, Milton Park, Abingdon, Oxon OX14 4RN

and by Routledge
711 Third Avenue, New York, NY 10017

Routledge is an imprint of the Taylor & Francis Group, an informa business

© 2015 John Clammer

British Library Cataloguing-in-Publication Data
A catalogue record for this book is available from the British Library

Library of Congress Cataloging-in-Publication Data
A record for this title is available from the Library of Congress.

ISBN: 978-1-138-02471-7 (hbk)
ISBN: 978-1-138-02472-4 (pbk)
ISBN: 978-1-315-77555-5 (ebk)

Typeset in Bembo
by Apex CoVantage, LLC

CONTENTS

PREFACE

The relationship of the creative arts to development is a very neglected topic. This book is the first to systematically review this relationship and to discuss the many ways in which the arts are (or should be) both a very significant part of what we might understand as holistic development, or what later in the book I called 'integral development', and how the promotion and appreciation of those arts contributes to the humanizing of the landscape of social change and globalization that we see all around us in the contemporary world. Indeed, it goes further, and suggests strongly that any conception of 'development' is vacuous without the recognition that culture, much of it constituted by those very arts, is the medium in which we live our daily lives, and so no sensible notion of social transformation is possible without recognizing that the development of culture is a key to any satisfactory human existence. Consequently the book goes far beyond (while incorporating) older 'culture and development' approaches, often conceived as being the ways in which culture can advance (or retard) development practices and interventions, to a holistic view of development that sees culture at the core of human being-in-the-world. By implication, the book is also about the potential transformation of the arts from their frequently socially irrelevant and narcissistic preoccupations and expressions, to becoming constructive ways in which people can act upon and appreciate their world and its natural and social environments in positive, creative and life-enhancing ways.

To this end, the book takes the reader through a series of chapters each concerned with a form of major artistic expression, including the visual arts, architecture, design, film, literature and theatre, and in each case explores the form in relation to both critiques of society and reconstruction of society and culture. Practical means of arts education for development are also explored, and each chapter is followed by a short list of key readings on its theme, and a listing of Internet and other resources that can be used to follow up in practical ways the ideas set out in that particular chapter. These are in addition to the extensive bibliography at the end of each chapter which lists all written sources consulted or recommended throughout.

The book builds on my earlier work which the interested reader is invited to consult to add more depth. For a detailed analysis, suggesting many hopefully innovative perspectives, on the broad issue of culture and development, see my *Culture, Development and Social Theory: Towards an Integrated Social Development,* Zed Books, 2012, and for a thorough analysis of issues of art and society from a more theoretical viewpoint (including such questions as the role of art movements as social movements), see my *Vision and Society: Towards a Sociology and Anthropology from Art,* Routledge, 2014.

Hopefully this book will open up new visions of the possible meanings of that protean word 'development', of fresh approaches to the achieving of the desirable results of that process, including not only expansion of economic opportunities, but also, sustainability, human rights, a responsible relationship to the environment, widespread social justice and the expanding of creative opportunities for the greatest number, and towards humanizing and indeed beautifying the whole landscape of development. This should suggest, as this book argues, ways of encouraging forms of social transformation and social being that are enriching, peaceful, exciting and deeply absorbing.

My companion in these efforts has once again been Miyoko Ogishima, and I thank her deeply for her constant inspiration, her provoking of my interest in areas of art that I had not previously explored such as weaving, an art in which she herself excels, for locating and exploring together endless fascinating remote galleries and museums all over Japan that I would have never have discovered on my own and for as always her somewhat impatient help with my struggles with a Japanese operating system computer and its mysteries.

1

ART, CULTURE AND DEVELOPMENT

What are the connections?

Few would disagree that global society currently faces unprecedented problems, ones indeed never seen before when taken together in human history or the bio-history of our planet: climate change, pollution, loss of biodiversity, massive levels of poverty, hyper-urbanization, population pressures, declining resources of the kinds that industrial civilization has relied on for its existence, conflicts fuelled by a massive international arms industry, terrorism and the rise of religious fundamentalisms, political repression in societies that once looked as if they were evolving towards democratization . . . the tragic list goes on. Yet all this and more is occurring in a world society of (overall) unprecedented wealth, technological know-how, communication networks (the Internet being only one of the most prominent), levels of urbanization and industrialization. Somewhere, in other words, there is a massive misfit between the intellectual, material and cultural resources available on our globe, and the continuing and deepening ecological, social and political challenges that now confront human society and the biosphere on which we ultimately entirely depend. With the target date for the fulfilment of the UN Millennium Goals upon us, it is very evident that many of those goals have not been met in much of the world (and indeed in some cases statistics show a retreat rather than an advance) and even when they have been at least partially fulfilled, they often coexist with bad human rights regimes, declining ecological sustainability, escalating social or religious conflict and retreats from democracy back into authoritarian regimes or failed states. Despite decades of 'development' we can hardly imagine that we live collectively on a secure and sustainable planet in which social, economic and cultural prospects and freedoms are expanding for a majority of its human population (to say nothing of the damage that that same 'development' may be inflicting on the very physical environment on which it depends).

Something has evidently gone wrong, but what? There are many potential answers, but one, not much heard in conventional development circles, is that the root cause is our civilization itself. This is the argument that a global civilization built on resource-extracting and polluting industrialization, unsustainable energy sources, (over)consumption, addiction to travel by oil-guzzling means, forms of agriculture and food production that are not only unsustainable in the long run, but may be actually hazardous to the health of those who consume their products, expensive and technologically driven models of health care, and is one which has not addressed some of its most pressing and persistent social problems such as poverty, ethnic, educational, economic and gender inequality, crime, unemployment and rising levels of addiction and psychological stress, is simply dysfunctional. It may indeed have produced amazing achievements (in technology, medicine, and science in particular), but at the cost of massive environmental destruction, unfairness between those (both individuals and nations) who have and those who do not, and amazingly, a total unwillingness to discern or define what its goals are. If these goals are just more of the same, then it is now very evident that we live on a doomed planet, one doomed by our own behaviour as a species (Diamond 2005). Some would indeed argue, as in the much discussed theory of the "Risk Society" promulgated by the German sociologist Ulrich Beck and others, that life in the contemporary world is now *more* risky than in the past, not less (Beck 1992, Strydom 2002). At least in the past we more or less knew what the risks were and how to protect ourselves. But now the risks themselves are nameless, or, if named, completely beyond the control of any individual: global warming, holes in the ozone layer, new diseases (AIDS, SARS, Bird Flu . . .), nuclear radiation, almost complete lack of knowledge of where our food comes from or what is actually in it. As one who personally lived through the meltdown of the Fukushima No.1 nuclear power plant in Japan in 2011 (considered the worst nuclear disaster since Chernobyl, and still not fully under control), I can testify to the truth of this. How does one protect oneself from an invisible and by normal humans, undetectable level of radiation, announced daily during the crisis and its aftermath by the media, in 'scientific' numbers that mean nothing to the average layperson?

If indeed it is our civilization (or at least, that of the affluent West, Japan, and those who seek to emulate it) that is the root problem, then it is this, rather than the individual issues that preoccupy development economists, agronomists, hydrologists, and the like, that needs attention. Not that the other 'smaller' issues are unimportant, but they need framing. This frame is the issue of culture. A civilization is defined largely in terms of its culture, both in a material sense (not only its technology, but its buildings, art, fashion and artefacts) – why else do we go to Paris, Madrid or Kyoto other than with the intention as tourists or visitors to visit the museums and cultural sites? We enjoy their expressive culture: music, theatre, dance and even their religious 'performances' whether these be actual religious services or rituals, or public dramatizations, such as the carrying of *Mikoshi* or palanquins or chariots of the local gods through the streets of very contemporary Japanese cities during shrine festivals, or the custom of Hindu devotees of the god Lord Murugan to carry on their own bodies lacerating cages or *kavadis* through the streets to the appropriate temple during the annual South Indian festival of Thaipusam. But somehow the study of culture and the study of development have drifted apart. This book is designed to show how they might be fruitfully brought together.

This is very important for at least two reasons – one conceptual and the other practical. The conceptual one of course is what we mean by the much overused term, but ill-defined word 'development'. Again clearly it has meant different things to different people, but almost always implies primarily economic development – growth, the expansion to the technological base of a society, increasing incomes (at least for some) and usually the assumption that the model of such economic development is a capitalist or 'neo-liberal' one. But such a definition once again ignores the basic question of what the development is ultimately *for*. Are the goals of human life simply acquisition and the maximization of personal material resources? Many would argue most certainly not, for several very good reasons. Firstly, because such a definition provides only a very impoverished picture of human existence – clearly we are not just acquiring animals, but also cultural and spiritual ones. Secondly, because it leaves out any discussion of our leisure life, our necessity for means of self and collective expression, and our need for beauty. The older and now rarely discussed 'Human Needs' theory of development dating from the 1980s (Dube 1984: 73–87) clearly recognized this, and all the lists of such needs that I have seen always include aesthetic, spiritual and expressive needs, as well as obviously material ones such as food or shelter. And thirdly, such a definition overlooks the possibility that the role of development might be not just more things, but the development *of* culture. In other words, the active promotion of all those forms of expressivity which not only enrich life (and are certainly psychologically necessary), but which point us to the sorts of societies in which we would actually like to live, and potentially can if we direct our development efforts in that direction. Interestingly in most Utopian societies, although they remain either as literary fictions or as small scale and often short-lived actual social experiments, cultural enrichment and its democratization so that everyone can be creative is almost always a goal. Hitherto, in most of the existing literature, small as it still is, the focus is on 'culture and development' (i.e. the role of culture in promoting development, a sort of handmaiden role) rather than the development *of* culture, or even more radically, culture *as* development. Our central question then is not so much one of technical development as it is of philosophical anthropology: what kind of humans do we want to be, and in what kind of society do we want to live?

Re-imagining development: culture, social change and human futures

In one of his major books, the well-known critic of corporate capitalism and its associated processes of globalization, David Korten, has written that "To create a just, sustainable, and compassionate post-corporate world we must face up to the need to create a new core culture, a new political center, and a new economic mainstream" in the pursuit of what he calls the shift to a "new integral culture that affirms life in all its dimensions" (Korten 1999: 261). I think that he is very right, but the problem is that he, like many other writers in the field of what might be called 'alternative development', while indeed discussing in detail the political and economic dimensions of a sustainable future, does not elaborate on what this "new core culture" might look like. But any discussion of holistic development must surely raise this question, not only of the political changes desirable (no doubt in the direction of democratization and participation), and the economic ones (in the direction of social justice, solidarity and environmental sustainability), but also of the cultural forms that might accompany and indeed support such political and economic initiatives, neither of which exist in a social vacuum and both of which are deeply informed by cultural values. Some, as we have suggested before, would go even further and argue that the roots of our current multi-dimensional crisis – persisting poverty, conflict, ecological degradation on an unprecedented scale, loss of both biological and cultural diversity and a cascading multitude of related problems – are to be found in our dysfunctional culture(s) and 'civilizations', that are out of touch with nature, have in many cases in practice severed themselves from their traditional spiritual roots, and in their commitment to the blind belief that endless growth and consumption can be sustained forever, seem to create endless new forms of alienation, inequality and social exclusion amongst their own members.

But if we stand back from this situation for a moment and ask ourselves what role culture should actually play in development (understood here as the process designed in principle to bring about human and ecological security, meaningfulness and well-being for the greatest number), and what a new "core culture" compatible with the sustainability and preservation (and perhaps restoration) of our planet might look like, very fresh and interesting possibilities arise, and with them new methodologies for approaching the practice of development.

In the past, culture has often been seen either as an impediment to 'development' (understood in an earlier discourse as 'modernization'), or as a means of delivering it more effectively. In this latter case, culture is seen as a body of knowledge often derived from anthropology, useful in understanding how best to impose a set of policy decisions on a target population, whether these be in agriculture, health, population planning, urbanization or other fields. This is perfectly legitimate up to a point: reasonable policies do need to be effectively implemented. But it also has fundamental weaknesses: a purely instrumental approach to culture tends to lead to the ignoring of the intrinsic value of the particular instance in question, which can easily lead on to the denigration of that culture; and it can also lead to the failure to recognize that there is a feedback loop between new policy initiatives and changes in culture. A new health system in a village does not just 'deliver' new therapeutic and pharmacological goods, but also changes conceptions of illness, of the body, of appropriate treatment; alters the links between religion and illness and profoundly changes what the medical anthropologist Arthur Kleinman has called "narratives of illness" – the ways in which people make sense of their own illnesses and explain it both to physicians and health-care professionals, and to others in their own community (Kleinman 1988). Cultural change is as a consequence often driven not by direct influence of other cultural forms (although of course this happens with the advent of TV, foreign movies, new fashions and the spread of alien popular cultures), but equally by changes in the *context* of the original culture: its relationship to itself now refracted through wider national, governmental or development policies designed to 'uplift' it, in which the old meaning systems no longer quite make sense or seem 'old fashioned' when compared with the new world views being promoted.

One quite natural response to this is to jump to the defence of the 'traditional' culture and to try to shield it from at least some of the erosive effects of globalization. But this is not only in practice difficult, but overlooks the fact that 'traditions' themselves are constructed and have a history. Another danger is to accept an implied uniformity in Korten's conception of a new core culture. Note that he uses the word 'culture' in the singular. What I assume he is suggesting is not of course a new and subtle form of cultural colonialism, but the identification of a set of core *values* held across a range of cultures and compatible with a wide range of actual cultural expressions, which when adhered to would eventuate in a sustainable and socially just future for the majority of humanity. Assuming this to be the case, we should attempt to identify what these values might be, and the nature of the practices and institutions that support them. The discussion of values has to be undertaken in the context of culture: culture is the source of our collective memories and our social imagination, and is both the depository of historical experiences and also the main resource for conceiving and mapping humane and viable futures for our planet. Culture is not just *what is* but also *what can be*. One piece of very empirical contemporary evidence for this is that, with our looming ecological crisis, almost all religious traditions have begun to explore their own scriptures and practices and the nature of many of their liturgies and rituals, to begin the process of re-orienting themselves in a more ecologically responsible direction (Gottlieb 2004).

We might agree that some of these cultural core values would be: the search for non-violent cultural expressions, including how they are embodied in films, popular cultures, sports and entertainment; the promotion of positive relationships between humans and nature that seeks a notion of human identity that transcends anthropocentrism; the recognition that culture contains and often conceals inequalities, hierarchies of power and domination, and often itself attempts to justify patterns of age, gender, class or ethnic discrimination, and that these need to be confronted and overcome; that culture cannot be separated from economics, but must also overcome the strange contemporary situation in which economics has become the master of culture rather than its servant; the promotion of a culture of responsibility rather than simply of rights and entitlements; the encouragement rather than the suppression of cultural and linguistic diversity and the recognition that in everyday terms, culture is life: it is the medium in which we spend our days. If ultimately development means the enhancement and protection of life, then it will be through culture that this is achieved. In fact it cannot really be otherwise. As Roger Gottlieb nicely puts it in another book on religion and ecology,

> We can repair the boat of human culture – which carries us, as it were, on the sea of life – only as we are sailing in it. There is no dry land – no life without culture – on which to switch to a totally different boat. We will have to

engage our past wisdom as well as respond in ways that could not have been conceived of generations ago.

(Gottlieb 2006: 21)

Development has come to be regarded as a technical process, to be directed by 'experts', and dominated by economics. I would prefer to argue that it is an art, one that involves a continuous balancing act between preserving existing cultural and biological diversity, drawing upon them and their component parts (in the case of culture, elements including arts, religion and modes of spirituality) in the attempt to conceive of better and more humane and sustainable futures, and developing the quality of culture itself as the actual content of our everyday lifeworlds. We may overcome material poverty, but without overcoming our cultural poverty our future in a state of 'affluence' may be one of boredom and alienation: yet another form of spiritual poverty. As a patient of Arthur Kleinman aptly put it, in words that are as applicable to development as they are to medicine: "We have powerful techniques, but no wisdom. When the techniques fail, we are left shipwrecked" (Kleinman 1988: 142).

This still leaves a number of questions unanswered, including that of exactly what constitutes culture, not in an abstract sense, but in very practical terms, and also what aspects of culture are most compatible with a holistic conception of development. For we can certainly argue that if development is not holistic, then it is not really development at all. If we see development in principle as the striving for the full realization of human potential compatible with full ecological responsibility, and with the proviso of course that that realization does not conflict with the legitimate interests of others but is compatible with the as-full-as-possible flowering of everybody, then it is evident that culture must play a central role, and that much of this culture must be expressive. And this is precisely where the arts enter the scene. Development is itself a form of culture, or certainly of social transformation, and as such cannot in reality be separated from discussions of culture. To do so is a form of sociological Cartesianism: not splitting body and mind in this case, but splitting society from its embodiment in cultural forms.

It is a sad fact that the existing literature on culture and development (and for that matter on culture and globalization – cf. Tomlinson 2000, Skelton and Allen 1999) manages almost entirely to talk about culture in an abstract sense without actually discussing its concrete manifestations in any way at all – an extraordinary lacuna. A number of prominent examples illustrate this very well. One of the few textbooks to specifically address the issue of culture and development – Susanne Schech and Jane Haggis' volume *Culture and Development: A Critical Introduction* (Schech and Haggis 2000) manages, in over 200 pages, to give no actual examples of cultural expression at all. Certainly discussed are definitions of culture, globalization, post-colonialism, ethnicity, gender, feminism, human rights, the invention of traditions and media and cultural imperialism, without, as far as I can detect, giving a single example of actual cultural expressions as embodied in art, craft, theatre, literature (oral or written) or dance. Here we have a fairly clear example of 'culture' being identified with social structure, and not with any of its expressive forms, including, amazingly, even popular culture, which has a great deal to do with issues such as ethnicity and feminism. The same can be said to be true of a whole range of texts addressing dimensions of culture and development, even if they do not use those terms specifically in their titles. There is no need to multiply too many examples, but this is equally true of major works in the anthropology of development (e.g. Olivier de Sardin 2005, Gardner and Lewis 1996), and in the sociology of development (e.g. Webster 1991) where even texts that bill themselves as actor-oriented approaches (e.g. Long 2001) are entirely innocent of any discussion of actual concrete expressions of culture, and of how that culture might have some significant bearing on the sociological issues that are discussed (poverty, peasant movements, agricultural change, the impact of urbanization and industrialization and so on). One of the very rare exceptions is Allen Kaplan's book *Development Practitioners and Social Process: Artists of the Invisible* (Kaplan 2002) in which the idea of narratives appears – actually listening to stories from the field, and in which the structure of the book itself is organized around themes such as intuition, discerning, co-creating and imagination, and which utilizes and recommends artistic practices such as drawing as an important part of the methodology of 'doing' development. The activities of the development practitioner or community developer he sees as essentially artistic, rather than as technical or managerial: "for it is through the practice of art that the imaginative faculty is exercised" (Kaplan 2002: 34). This book is an attempt to fill that vast silence identified by Kaplan and absent from almost all development discourses and theory.

In practice then, as we must all be aware, culture refers to what we actually *do:* it is not an abstract concept at all. It is reflected not only in the so-called 'high arts' (although these – classical music, painting and sculpture, ballet and other forms of dance, theatre and opera – are consumed and practiced by many), but very much so in popular culture (comics, music, dance forms, films, television content, fashion) and what are often dismissively categorized as 'crafts' including pottery, weaving and other textile arts, carving, 'folk' music and quite possibly the undoubted arts of gardening and cooking. Many cultural preferences in fact define the boundaries of sub-cultures: jazz for example. Other art forms, such as photography and architecture, cut across all these boundaries, and have profound if often undefined influence on everyday life through such media as advertising (which, despite its obvious marketing/capitalist intentions, quite often attains high artistic standards), and the shaping of social interaction and relationships to the environment through the effects of built spaces and constructions.

Absenting the arts from discussions of development is consequently to create a major gap, and the lack of consideration of such expressive forms of culture may well have a lot to do with both the failure of many well-intentioned development projects that fail because they do not touch the well springs of people's emotional lives, and with the barrenness and sheer ugliness of many of the landscapes (particularly urban ones) that result from development, to say nothing of the destruction of organic cultures that often existed before 'development' swept away cultural diversity in much the same way that it tends to destroy biological diversity. There is in any case, the substantial argument that the arts are a universal and integral part of all societies in history, and that they have an important and indeed essential function, both in the training of the mind, which is not separate from the expansion of forms of sensory awareness and expressivity (Eisner 2002), and as a critical element in evolution, where beauty as well as material necessity and physical pressures, drive both the complexity and the domestication of human cultures (Dutton 2010, Rothenberg 2012). The Marxist critic Ernst Fischer has argued that while art is often distorted and commodified under capitalism, it remains a necessity in all human cultures and is a major way in which we both discover and represent back to ourselves reality (Fischer 2010). Its absence then from development studies discourse is to leave out a profound element in human experience, history and social organization, since such cultural expressions not only are implicated with class, as Pierre Bourdieu has shown vividly for both the arts in general (Bourdieu 1984) and specifically for photography (Bourdieu 1965), but these cultural expressions are intensely political, as demonstrated in recent and contemporary debates about 'multiculturalism' (for a good summary and discussion see Ivison 2010), representation of other cultures (Said 1978) and indeed the representation in the popular media of development itself (Lewis, Rodgers and Woolcock 2013), and the relationship between culture and colonialism and the continuing possibility or reality of cultural imperialism today, even if the official age of empires is over (Hamm and Smandych 2005). Many of the contemporary struggles around the world over 'identity' (especially of minorities, political, ethnic, religious, sexual) are actually about culture – the right to the use of a particular language in many cases and the right to express that threatened culture through traditional arts, both visual and performative.

Stories, narratives, images and expressive performance are central to human life. It can certainly be argued that imagination rather than reason is the main faculty of human interaction with the world, an imagination expressed in myriad forms, many of them artistic, and which in turn spill over into what might be termed 'social imaginaries' – alternative ways of organizing society that lead in many cases not just to utopian schemes (important as they are), but to very practical interventions in design, architecture, education, fashion (itself signifying and reflecting important shifts in gender relations, self-images and empowerment) and social organization itself, both of sub-cultures and in turn of the wider society, often taking its lead from avant-gardes defined mainly in artistic terms. A very good example of this would be the impact of the so-called 'Bloomsbury Group' in early and mid-twentieth-century Britain, a group that included accomplished writers (Virginia Woolf and Lytton Strachey being the most prominent), painters (including Vanessa Bell, Duncan Grant and Roger Fry – who was also a prominent art critic) and the world renowned economist John Maynard Keynes – who was also a major promoter of theatre in Britain and who married the prima ballerina of the famous Ballets Russe, Lydia Lopokova. The Bloomsbury Group also had a major impact on design in furniture, book production, wallpaper and other dimensions through the Omega Workshops created and run by the group. In the penumbra of the core Bloomsbury

Group were such luminaries as the painter Walter Sickert, the novelists Aldous Huxley and E. M. Forster and the cartoonist and satirist Max Beerbohm, amongst many others. Collectively the Bloomsbury Group has had a huge influence on painting, design, literature, economics, theatre and lifestyles in general, despite its small size and generally upper class (between the wars Britain was still class-ridden) social composition. (For an excellent overview of the arts of the group see Shone 2002).

Situating the arts

The purpose of this book is to relocate the arts (visual and performative) in relation to development, to argue for their full inclusion in development discourse (especially those parts that do purport to discuss 'culture and development'), and to demonstrate that the arts have vital roles to play not only as vehicles for other forms of development (for example the delivery of health care or family planning programmes), but as an essential part of any holistic or integrated conception of development as a whole. I have argued elsewhere at length for such a holistic conception of development (Clammer 2012) and here want to expand at length on the role of the arts specifically in such an (ideal) development process.

Anthropologists concerned with development issues have turned in recent years to the re-discovery and study of what is now being called 'Indigenous Knowledge' (for example Sillitoe 1998), particularly as it relates to such fields as medicine, agriculture and ecology. But once again missing entirely from such discussions is any concern with indigenous arts, even though these are profoundly implicated in processes of healing, planting, harvesting and ritual, as well as often reflecting gender distinctions within the society (who paints? who pots? who weaves?). As Victor Turner demonstrated long ago (Turner 1969, 1982), ritual is a vital form of expressivity and performance in many societies, and it has important social functions, whether of social solidarity, initiation and status transformation, healing, supplication, emotional stimulation and, let's admit it, entertainment. Indigenous knowledge then needs to be balanced with indigenous expressivity. Or, as the Thai social critic, activist, and promoter of what he terms "engaged Buddhism" Sulak Sivaraksa puts it, "the crucial dimensions of life are not economic but existential. They relate to our needs for leisure, contemplation, love, community and self-realization" (Sulak 1992: 36).

It is in culture that these existential dimensions are embodied and to a great extent provide the medium through which we seek answers to those fundamental questions. Note that here I am using the word 'culture' in its quite everyday sense: essentially as practice – in other words what we *do* – and abstracting from this the particular set of human activities known collectively as 'the arts'. We can be well aware that culture is dynamic and ever-shifting and articulates closely with the political economy of any society (see Clammer 2012: 33–57 for a detailed discussion), and that the notion of 'art' as a distinct category of cultural practice did not emerge in the West until around the seventeenth century and still recognize that everyday life is pervaded by (even made up of) cultural practices or practices that are culturally shaped (even sleeping), and that many of these practices constitute what at this point in historical time are collectively known as art. When people talk of art as 'contested' or as a field of struggle, they do not mean that there is debate over whether the arts exist. Rather they are either talking about the *boundaries* of art (as with Marcel Duchamp's (in)famous urinal, submitted as art [under the title of *Fountain*, and signed "R. Mutt"], at the epoch making Armory show in New York in 1913), or of *whose* art should be exhibited and whose is excluded, or indeed included, as with the highly controversial Whitney Museum biennial in New York in 1993 which exhibited, contrary to most galleries' conventions, a high percentage of art by women and ethnic minorities, and included 'art' thought by many to be no such thing (videos, installations, assemblage), which bore little relation to the traditional aesthetics of 'fine art'.

These issues have been complicated by globalization – a situation in which art and artists frequently migrate across national boundaries, in which elements of performance in one culture are appropriated by another (in dance, theatre and music in particular) and then sometimes reflected back to the culture of origin in a very changed form. Nevertheless, certain things can be said with a high degree of certainty: that culture is where we have what Jeremy Rifkin calls "deep play"(Rifkin 2004: 141), and that play is both serious and legitimate (especially for adults); that culture is the realm in which a society's most fundamental values are exhibited; and that subjectivities both form and are formed by participation in culture, and those subjectivities do not remain as individual attributes, but express themselves socially – by defining oneself for example as an 'artist', as a 'poet', as a jazz lover, or whatever larger social categories are available in that particular culture and historical epoch. Some sociologists such as Erving Goffman have indeed argued that all social action can be thought of in a sense as acting, and the creation of social roles and the acting of them out constitutes a form of theatre. 'Real' theatre is consequently just a kind of distillation of what we all do every day, transposed to a particular setting (a literal stage) (Goffman 1959).

In an important book devoted to the re-analysis of development theory, Jan Nederveen Pieterse (2001) argues specifically for the centrality of culture in the context of what he calls throughout his book 'alternative development', an important idea given the failure of so much conventional development. For Nederveen Pieterse the sphere of culture is important as it is an arena of choice, where agency often prevails over structure, and where alternatives and resistances can be formulated and practiced, while keeping in mind that it must also be constantly subject to critique, as 'culture' can embody the anti-human and the anti-nature to the same degree that it can embody exactly the opposite. The country of Beethoven also produced the Nazis. The possession of 'culture' is no guarantee against barbarism, but may indeed be used to justify it, as in Hitler's move against what he termed *Entartete Kunst* or 'degenerate art', much of it included in a show in Munich in 1937 which contained works by artists now considered amongst the major figures of modern art in Europe, including Chagall, Otto Dix, Max Beckmann, Paul Klee, Ernst Ludwig Kirchner and many others (Altshuler 1994: 136–149). It is often forgotten that art movements are also cultural movements, and cultural movements very frequently change society (Clammer 2014: 95–119).

A number of leading scholars in the humanities have argued specifically that in an age of increasing managerialism, scientism and virtual worship of technology, the humanities should play an increasingly vital role as carriers of alternative values. Indeed the word 'humanities' itself obviously implies the humanization of life and the inclusion within it of democratic values, imagination, ethics, dialogue and an inclusive notion of citizenship (Nussbaum 2010). As we face the probable problems of 'transition' – from an oil-driven to a potentially post-petroleum economy, from a high consumption one to a modest- or low-consumption one, from the reckless exploitation of nature to its conservation and appreciation, such values will only increase in importance. If we imagine what a 'post-development' society might look like, in every scenario known to me, the arts play a vital and democratic role, practiced by all in a setting of low consumption, ecological responsibility, democratic decentralization politically and low conflict (for two recent examples, the latter by quite a surprising author in this context, see Callenbach 2004 and Harvey 2002: 257–281).

In a previous work I attempted to substantially expand the understanding of the relationships between culture and development by introducing such elements as the emotions; the psychology of development; the importance of narratives and stories in the understanding of how development actually affects its recipients, whether as beneficiaries or as victims; trauma; the links between culture and climate and, significantly in relation to this book, the notion of the 'aesthetics of development' (Clammer 2012: 220–241). This idea includes the necessity for development studies not only to discuss the very important but neglected field of development ethics, but also how aesthetic transformations – in subjectivities, in vision, in fashion, in patterns of entertainment and forms of expression – accompany the social and economic changes encapsulated in the term 'development'. Social historians and social theorists should know this from studies of modernity, since modernity (and its putative successor post-modernism) are themselves to a great extent defined in terms of cultural shifts (e.g. Gay 2009). There is indeed a large body of evidence to show the unavoidable relationship between the arts and society, and the impact that the arts themselves have on social forms, hierarchies and practices, including their role in processes of catharsis, emotional well-being, the moral improvement of civilization, their use as an instrument of politics and their role in both social stratification and individual and collective identity formation (Belfiore and Bennett 2010). What is important specifically in development studies is the relation between such shifts and the social processes (e.g. changes in gender relations, perceptions or classifications of 'race') which intersect with them at all levels, and their impact on issues of social justice. In that context, I introduced the idea of 'visual justice' to supplement the older idea of social justice, and indeed as an important and neglected part of it. Why should only the rich enjoy beauty – whether in the forms of access to art and theatre, or in the form of attractive dwellings, interior design or of their general environment for living, from which the poor are often excluded? Why does so much development, in the sense for example of urban development, have to be so ugly? It is certainly not the case that the poor in many societies, even if socially excluded, lack access to either aesthetic or natural beauty, but it is certainly true that either their access is limited, or the often beautiful products of their own art and craft traditions are undervalued and certainly never gain access to the so-called 'art world' except on rare occasions. Such artefacts are much more likely to appear in an ethnographic museum than in an art gallery.

In response to this of course many artists have devoted their work to uncovering and representing social injustice and corruption, through the visual arts. Significant examples in the West include the German artists Käthe Kollwitz and her engravings of the conditions of the working classes in early twentieth-century Germany, or the highly satirical paintings of George Grosz, almost brutal in their depiction of greed, corruption and moral decline in the post–World War One Weimar Republic. In Latin America such historically significant figures as the famous Mexican muralist and political activist Diego Rivera, and many subsequent painters in Guatemala, El Salvador, Cuba and other places likewise used their art as a form of social critique. It has been in theatre that this tendency is even more marked, with examples including the enormously influential playwright and director Bertolt Brecht again in Germany, or the work of (and stemming from) the seminal practices of the Brazilian Augusto Boal, which will be discussed in detail in a subsequent chapter. This principle can be found in literature too, not only in the more obvious form of the novel, but very much in poetry, where leading poets such as the Chilean poet, politician and activist Pablo Neruda, have argued that poetry is not just 'text', but transformative energy embodied in writing – and reading and public declamation, and a deep method of cultural critique through the stimulation of the imagination (on Neruda see Feinstein 2005). Or as the recently deceased and very prominent German artist Joseph Bueys has aptly put it:

> As our ageing old order muddles its way towards death, it is only by radically widening our conceptual understanding to embrace art, that we will be able to receive the powerful inspiration of art. And it is only such inspiration of creative art that can serve as evolutionary midwife to aid the birth of a new society. Such a society, celebrating liberty, equality and fraternity, would itself be a great work of art, and every person in it a deeply fulfilled artist.
>
> *(Bueys 1977: 127)*

This is equally applicable, as Kaplan has suggested, for the development practitioner, and of course for those developing, or worse 'being developed', since as we will discuss in the next chapter, art is not only a means of self and communal expression and empowerment and exercise of the imaginative (and indeed critical) faculty, but also has multiple practical functions in poverty alleviation, gender relations, the formation and sustaining of local economies and many other fields.

Cases in point

Many of these points can be illustrated with actual examples drawn both from the field and from art history. A good practical case can be seen in the work of the

Kolkata-based Indian artist Amitava Bhattacharya, who, in addition to his own artistic practice (as a painter, utilizing many techniques from East Asian brush painting, and trained in part in Beijing) spends large amounts of time encouraging art practices (painting, drawing, murals, metal-work and other media) in the often tragically poor and marginalized tribal areas of Northeast and East India, home also to many communities of *Dalits* or so-called 'untouchables', so low in the hierarchy of Indian castes that they are actually outside it. One of Bhattacharya's projects has been in the tribal hamlets of the Chattisgarh district of Madhya Pradesh state in North-Central India (described in his self-published book *A Diary of An Art Master*, 2013). While forms of indigenous arts have been practiced (such as the decoration of the exteriors of houses, usually done by women) children in the villages and the severely inadequate schools had never had the opportunity to practice art in any form (and were too poor to acquire the materials necessary). But when introduced to painting, glass painting and murals they rapidly and spontaneously showed huge creativity, producing amazingly vivid work, most of it reflecting their own life conditions, the environment around them and the social problems that they constantly encountered. Was this just a one-off project, destined to die out as soon as the artist left to return to Kolkata? It seems not, since the springs of creativity once unleashed are hard to bottle up again and continue to express themselves in numerous imaginative ways.

For the source of positive social change is not economics or politics in the last analysis – it is creativity and imagination (from which by the way both economic ideas and political forms themselves emerge). The possibility of envisaging another world is the root of the future. Decades of 'development' in India and throughout much of the world have not always brought about the benefits promised. Poverty, deprivation and marginalization continue and in many cases have increased. The experience of development for many has been one of violence and up-rooting, not a peaceful transition to a richer, more secure, healthier and happier world.

This very negative experience has tragically been the fate of many of the *Adivasi* (known as 'tribals' in South Asian bureaucratic terminology) communities in India, and not of these alone: many *Dalits* ('Untouchables') and other socially marginalized groups have had similar experiences – at the worst loss of traditional land to mining, dams and other mega-projects, at best continuing poverty, lack of access to health care and education, and very little participation in the 'India Shining' promised by the political and economic leadership. But despite this, the experiences recorded in the diary of the painter Amitava Bhattacharya's (Bhattacharya 2013) fertile attempt to introduce art to the children of remote villages in the state of Madhya Pradesh shows that behind the deprivation lies a whole continent of humanity – of creativity, close links to nature, warmth, humour, hope and imagination, simply waiting to be released.

Despite its huge social problems, one encouraging thing about India is that it is also full of social energy, especially in the NGO sector where many groups are working to stimulate and preserve local textile production, handicrafts, and indigenous theatre and music (see resource listings for some examples). Art in India indeed, since the colonial period, has always been a medium of struggle and opposition against foreign domination, a means of seeking for an authentic identity, and a way of keeping traditions alive and maintaining respect for the village societies from which most Indians have come and which still harbour 60% of the Indian population (Mitter 2007). Much the same can be said of Latin America, a region plagued both with underdevelopment and a succession of brutal military and totalitarian regimes, where art has been a major form of social protest. This has been true in painting including the work of the great Mexican muralists Orozco, Rivera and Siquerios, for whom art was simultaneously a mode of protest against oppression, a vehicle of public education in a largely illiterate society (in the 1920–40s), and an exhortation to modernization and development (Rochfort 1993), and elsewhere in Latin America by painters in such politically difficult societies as Nicaragua, Honduras and Brazil (Sullivan 2006). Art as a tool of social development – in relation not only to promoting revolution, but in encouraging socially acceptable forms of behaviour in relation to health, fitness and sport; literacy, immunization campaigns and maternal health; encouraging urban farming and warning against mosquito-borne diseases – has had an especially significant role in the socialist societies of Latin America and the Caribbean. This is very true in Cuba, where the art of the poster has flourished as a means of social and political communication, and as a form of public art in its own right (Cushing 2003). And the same is true of other genres which we will explore later in the book – poetry, the novel, oral literature and song, film, theatre, music and photography. The links between art and modernity are now very clear, and much the same can be said of the links between art and revolution, as the historical experience of both China and the former Soviet Union attest. What needs to be strengthened is the analysis of the relationship between art and development, the theme of this book.

Theorizing art and development

One danger however needs to be noted and headed off at the start. This is the danger of assimilating what is considered to be 'art' to purely Western aesthetic paradigms, and the consequent 'Othering' of other forms of art practice or forms that relegate them to the realm of the 'exotic'. In this book we will be promoting what might be called genuine aesthetic democracy – the equal evaluation of all forms of art and craft that emerge genuinely from the soils of cultures. This latter point is also important, since while art may indeed represent an important form of resistance – to colonialism, the hegemony of the market, a particular oppressive political ideology or practice – it is easily co-opted, especially into the market, as so much contemporary art in the West so clearly reveals. When it does this it of course loses its critical edge, and is no longer the voice of the people speaking through images or performance, but becomes another commodified aspect of that market and no longer an expression of true autonomous and indigenous development.

The aesthetic equality of forms of art found in different cultures must then be our starting point. This is not of course to deny judgments of quality *within* any particular art form (someone's pots or carvings may indeed be better than someone else's in the same village), but to argue in principle for what Ella Shohat and Robert Stam call a "polycentric aesthetics", one that does not relegate the art of the Other to some distant time zone, which accepts that there are different avant-gardes (in Asian art and in Latin American art for example) which while they may be related to the Western forms are not derivative from or parasitic in relation to it, and that Western art has been as much influenced by the discovery of alternative art forms (French painting initially by the discovery of Japanese art, especially the wood-block prints, and later, as famously with Picasso, by the discovery of African sculpture, for example) as has non-Western art by the West (Shohat and Stam 2002: 37–59). The result is certainly a polycentric understanding of aesthetics, applied to such genres as film and writing as much as to painting and other forms of visual art, and even the possibility, indeed reality, of their being many entirely new aesthetic concepts and practices emerging from the art practices and discourses of the developing world – such new notions as 'the aesthetics of hunger', 'nomadic aesthetics', 'Tropicalia', the '*Cine imperfecto*', Carnival and the now better known 'magical realism' (Shohat and Stam 2002: 41). For while many have written about the 'colonization of the mind' (e.g. Nandy 2003) it is also important to remember that there can be an equally pernicious 'colonization of the senses' – a process that does not necessarily end with the termination of formal colonialism, but continues through the avenues of advertising and popular culture so characteristic of global capitalism.

The study of art in relation to development is not then to assume a fixed category of 'art' that must somehow be brought into a dialogue with 'development'. There are many forms of art practice, and one underlying theme of this book will be to draw attention to these 'alternative arts' (although they are not alternative at all in relation to their native setting of course, but entirely organic) and by so doing to promote what might be thought of as comparative aesthetics, rather than any fixed or elitist view of what constitutes art. There are also of course many alternative forms of 'development'. This book should not be read as a cook book, one full of recipes to simply bring together the arts and development, but rather as a dialogue between two dynamic and ever-shifting dimensions of culture: the constantly re-negotiated notion of art that shifts across cultures and between generations within cultures, and the equally evolving question of what constitutes 'development'. The result will hopefully be a kind of multi-vocal (and embodied, visual and aural) conversation that will point both to a redefinition of development that places culture at its core and allows new stories and imaginative possibilities to arise, and which leads not only to a deepened appreciation of art in this process, but points art to a highly significant social role in addressing the critical issues of ecology, human rights, conflict, resources and injustice, poverty and injustices that still plague our world, and which purely technological solutions have proven unequal to solving. Assuming, that is, that 'solving' is the right approach to the perennial circumstances of being human, to the great existential questions that are beyond any managerial capacity to address. These are precisely the issues that the arts have arisen to address, so listening to them may help us significantly rethink what it is we really want in our ideal society – the creation of which is presumably the desirable outcome of 'development'.

Key readings

While all of the literature cited in the chapter is valuable a few texts stand out as essential reading. On "Risk Society" readers should consult the foundational text, Ulrich Beck's 1992 volume *Risk Society: Towards a New Modernity*, London: Sage, which sets out the essential issues. For a more extensive discussion of the relations between risk and environmental change go to Piet Strydom's 2002 book *Risk, Environment and Society: Ongoing Debates, Current Issues and Future Prospects*, Buckingham: Open University Press. For detailed discussion of the nature of culture in relation to development (including issues of aesthetics, the emotions, suffering and illness) see John Clammer, *Culture, Development and Social Theory: Towards an Integrated Social Development*, London and New York: Zed Books, 2012. For an in-depth analysis of the relations between art and society (especially the visual arts), including the ways in which art movements can be seen as important social movements, see also John Clammer's 2014 *Vision and Society: For a Sociology and Anthropology from Art*, London and New York: Routledge. While it does not discuss the arts at all, although billing itself as a textbook on culture and development, the volume *Culture and Development: A Critical Introduction* by Susanne Schech and Jane Haggis (Oxford and Malden, MA: Blackwell, 2000) is a useful introduction to the general issues. Less systematic but much more original in its approach is Allen Kaplan's 2002 book *Development Practitioners and Social Process: Artists of the Invisible*, London, Pluto Press. A classic work on art and society, in this case from a Marxist perspective is Ernst Fischer's 2010 *The Necessity of Art*, London and New York: Verso, translated from the German by Anna Bostock and with an introduction by the major art critic and novelist John Berger. For locating art in much longer processes of human evolution go to the entertaining and accessible book *The Art Instinct: Beauty, Pleasure and Human Evolution* by Denis Dutton (New York, Berlin and London: Bloomsbury Press, 2010).

Resources

In addition to the readings there are a number of organizations and websites that can be visited online. For a major listing of NGOs, social movements and civil society organizations go to the resources listed in Paul Hawken's book *Blessed Unrest: How the Largest Social Movement in History is Restoring Grace, Justice, and Beauty to the World*, New York: Penguin Books, 2007 and the constantly updated links to be found at www.wiserearth.org and www.naturalcapitalproject.org both of which will lead you to resources related to many issues including arts activism, arts education, arts therapy, literature and performing arts. One of the leading arts activist groups, the feminist Guerrilla Girls who bill themselves as the "conscience of the art world", can be accessed at www.guerrillagirls.com and their activities followed. Amongst the groups working specifically on art and development are the Art for Development network at www.art4development.net and the Power of Hope at www.powerof hope.org. Working on art and sustainability is the Center for Art, New Ventures and Sustainable Development (CANVAS) at www.canvas.ph based in the Philippines, and another regional organization is the South African based Arts and Media Access Centre (AMAC) in Cape Town, and addressing the particular issues of Latino artists is the National Association of Latino Arts and Culture at www.nalac. org while others can be located in the Middle East (Gudran Association for Art and Development in Egypt: http://gudran.com/main/) and in Japan, including Survivart (http://survivart.net).

DISCUSSION QUESTIONS

1. This chapter argues that culture is the 'frame' through which we see and respond to issues of development. What aspects of culture are especially relevant to the analysis and conceptualization of development, and how do they specifically fit into this frame?
2. Distinguish the development *of* culture from culture *and* development. How do they differ and why should the former be promoted?
3. Research examples of the ways in which one or more of the arts have been utilized to promote social justice, empowerment and/or positive and humane social change.

References

Altshuler, Bruce (1994) *The Avant-Garde in Exhibition: New Art in the 20th Century.* New York: Harry N. Abrams, Inc.

Beck, Ulrich (1992) *Risk Society: Towards a New Modernity.* London: Sage.

Belfiore, Elenora and Oliver Bennett (2010) *The Social Impact of the Arts: An Intellectual History.* London and New York: Palgrave Macmillan.

Bhattacharya, Amitava (2013) *A Diary of an Art Master.* With an introduction by John Clammer. Kolkata: Privately Printed.

Bourdieu, Pierre (1965) *Un art moyen: Essai sur les usages sociaux de la photographie.* Paris: Minuit.

Bourdieu, Pierre (1984) *Distinction: A Social Critique of the Judgment of Taste.* Trans. Richard Nice. Cambridge, MA: Harvard University Press.

Bueys, Joseph (1977) "Admission of a Living Being". Talk at Kassel Documenta, quoted in Ulrich Roesch (ed.) (2004) *Vision and Action for Another World.* Calcutta: Earthcare Books.

Callenbach, Ernest (2004) *Ecotopia.* Berkeley: Banyan Tree Books.

Clammer, John (2012) *Culture, Development and Social Theory: Towards an Integrated Social Development.* London and New York: Zed Books.

Clammer, John (2014) *Vision and Society: For a Sociology and Anthropology from Art.* London and New York: Routledge.

Cushing, Lincoln (2003) *¡Revolucion!: Cuban Poster Art*. San Francisco: Chronicle Books.

Diamond, Jared (2005) *Collapse: How Societies Choose to Fail or Succeed*. New York: Penguin.

Dube, S. C. (1984) *Development Perspectives for the 1980s*. Kuala Lumpur: Pelanduk Publications for the United Nations Asian and Pacific Development Centre.

Dutton, Denis (2010) *The Art Instinct: Beauty, Pleasure, and Human Evolution*. New York, Berlin and London: Bloomsbury Press.

Eisner, Elliot, W. (2002) *The Arts and the Creation of Mind*. New Haven and London: Yale University Press.

Feinstein, Adam (2005) *Pablo Neruda: A Passion for Life*. London: Bloomsbury.

Fischer, Ernst (2010) *The Necessity of Art*. Trans. Anna Bostock, with an introduction by John Berger. London and New York: Verso.

Gardner, Kathy and David Lewis (1996) *Anthropology, Development and the Post-Modern Challenge*. London and Chicago: Pluto Press.

Gay, Peter (2009) *Modernism: The Lure of Heresy from Baudelaire to Beckett and Beyond*. London: Vintage Books.

Goffman, Erving (1959) *The Presentation of Self in Everyday Life*. New York: Anchor Books.

Gottlieb, Roger S. (ed.) (2004) *This Sacred Earth: Religion, Nature, Environment*. New York and London: Routledge.

Gottlieb, Roger S. (2006) *A Greener Faith: Religious Environmentalism and Our Planet's Future*. New York: Oxford University Press.

Hamm, Bernd and Russell Smandych (eds.) (2005) *Cultural Imperialism: Essays on the Political Economy of Cultural Domination*. Peterborough: Broadview Press.

Harvey, David (2002) *Spaces of Hope*. Edinburgh: Edinburgh University Press.

Ivison, Duncan (ed.) (2010) *The Ashgate Research Companion to Multiculturalism*. Farnham: Ashgate.

Kaplan, Allen (2002) *Development Practitioners and Social Process: Artists of the Invisible*. London: Pluto Press.

Kleinman, Arthur (1988) *The Illness Narratives: Suffering, Healing and the Human Condition*. New York: Basic Books.

Korten, David C. (1999) *The Post-Corporate World: Life After Capitalism*. West Hartford, CT and New York: Kumarian.

Lewis, David, Dennis Rodgers and Michael Woolcock (eds.) (2013) *Popular Representations of Development: Insights from Novels, Films, Television and Social Media*. London and New York: Routledge.

Long, Norman (2001) *Development Sociology: Actor Perspectives*. London and New York: Routledge.

Mitter, Partha (2007) *The Triumph of Modernism: Indian Artists and the Avant-garde, 1922–1947*. New Delhi: Oxford University Press.

Nandy, Ashis (2003) "The Colonization of the Mind". In Majid Rahnema with Victoria Bawtree (eds.) *The Post-Development Reader*. London and New Jersey: Zed Books, pp. 168–178.

Nederveen Pieterse, Jan (2001) *Development Theory: Deconstructions/Reconstructions*. London and Thousand Oaks, CA: Sage.

Nussbaum, Martha C. (2010) *Not for Profit: Why Democracy Needs the Humanities*. Princeton and Oxford: Princeton University Press.

Olivier de Sardin, Jean-Pierre (2005) *Anthropology and Development: Understanding Contemporary Social Change*. Trans. Antoinette Tidjani-Alou. London and New York: Zed Books.

Rifkin, Jeremy (2004) "The Age of Access". In Jerome Bindé (ed.) *The Future of Values*. New York and Oxford: Berghahn Books and Paris: UNESCO Publishing, pp. 129–141.

Rochfort, Desmond (1993) *Mexican Muralists: Orozco, Rivera, Siqueiros.* San Francisco: Chronicle Books.

Rothenberg, David (2012) *Survival of the Beautiful: Art, Science and Evolution.* New York, Berlin and London: Bloomsbury Press.

Said, Edward W. (1978) *Orientalism.* London: Penguin Books.

Schech, Susanne and Jane Haggis (2000) *Culture and Development: A Critical Introduction.* Oxford and Malden, MA: Blackwell.

Shohat, Ella and Robert Stam (2002) "Narrativizing Visual Culture: Towards a polycentric aesthetics". In Nicholas Mirzoeff (ed.) *The Visual Cultures Reader.* 2nd edition. London and New York: Routledge, pp. 37–59.

Shone, Richard (2002) *The Art of Bloomsbury.* Princeton: Princeton University Press.

Sillitoe, Paul (1998) "The Development of Indigenous Knowledge: A New Applied Anthropology". *Current Anthropology,* 39, 2, 223–52.

Skelton, Tracy and Tim Allen (eds.) (1999) *Culture and Global Change.* London and New York: Routledge.

Strydom, Piet (2002) *Risk, Environment and Society: Ongoing Debates, Current Issues and Future Prospects.* Buckingham: Open University Press.

Sulak, Sivaraksa (1992) *Seeds of Peace: A Buddhist Vision for Renewing Society.* Berkeley: Parallax Press.

Sullivan, Edward J. (2006) *Latin American Art in the Twentieth Century.* London: Phaidon Press.

Tomlinson, John (2000) *Globalization and Culture.* Cambridge: Polity Press.

Turner, Victor (1969) *The Ritual Process: Structure and Anti-Structure.* Chicago: Aldine.

Turner, Victor (1982) *From Ritual to Theatre: The Human Seriousness of Play.* New York: PAJ Publications.

Webster, Andrew (1991) *Introduction to the Sociology of Development.* London: Macmillan.

2

ART AS SOCIAL ENTERPRISE

The creative sector in relation to poverty, policy and social development

Let us then turn to an examination of more direct relationships between art and development. It is by now quite clear that despite decades of 'development', many of the major problems that plague our world still exist, or in many cases have worsened: conflict, poverty, resource depletion, hyper-urbanization, climate change, new disease vectors, pollution and loss of biodiversity to name some of the main ones. The blame for this cannot be ascribed to any one actor or group of actors: in practice almost all of us are implicated at some level or to some degree. But at the same time, analysis does reveal some of the main factors at work. Some of these are clearly political, others more sociological (ethnic and religious differences and tensions for example), and others economic (including, very significantly, the negative aspects of economic globalization, including its relationship to such factors as migration, de-skilling, the hollowing out of economies). While these (and other elements) do represent the 'objective' structures of our current world system, there are also intellectual factors at work. Here I would single out two of these. On the one hand there has been the very strong tendency to approach development as pre-eminently an economic issue, and consequently to analyse it almost entirely from the perspective of economics to the occlusion of other approaches, including the sociological and the cultural. The Columbia University economist Jeffrey Sachs for example has produced two (paradoxically best-selling) books on poverty (and its solutions) barely even mentioning sociological, cultural, religious, or value issues (Sachs 2005, 2008). On the other, there has been the tendency of 'Third Sector' approaches to solving global problems, to focus on the world of traditional NGOs and NPOs to the exclusion of other forms of social movements which have somehow fallen outside of the framework even of sociology and other disciplines that are allegedly devoted to the analysis of society. To take again one example, a relatively recent major book on social movements, fairly typical of its genre (Buechler 2000), does not at all discuss cultural, artistic or religious movements although historical evidence shows very clearly that all of these (as well as gender and ethnic based movements) have been major engines of social change. (See Clammer 2014: 95–119 for a detailed discussion of art movements as highly significant social movements.)

In this chapter we will re-orient discussion to achieve at least three ends: deepening understanding about the relationships between culture and development; drawing attention to the significance of culturally based social movements that often fall outside of the traditional NGO sector; and discussing the extent to which these movements impact thinking and policy about a range of factors including poverty alleviation, income and employment generation, gender in relation to development (and indeed to the arts), the strengthening of social or solidarity economies and communities and deepening our awareness of the enriching role of cultural production in development. I have argued elsewhere (Clammer 2012) for the necessity of taking seriously a cultural approach to development, not only or mainly as a vehicle for delivering other development goods (say, health systems or new agricultural techniques), but as a highly desirable end in itself, both because the outcome of development should presumably be an enriched and fulfilling life, but also because it is the neglect of cultural factors that has to a great extent led us into our current global crisis. If it is our civilization and its values and practices that are at the root of our problems no lasting change can occur without addressing, and where necessary changing, the nature of that civilization and its enormously negative impacts on nature, social justice and happiness (while certainly also being happy to laud its enormous achievements especially in such fields as technology, medicine and the arts).

The development of culture

The focus then in this chapter is not simply that of 'culture and development', but rather of the 'development of culture' as a means to achieving many of the goals of a holistic conception of development. How do the arts contribute to this? Let us start by making at least a partial catalogue.

1. Poverty alleviation. While precise figures are hard to determine, it is estimated that at least 20–30 million people in Asia alone live from art and craft production. These figures are greatly expanded when one also includes middlemen, emporium keepers, gallerists, suppliers of raw materials, weavers, people and groups working in the performing arts (dance groups, theatres, puppeteers, shadow play artists for example) and musicians. The individuals involved may define themselves specifically as artists or craftspeople, or may see their artistic production as a supplement to farming or some other income generating activity. My own work in South and Southeast Asia in particular paints a very mixed picture of the viability of many of these art practices. Many (such as weaving in India) are threatened by cheaper mass produced textiles, others by their dependency on a fickle tourist market for the sale of their products, yet others by changing tastes amongst potential middle-class buyers of textiles and art and craft products, and still more by the aesthetic judgments of the mainstream

'art world' which may or may not classify their work as 'art' at all, a problem faced worldwide by community arts projects and movements (for a very good example see Crehan 2011). For many indigenous artists and craftspeople their work is their main source of income, or in many cases that I have encountered, would like it to be, but find it not economically feasible to rely solely on their artistic production for their living, but have also to engage in farming or undertake wage labour outside of their vocation. With more and more people being drawn out of more traditional livelihoods into cities, industry and often marginal and unstable economic activities, studies show that the encouragement of the art/craft sector both prevents such migration on the one hand, and creates economically viable livelihoods for people with artistic skills on the other. It is very surprising that in poverty alleviation projects around the world, little attention is paid to developing the 'creative sector' and assisting marketing, appreciation and showing of such work. Probably the main source of such encouragement has come from the fair trade movement, which often includes handicrafts amongst its marketed products (Litvinoff and Madeley 2007).

2. Empowerment, self-esteem and social imagination. Studies of community arts projects worldwide (in ghettoized areas of US cities for example Kids of Survival [Lucie-Smith 1995: 229–231]) including ones focused on visual arts, on activist theatre (Landy and Montgomery 2012) and on other hybrid forms such as fire-shows, circuses and multimedia presentations, show that such projects have a huge positive effect on feelings of increasing control of their environment on the part of people living in previously unattractive or unsafe neighbourhoods, create a sense of autonomy and creativity when high levels of participation and in-put are encouraged and build self-esteem when people (often children) discover that they have talents and unsuspected (because never encouraged) abilities, as we saw in the previous chapter. These have knock-on effects by stimulating imagination, suggesting alternatives, enabling people to rethink their physical, social and build environments, and consequently have political implications. This can occur not only in settings of direct citizen participation, but also in the context of public transport, hospitals, monuments, parks and the creation of spaces which encourage the development and use of the 'convivial city' (Miles 2000).

3. Community building. A result of such activity is often an increase in social solidarity, a sense of community, a decline in social and racial divides and sense of pride in a neighbourhood in which one has had a creative role in shaping. In community art projects where murals and other very public art outcomes have been created, little or no vandalism occurs directed at the art, even when it is still common in relation to other objects or spaces.

4. Solidarity economy. The notion of solidarity economy, or what is also sometimes called 'social economy', has entered development discourse late, but is now a rapidly expanding movement of both ideas and activities and is being expounded in a fast growing literature (for example Arruda 2009, Gibson-Graham, Cameron and Healy 2013, Lewis and Conaty 2012, Jayasooria 2013).

Almost all theories of solidarity economy assume a sense of community. Yet in practice in the contemporary world, such real communities are hard to find and where they exist are often in the process of disintegration. Three factors point to a strong congruence between art/craft production and solidarity or social economies: the fact that much artistic production, especially in 'developing' countries, is communal; that community art projects, as suggested above, strengthen a sense of community; and that fair trade relationships between art/ craft producers and consumers create a sense of solidarity across national, class and ethnic boundaries. An important aspect of many art/craft producing communities is that women play a major role (unlike, say in the 'fine art' communities of the West) and so gender empowerment and economic independence is also a significant link between craft production and the creation of economies of solidarity (Bartra 2003), a subject that we will return to in more detail below.

For these four reasons alone, quite apart from the intrinsic joy of making, seeing and using beautiful objects, the art/craft sector is highly significant – as an economic sector in its own right, as an important part of the social structure of many societies and social groups in Asia, Africa and Latin America, and I will illustrate this with a number of examples and cases.

Cases in point

Although art practices have not yet entered the mainstream of development thinking, numerous, often very small and localized, examples exist. These range across the whole spectrum of the arts and some representative examples can be listed here (only a tiny selection of the numerous examples actually in existence, some short-lived, others persisting over long periods of time).

a. Attempts to encourage and market local textiles in Bengal, Rajasthan and other localities in India. India has an ancient and vibrant countrywide tradition of weaving and other textile creation crafts. These were actively encouraged by Gandhi in his attempts to promote village industries and overcome Indian colonial dependence on imported textiles, mainly from the UK, but paradoxically utilizing cotton and silk sourced from India. Today, many of these village and cottage industries are falling into disuse as contemporary Indians increasingly wear Western style fashions and/or mass produced factory made textiles. However there are many NGOs and local marketing movements attempting, if not to totally arrest this trend, at least to promote their sale, use as furnishings if not for wear, and to even promote them to the tourist and international markets. Good examples would be the Sasha Association for Craft Producers in Kolkata and the Crafts Council of India. Similar NGOs and Third Sector and fair trade organizations can also be found in neighbouring Bangladesh, Nepal and Sri Lanka.

b. Similar movements can be found in Southeast Asia, a prominent example being that of the Japanese textile artist Morimoto Kikuo, who has single-handedly created a movement in war- and holocaust-devastated Cambodia to re-teach weaving to local women as a way of simultaneously giving them an income-generating skill and preserving one of the most beautiful of all Cambodian crafts. His weaving school required silk, leading to the revival of silk farms as a consistent source of high quality supply, creating yet further employment, and of course the income generated from the marketing of the very high quality goods – clothes, furnishings (cushion covers etc.), bags, wall hangings, handkerchiefs, etc. produced by the women (with the additional sociological effect of female empowerment, financial independence and re-skilling). Based in the city of Seam Riep, the location of the world-famous temple complex of Angkor Wat, his atelier is not only very well situated for the tourist trade, but is symbolically in what is regarded as the cultural navel of Cambodia. Angkor Wat itself has proved to be an interesting case of artistic re-skilling. The Angkor archaeological park covers a large area just outside of the city of Seam Riep, and includes many famous UNESCO World Heritage sites, including the central temple complex and many subsidiary temples, many of them still not fully excavated. The whole city was 'lost' in the jungle until rediscovered and cleared during the early French colonial period in Indochina. Archaeologists from Tokyo's Sophia University, who have long been working at the site, discovered, as a result of repairing monsoon rain damage to the main causeway across the lake in which the main temple stands on an artificial island, the extraordinary techniques which the original builders (mainly ninth to eleventh centuries) had used. The decision to rebuild using the same techniques meant that these had to be taught or re-taught to the local artisans, and from this has stemmed an entire project to re-vitalize the economies of the local villages through a combination of re-skilling in traditional stone masonry techniques, the re-creation and promotion of local crafts such as basket-weaving for both use and sale to tourists, and eco-tourism including home-stays in village houses. Here we see a synergy, in which one craft-based activity feeds another, and one which incorporates both men (as stone masons) and women (as the primary handicraft producers and home-stay hostesses), which has led to employment and many new economic activities and rises in incomes, has kept villagers from migrating to Phnom Penh or even neighbouring Siem Riep, has led to re-skilling in now largely lost traditional techniques, has maintained the traditional village communities and has indeed helped greatly to restore them after the massive disruptions and displacements of the brutal Khmer Rouge period, and has the additional advantage of helping to maintain one of the world's most amazing and beautiful cultural sites.

c. In visual arts there is probably less work, but one outstanding example is the work mentioned in the previous chapter of the Bengali painter Amitava Bhattacharya and his wife Anita, to promote art amongst highly disadvantaged and marginalized tribal children in Northeast India. Living in remote locations, in considerable poverty, with little in the way of health services, education or employment beyond subsistence farming, and considered as of extremely low social status in hierarchical Indian society, Bhattacharya took to working with these children, supplying them with basic art equipment (most had not access to or had even ever seen, paints, paper, canvas, or other conventional art materials), and the idea that they too could produce art. And indeed they did – paintings, drawings, murals and constructions, usually based on their own perception of their social situation, marginalization and oppression, but also reflecting and externalizing their dreams, hopes and desires for a better and different future, as individuals and for their community. Bhattacharya's work in a number of communities in Bengal, Orissa, Madhya Pradesh and Bihar clearly released huge quantities of imagination, excitement, fun and what might be called a rudimentary form of social analysis on the part of the children (and indeed many of the adults) and gave them a whole new way of visualizing and examining their world. Other work has been done with adults, for example the workshops with Dalit ('Untouchable') artists by the activist Ajit Muriken in Mumbai and Kerala and the embodiment of their work in exhibitions, calendars and other forms, again creating both income generating opportunities, self-respect and a mode of visual representation of the exclusions and humiliations of Dalit experience. There is again a strong sociological component to many of these endeavours, and even an ecological one. For example in Tirupati, a famous temple town in South India, also well known for its wood carvers (mainly of religious figures from the Hindu pantheon), there are also communities – in effect communes – of female artists who paint on textiles, work collectively with different women working on different parts of a total textile picture (some drawing the basic designs, others colouring, yet others providing the calligraphy in Sanskrit or local languages embodied in the work) and with the community only using natural unbleached cotton or silk as their basic 'canvas', and making their own pigments and dyes entirely from natural products. Here we see communal art production, women forming a community of solidarity in a patriarchal society, generating income, utilizing locally available environmentally friendly products, while keeping alive a local tradition and forms of solidarity economy. Elsewhere in Eastern India (again in the states of Bengal, Orissa and Bihar in particular) a traditional form of painting, based not on individual production but on family and community work (something akin to the workshops of Renaissance Italy) known as *Patta* art, exists on a large scale and is a major source of livelihoods for the artist communities, as their works are bought both by locals and pilgrims, especially those attending the great Jagannatha temple festivals, and by tourists, both Indian and foreign, and are recognized on the national stage, more than one *Patta* painter having received prestigious awards (Bundgaard 1999).

d.   If one extends the range of examples to other craft/art forms such as basket weaving, pottery and ceramics, metal working, wood carving, embroidery, temple decoration and carving, unusual forms such as the sand painters of Bagan in Myanmar (an art form consisting of creating pictures, usually on Buddhist themes, by sprinkling coloured sand on a textile surface coated with a glue to make it adhere), then the remarkable range and number of craft/art produc- ers and the range and quality of their products becomes apparent. Here I have drawn examples from Asia, but equally valid examples can be found in Latin America and the Caribbean (Bartra 2003), and Africa (Kasfir 1999), and of course in places where there has long been a recognized craft/art tradition (Bali for example), as well as in the 'developed' world where there is either a long- standing tradition of crafts (Japan for example) or where traditional crafts have revived (the UK for example) or where they have entered into a very fruitful dialogue with contemporary art (Buszek 2011).

e.   The visual arts of course do not exhaust the category of art, although the arte- facts of craft production are most easily marketed, and art naturally includes the performing arts. Here we find many genres in existence, often underfunded and working in difficult situations. They include theatre and dance or very frequently hybrid forms of these such as the dance dramas of South India (Hollander 2013), the shadow plays of Indonesia and activist drama designed specifically to gener- ate social and political awareness. A distinguished South Asian example is the group Jana Sanskriti which employs local idioms to raise awareness of social, political, health, environmental and other issues amongst rural populations in India (Ganguly 2010). Many other examples of 'Applied Theatre' exist, in Asia, Africa and Latin America (for a detailed bibliography see Landy and Montgom- ery 2012), many of them drawing their original inspiration from the seminal text by Augusto Boal, *Theatre of the Oppressed*, (originally published in Spanish in 1974, but since then in many translations and new editions the most recent in English being Boal 2008). Theatre has proved to be a very effective (and enter- taining) way of conveying social messages, especially to illiterate or semi-literate populations and in locales where there is little entertainment, probably no elec- tricity, and intermittent intercourse with the wider world because of social or geographical isolation. It is, furthermore, often a familiar genre, as many South and Southeast Asia cultures have ancient traditions of forms of theatre often related to religious festivals or events. This is important because the symbiosis between theatre and religion creates a relationship of mutual support, beneficial to both, and creating an 'audience' for both, that might otherwise fade away. Not all forms of performing art are brought to communities from the outside – many arise spontaneously from within: village poets, work songs sung in the fields, while fishing or well digging, dance forms, debates in verse such as the Tagalog (Philippine) *balagtasan* or the form of poetic 'duels' known as *Dondang Sayang* amongst the Baba or Peranakan Chinese of Singapore, Malaysia and Indonesia (Thomas 1986), or the shadow plays and puppet theatres of Bali, Java and other locations in Indonesia. The recent innovations have been the linking of these traditional forms of performance to current development issues, since these forms are both indigenous to the local communities in question and adaptable to promoting easily assimilated social messages.

f.   Many other cases in point combine many genres into multimedia and activ- ist forms, without compromising the artistic quality of the productions. In their unfortunately rather hard to find book *Re-enchanting the World,* Hamilton Faria and Pedro Garcia (n.d.) describe many such projects. One is the Ballet Stagium in Brazil that works 'without words' on projects bringing together dance and education for poor children (and their parents) through both performances and workshops, including in the villages along the banks of the São Francisco river in Brazil's remote northeast, and works with street children, prisoners, hospitals and other agencies to promote self-esteem and awareness of rights. Another project in the Brazilian northeast in Alagoas State is the Project Alagoas Present!, a project developed by the artist Marta Arruda linking art, rights, education and development through classes and workshops in ceramics, clay, collage, drawing, mural painting and other media, and promotes conferences and performances of local folk dances. A third Brazilian case is that of the movement "Artists for Nature", an NGO that brings together artists and educators and produces both art works and many socially activist interventions including promoting and creating ecological parks, persuading the government to create a National Park in the Brazilian central region, and holding campaigns, demonstrations and conferences for art teachers and teachers of ecology. The movement was started by the artist and writer Bené Fonteles, the partner of the well-known Brazilian composer and singer Gilberto Gil. In India, where wells are very important in the semi-arid regions of the South and West especially, a novel project involving an artist, a dancer and a photographer called "Wells of Life" has appeared in an attempt to bring together symbolic associations between wells, art in its socio-historical context, local communities and their traditional well-digging songs, potters who relied on the water from the now often dried up wells, and to reconnect local people to the Earth and water in an area of India now undergoing intensive urbanization (the city of Bangalore where the project is located being one of India's fastest growing cities, with all the attendant problems of traffic congestion, pollution, lack of utilities, slums and communal tensions). Such examples also exist in the developed world – the itinerant theatres of Montreuil with their roots in a very old festival discontinued because of economic difficulties, with the result that the theatre people simply took their shows out of the theatres into the streets and cafes. A final example (many others are listed in the book) is the Shalom Salam Paz, a movement in Brazil bringing together artists from the Jewish and Arab communities and involving visual arts, poetry, dance and music, with the long-term intention of establishing a "Museum Without Frontiers" on the line that divides Jewish West and Arab East Jerusalem (Faria and Garcia, n.d. pp. 53–94).

g. Finally, literature. Literature can take many forms: written, recited, or 'multimedia' as in the storytelling of Bihar and parts of Bengal and Orissa in India, where the oral recitation is accompanied by the gradual unrolling of a picture scroll illustrating visually the spoken narrative. A similar tradition is found in parts of Indonesia and elsewhere in Southeast Asia. Vast volumes of 'folk literature' exist throughout Asia, some of it in the form of ancient legends, much of it more modern or entirely contemporary, and some specifically in the form of social commentary and criticism. A very good example of the latter is the Oriya (East India) writer, the recently deceased and prolific Chitta Ranjan Das (discussed in detail in chapter six), who wrote extensively on contemporary social issues, worked actively to promote and encourage the local Oriya literature, and utilized literature as a vehicle for consciousness raising. Asia is full of 'vernacular' literature, mostly unknown to those who only read the 'metropolitan' languages and mostly un-translated, this literature is a huge store-house of imagination, social comment, social analysis (especially of gender, class and caste) and is increasingly aware of emerging global issues such as climate change as they appear at the local level. Oral literature, which, like dance, is often an ephemeral medium, only present when performed, has important roles often unsuspected. For example the field songs of village women in Karnataka (South India) are a form of collective poetry sung while harvesting or working on the land, and prove to be a rich form of social and gender criticism, often unheard by the men to whom it refers, and which evolves over time with changing social, economic and environmental circumstances. These oral forms are important in themselves as cultural expressions (and as media of protest, humour and memory), but also as a main means by which the history of a community is kept alive and transmitted from one generation to the next, and in which history being structured in a particular way by the means of narrative exposition chosen, also is a structuring element in the organization of a society. History and historical narratives live in the present in that they organize perceptions and images of the past in particular ways, and so create concepts of identity in the present (on oral history see Tonkin 1995, and on traditional storytellers see Stoller 1997).

Policy and practice

In terms of policy and practices devoted to poverty alleviation, community building, gender empowerment and preservation of traditional cultures while stimulating new forms of cultural expression, it is clear that the art/craft sector creates many possibilities. In North America people working in these and related fields have been dubbed 'cultural creatives', and are estimated to comprise a surprisingly large percentage of the working population, especially if such activities as film and TV production, radio, museums and galleries, journalism, teaching of art and performance, publishing, writing and photography are factored in. The US-based urban sociologist Sharon Zukin (Zukin 1995) has estimated that a very high percentage of the economy of New York City is cultural production and consumption, and this is true too of not only other major cities in the 'developed' world – London, Paris, Berlin, Seoul, Tokyo, Singapore – for example, that are well known as centres of the arts, but of cities and regions in the 'developing' world as well, where such activities are however often 'invisible' to both the wider art world, and to development practitioners and theorists. Cultural creatives are certainly not a monopoly of the industrially advanced economies.

This fact has many implications for development policy and practice of which some of the major ones are as follows:

a. Cultural policy. In many 'developing' societies cultural policy (as opposed to economic policy) is frequently weak, underfunded and of low national priority. This is despite the fact that, as the work of Zukin and others shows quite clearly, the 'creative' sector is in fact an important part of the economy. The usual context in which this is recognized is tourism. But tourism alone, especially when it is concerned mainly with outsiders making brief visits, is an inadequate basis for cultural development. It may, and frequently does, lead to the deterioration rather than enhancement of local creative cultures, encouraging the production simply of what tourists are thought to want to see, purchase or consume, to the detriment of the deepening of integral and authentic cultural expressions. But countries that set out on a path of rapid economic development, industrialization and urbanization, such as Singapore, soon realized that without a real cultural base their own society is impoverished, shallow and sterile, and additionally, that even the tourists don't come or don't stay long if all they are offered is a packaged, predictable and essentially inauthentic version of local culture(s). Cultural policy then, rather than being peripheral to overall social development, should be a major and integral part of it.

b. Poverty alleviation and income generation. As suggested above, income generation is greatly enhanced by the encouragement of the creative sector. Craft/art production creates employment, generates income, provides meaningful work, tends to keep people in their communities rather than encouraging migration to large cities, retains skills, empowers women, and contributes to the maintenance, preservation and reproduction of culture. It is remarkable that most conventional approaches to poverty alleviation ignore the cultural and sociological dimensions, and it for this reason that many of them fail in their objectives. It should be remembered that poverty is not only material deprivation, but includes psychic and emotional deprivation as well. It is significant that in the 'basic needs' approaches to development, meeting these cultural and non-material needs always occupy a major place.

c. Solidarity economy. In a high percentage of cases studied, craft/art producing methods are communal and already share many of the features of solidarity or social economies — in fact in many cases *are* solidarity economies. As I have argued elsewhere (e.g. Clammer 2013), it is regrettable that one of the ignored sources for the study of solidarity economies (and of art producing communities) has been the field of anthropology (the sub-field of economic anthropology in the case of solidarity economy), examples of which exist or have existed and are widely described in the ethnographic literature, and of the anthropology of art in the case of art and craft production. In a world in which traditional cultural expressions are being eroded or destroyed, and in which the need for solidarity economies is becoming more and more apparent, models for such economies do exist and are frequently found in art/craft producing communities or in the networks of marketing that have sprung up to disseminate their products. An interesting case in point is the "Natural Desi" marketing network in South India, a communal women-run marketing network that sources and buys only *khadi* or organically produced home-spun textiles and sells them through their outlets in major cities such as Bangalore. The materials that they buy are themselves in many cases made by women, so the circle is complete. So even where a fully fledged solidarity economy may not yet exist, such fair trade networks provide prototypes of what might be done on an even larger scale. Part of the problem is persuading urban and affluent consumers (and the media which shape their consumption choices) to purchase craft products and to see them as equally fashionable and attractive as brand-name and mass produced alternatives.

d. Sustainability. As we are all aware, the current buzzword is 'sustainability', a word now very much over-used and often with little real content. But for communities, society as a whole and the environment to be truly sustainable, serious changes in practices of production, consumption, disposal of wastes and attitudes to nature will have to be undertaken. Such changes might include environmentally responsible production, recycling, use of organic products not requiring chemical input, responsible consumption, including the purchase of long-lasting, functional and aesthetically pleasing objects, clothing, utensils, decorations, foods, and architecture. Many of these are already available from the craft/art sector, but are often not easily obtainable because of both weak marketing structures and consumer preference. In most of the examples cited in this chapter, indeed in virtually all of them, sustainable practices are already the norm. This means, amongst other things, that this sector is not only already responsible, but provides a model for much of the rest of society to emulate.

e. Re-skilling rather than de-skilling. New skills requirements of course constantly emerge as a result of technological and associated economic changes. But the evidence is that in industrializing societies (with their attendant urbanization), many skills are lost and with them forms of indigenous and traditional knowledge that are very hard or impossible to recover once gone. Yet, as we know, vast amounts of knowledge and information exist in indigenous societies and in creative sectors in developed ones, not only in relation to craft/art production, but in fields such as health, agriculture, house construction, fisheries, biodiversity protection, forestry and other fields. Without sounding over-dramatic, it may well be that much of the future of humankind depends on the retention of this kind of indigenous knowledge and skills. They are often found in a holistic package, the same people who produce the art also having extensive knowledge of traditional medical practices, natural agriculture, sustainable house construction and so forth The notion of 'IK' as a result needs expanding to include artistic and craft skills as much as it does to ones pertaining to those more traditionally studied (at least amongst anthropologists) areas of know-how and activity.

Culture and development and the development of culture

One of the key targets of development assistance should always be vulnerable individuals, communities and social groups – vulnerable that is to displacement, loss of livelihood, destruction of their social and cultural capital and disruption of their chosen lifestyle. But far from protecting such groups, a great deal of 'development' actually accelerates these negative and destructive processes. What we have been suggesting in this chapter is the promotion, protection and enhancement of the lives of individuals and communities whose livelihood is based on art and craft production, in all its varied forms. Cultural policy should therefore be a central part of any development policy, whether internally generated or imposed from without by funding agencies, NGOs or multilateral institutions.

Studies conducted around the globe have consistently shown that what people desire from 'development' is by no means simply an increase in material wealth. What they also seek and desire is cultural enrichment and the improvement and deepening of the quality of social relationships. This ignoring of the cultural element in development is one of the main reasons for its frequent and predictable failures. Here I argue that the nurturing and promotion of arts, crafts and performance genres is a mechanism to raise many millions from poverty while enhancing and safe-guarding a large and in many cases disappearing part of humankind's total cultural legacy, while also supporting an authentic aesthetic outside of the market nexus, and with the additional advantage of enhancing the dignity of handiwork in an increasingly mechanized, technological and 'virtual' world (Crawford 2010). When effectively carried out, such a policy has multiple effects, including poverty alleviation, support of traditional cultural heritages, including what UNESCO defines as "intangible cultural heritage", the promotion and preservation of cultural diversity, which we might argue, is as important to a satisfactory human future as the preservation of biological diversity, the promotion of dialogue between civilizations and contributing to the genuine sustainability of human cultures into the threatening and uncertain future now unfolding. By situating culture at the heart of development discourse the true wealth of the world is safeguarded and what Bill McKibben (2007) has called the "deep economy" of the globe is strengthened, promoting a culturally richer future as we make the probable transition to a post-petroleum and possible post-capitalist society.

So hopefully we have established that far from standing in a peripheral relationship to development, the arts actually play a vital role in any holistic conception of social progress. If we see the development of culture as part of any total development package, then we are able to re-situate culture in the place that it should rightfully occupy, not as simply the handmaiden of economics, but in fact as its defining purpose, frame and source of values. The sociological impact of arts development is also highly significant, especially in its impact on such diverse areas as gender, identity and conflict prevention and resolution. Let us now examine some of these dimensions to see how they work out in practice.

The arts are gendered. The so-called 'High Arts' (with the exceptions of ballet and opera) tend to be heavily male dominated, especially in the visual arts. That is not to say that female artists do not exist – they most certainly do (see for example Grosenick 2003) and there are activist groups such as the Guerrilla Girls in the United States that devote themselves to publicizing the under-representation of women artists in galleries, museums and art histories. But to a great extent in the craft arts the situation is reversed, and women prove to play a major role as original designers and producers, and also as extenders of the boundaries of art, as an increasing amount of contemporary art utilizes craft materials and techniques, including media such as knitting, baking, weaving and sewing, as well as pottery and ceramics, that were previously thought of as existing in the world of 'crafts', but not of art (Buszek 2011). The recognition of the gendered nature of much craft art production has many consequences: it renders visible the previously invisible artists of great creativity and skill, it improves the conditions of existence and gives women an important form of agency and autonomy and of course it has huge economic impact, not only on women's lives, but on their entire families and communities. The series of case studies from Latin America and the Caribbean collected in Eli Bartra's volume *Crafting Gender* (Bartra 2003) demonstrates these factors very well. In that book studies of craft production in Mexico, Suriname, Puerto Rico, Panama, Ecuador, Columbia and Argentina all point to a common pattern: the significant role of female 'folk artists' in a whole range of media – pottery, embroidery, carving, weaving and painting. These vibrant arts prove to have many functions – economic through sales locally, to tourists and in the international market; visibility as their art products begin to appear in the art galleries, museums and books and magazines of the global North; agency for the women artists themselves and of course the production of beautiful and functional objects or clothing that may be used in everyday contexts or collected for display. But beyond this level, there are many others, as the cases also show the 'higher level' implications of local art production. These include the integration of the arts into everyday life, far removed from their sequestration in the galleries and museums of the First World, introduce whole new categories into the field of aesthetics (especially the area of what is sometimes called 'Ethno-aesthetics'), maintain cultural resilience and continuity in the face of globalization and other forms of social change, sustain cultural identity and even contribute to the peace process in violent societies such as Columbia, by "providing a traditional vision of the world that acts as a counterweight to the violence of contemporary life" (Duncan 2003: 140).

The economic, psychological and creative empowerment of women is one important dimension of the role of craft arts, but not the only one. They are also an important element in the empowerment of ethnic and cultural minorities, since crafts are not just 'objects', but also an important element in identity politics. To take just one example: if one walks the streets of Yangon (Rangoon), the principle city of Myanmar (Burma), a society in which by government decree almost everyone (except foreigners and ethnic Chinese) wears their traditional ethnic costume, one's cultural identity is immediately apparent to anyone who can read the code. Burmese of both genders will wear their national costume daily and the many minorities (Karen, Chin, Hmong, Rohingya and so forth) will wear their appropriate style of sarongs and blouses. This of course is also a double-edged sword: it establishes cultural identity in a positive and very attractive way, but it also, in an until recently highly authoritarian society, makes minority status instantly recognizable. As tension and violence has now broken out between the Burmese Buddhists and the Muslim Rohingya in the west of the country, this instant recognizability can be very dangerous, as it was in the recent past between the Burmese and the largely Christian Kachin peoples of the mountainous borderlands abutting onto Thailand in the east. Interestingly when states have tried to create a sense of artificial 'nation-building' through artistic means, these rarely if ever work unless they have truly indigenous roots, a case in point being the farcical attempt by the Singapore government not only to create a unifying 'national ideology' in that highly multi-ethnic state, but to create a national costume incorporating elements of traditional Chinese, Malay and Indian dress. The resulting hybrid of course was worn by nobody.

A significant area of art activity, both in the visual arts and in theatre, has been art therapy: the use of artistic activities to address a whole range of emotional, psychological and physical problems in sufferers. For the most part such therapy has been directed at individuals, and ultimately of course its effectiveness will be measured by its value in helping actual people overcome or modify their difficulties, rather than at a community level, especially in the context of development. The field of 'community arts' has proved to be effective in reducing ethnic tensions in racially mixed neighbourhoods, increasing feelings of security and identification with an area such as a housing estate, reducing crime and promoting a sense of conviviality (Crehan 2011). But it has mostly been tried in the context of the 'developed' world – in the UK for example – rather than in the developing world. But where it has been tried, or has spontaneously arisen, its effects have been very encouraging. Examples would include not only the Adivasi as mentioned above, but also instances of refugee art and art in post-conflict situations (or indeed in situations of ongoing conflict). One conspicuous example of refugee art would be the music of the band that emerged from the vicious civil war in Sierra Leone and which after starting in a refugee camp for self-entertainment and for the pleasure of fellow inmates, has become world famous – the Refugee All Stars. Another relates to the creation of dramas in Palestinian refugee camps in the Middle East, where theatre has been used by the inmates themselves to critique and protest their own situation and the political circumstances that have brought them there, and to propose alternative forms of politics – or of forms of cultural action beyond normal politics – a way of addressing their bleak conditions and lack of apparent hopeful futures (Wickstrom 2012).

In conflict and post-conflict situations the socially healing power of art is also visible. A beautiful example of this is in Rwanda, a society decimated and traumatized by the 1994 genocide, in which up to one million people were brutally killed, many of them neighbours and family. In 2007 the Ugandan born but Rwandan-resident artist Colin Sekajugo set up Ivuka Arts Kigali, a centre which has multiple effects in reviving art practice in Rwanda including promoting contemporary art, especially painting; running art classes for orphans of the genocide; creating a dance troupe for disadvantaged children and running a jewellery cooperative for and with poor women. This one centre has now spawned at least three other art centres in Kigali – the Inema Arts Centre, Bwiza Arts Kigali and Uburanga Arts, and Sekajugo himself has also founded a similar programme in Uganda – the Weaver Bird Arts Community in Masaka. The resulting work is shown locally and increasingly internationally (there have been shows in London, Edinburgh and New York) and sales of jewellery by local women from the cooperative is an important source of income for disadvantaged poor women, many of whom are also widows of the genocide (Brownell 2013). The flourishing of contemporary African art in general (across a whole range of genres – painting, carving, music, truck art [decoration of cargo vehicles and buses], coffins, concrete art [making and decorating compound walls and gates], metal-work, flour-sack art and advertising and sign painting) has been significant, not only for its aesthetic interest, but equally as art has become a vehicle for political activism (especially in South Africa), critique of the lingering influences of colonialism, and as a protest against and documentation of the problems of African urban life, such as AIDS, prostitution and even such mundane matters as pot-holed roads, as in the work of the now internationally recognized Congolese painter Cheri Samba (Kasfir 1999: 27).

The relationship between art and peace turns out to be an important one. In the Middle East context the well-known scholar Edward Said (of Christian Arab descent), and the Jewish conductor Daniel Barenboim organized a music workshop in Weimar on the occasion of that small but culturally highly significant German city becoming that year's Cultural Capital of Europe, bringing together young Arab and Israeli musicians and a small number of German ones, to rehearse and play together as a single orchestra (Barenboim and Said 2004). In Israel itself, art has proved to be an important element in peace education between Jews and Arabs, both in teaching peace through art and utilizing artists as teachers, much art being non-verbal and so beyond the categories of language, race, and religion that have so be-devilled the endlessly stalled peace process in the region (Feuerverger 2001). Craft activities have had a similar relationship to peace and to protest, especially anti-war protest and movements against sweat shops (very typical of textile production in the Third World) with movements such as Peace Knits, Cast Off Knitters and the Revolutionary Knitting Circle (Buszek 2011: 207–8, 216) active in the UK, USA and Denmark. In his major work *The Moral Imagination: The Art and Soul of Building Peace,* the peace scholar and facilitator John Paul Lederach (Lederach 2005) argues for the central role of the arts in peace building. This can take a number of forms – through encouraging the form of imagination that allows us to reshape the past and present, bring new things into existence and transform thinking and feeling through recognizing the power of images through which meaning is created and conceptualized; by transcending the categories that languages impose on our discourse; by encouraging adaptability; by moving beyond purely analytical categories into a more sensuous relationship to reality and by recognizing that social change is an aesthetic as well as a 'technical' process. As he suggests, in the context of peace-building

> We need to envision ourselves as artists. We need a return to aesthetics . . . Time and time again, social change that sticks and makes a difference has behind it the artist's intuition: the complexity of human experience captured in a simple image and in a way that moves individuals and whole societies.
>
> *(Lederach 2005: 73)*

This he illustrates through a number of situations (Northern Ireland, USA, Burkina Faso, Mali and Sarajevo) in which art – song, dance and music – defused tense conflict situations and negotiations, allowed participants to express emotions rather than arguments and allowed true feelings of grief, regret and sorrow to surface, leading to the possibility of real reconciliation (Lederach 2005: 152–162).

The more conventional approaches to poverty alleviation, conflict resolution, gender justice and ecology have not really worked. If they had, our global crisis might have been deflected, but this has clearly not happened. But why not? There are several answers. With the critical issue of climate change for instance we see lack of political will and the retreat into long outmoded national boundaries, when the problem itself is truly global. But it may be that the traditional paradigm of development is wrong, so it never quite hits the mark. What we are suggesting here is that a deep engagement with culture is missing, and that this blindness to the full complexity, emotional and existential depth of human life is why, despite addressing the great moral and practical issues of our day, development does not 'work'. It leaves untouched the basic well springs of human life, emotions and expressivity. Only by incorporating these into development will real progress towards social justice, ecological responsibility and the creation of a truly convivial society be possible.

Key readings

For a general introduction to fair trade practices see Miles Litvinoff and John Madeley (2007) *50 Reasons to Buy Fair Trade*, London and Ann Arbor, MI: Pluto Press. On community art, although mainly concerned with UK examples, Kate Crehan's 2011 book *Community Art: An Anthropological Perspective*, Oxford and New York: Berg, is the best contemporary reading and contains a good bibliography. On public art in general and its relation to urbanization see Malcolm Miles (2000) *Art, Space and the City: Public Art and Urban Futures*, London and New York: Routledge. On craft production and gender see Eli Bartra's edited volume *Crafting Gender: Women and Folk Art in Latin America and the Caribbean*, Durham, NC and London: Duke University Press, 2003. On 'deep economy' definitely read Bill McKibben (2007) *Deep Economy: The Wealth of Communities and the Durable Future*, New York: Holt, which, while it does not phrase itself in terms of solidarity or social economy, is actually one of the most readable and useful guides to economies arising from communities themselves rather than imposed by the 'big' national and international economies.

Resources

There are a number of sites that you can visit to explore some of these themes. KAMALA, the Crafts Council of India which promotes traditional textiles, natural fibres, terracotta and craft work in stone, metal and wood and which has a retail outlet in the Rajiv Gandhi Handicrafts Bhawan in New Delhi can be accessed through www.craftscouncilofindia.org. India also has a number of private orga- nizations devoted to handicraft promotion as a tool of poverty alleviation. These include the Sasha Association of Craft Producers in Kolkata (http://www.sasha world.com), and based in the UK the One Village organization that partners with craft makers' cooperatives in India (onevillage.com) and the fair trade organiza- tion Chandni Chowk at www.chandnichowk.co.uk. The work of Morimoto Kikuo at the Institute for Khmer Traditional Textiles in Cambodia can be researched through http://iktt.esprit-libre.org/en/2004/04/morimoto-kikuo-biography.html The Vikas Adhyayan Kendra in Mumbai, India, which promotes Dalit art can be found at www.vakindia.org. Many of the organizations listed in the previous chap- ter can also be consulted. There are also organizations devoted to the promotion of natural fibres and textiles and handicrafts made from them, often in conjunction with organic farming. A very good example in Japan is the Shouwamura organiza- tion that can be accessed at www.vill.showa.fukushima.jp although at the moment their website is only in Japanese.

DISCUSSION QUESTIONS

1. How can the promotion of the arts (including the so-called 'crafts') con- tribute to poverty alleviation, re-skilling and empowerment?
2. Research more cases that show models for the creation and organization of art and craft promotion organizations that can directly or indirectly contribute to development. Pay particular attention to their cultural appropriateness.
3. In what practical ways should development policy, both local and inter- national, incorporate cultural factors, and suggest ways in which this might be done.

References

Arruda, Marcos (ed.) (2009) *A Non-Patriarchal Economy is Possible: Looking at Solidarity Econ- omy from Different Cultural Facets.* Rio de Janeiro: Alliance for a Responsible, Plural and Solidarity-Based Economy (ALOE).

Barenboim, Daniel and Edward W. Said (2004) *Parallels and Paradoxes: Explorations in Music and Society.* London: Bloomsbury.

Bartra, Eli (ed.) (2003) *Crafting Gender: Woman and Folk Art in Latin America and the Caribbean.* Durham, NC and London: Duke University Press.

Boal, Augusto (2008) *Theatre of the Oppressed*. London: Pluto Press.

Brownell, Ginanne (2013) "Studio space as catalyst in Rwanda". *International New York Times,* October 17, p. S5.

Buechler, Steven M. (2000) *Social Movements in Advanced Capitalism: The Political Economy and Cultural Construction of Social Activism*. New York: Oxford University Press.

Bundgaard, Helle (1999) *Indian Art Worlds in Contention: Local, Regional and National Discourses on Orissan Patta Paintings*. Richmond: Curzon Press for the Nordic Institute of Asian Studies.

Buszek, Maria Elena (ed.) (2011) *Extra/Ordinary: Craft and Contemporary Art*. Durham, NC and London: Duke University Press.

Clammer, John (2012) *Culture, Development and Social Theory: Towards an Integrated Social Development*. London and New York: Zed Books.

Clammer, John (2013) "Learning from Experience: Anthropology and Solidarity Economics". In Denison Jayasooria (ed.) *Developments in Solidarity Economy in Asia*. Kuala Lumpur: Centre for Social Entrepreneurship, Binary University, pp. 64–70.

Clammer, John (2014) *Vision and Society: Towards a Sociology and Anthropology from Art*. London and New York: Routledge.

Crawford, Matthew (2010) *The Case for Working With Your Hands*. London and New York: Penguin Books.

Crehan, Kate (2011) *Community Art: An Anthropological Perspective*. Oxford and New York: Berg.

Duncan, Roland J. (2003) "Women's Folk Art in La Chamba, Columbia". In Eli Bartra (ed.) *Crafting Gender: Women and Folk Art in Latin America and the Caribbean*. Durham, NC and London: Duke University Press, pp. 126–154.

Faria, Hamilton and Pedro Garcia (n.d.) *Re-enchanting the World*. Bangalore: Pipal Tree.

Feuerverger, Grace (2001) *Oasis of Dreams: Teaching and Learning Peace in a Jewish-Palestinian Village in Israel*. New York and London: RoutledgeFalmer.

Ganguly, Sanjoy. (2010) *Jana Sanskriti: Forum Theatre and Democracy in India*. New York: Routledge.

Gibson-Graham, J. K., Jenny Cameron and Stephen Healy (2013) *Take Back the Economy: An Ethical Guide to Demystifying the Economy and Creating a More Just and Sustainable World*. Minneapolis: University of Minnesota Press.

Grosenick, Uta (ed.) (2003) *Women Artists in the 20th and 21st Century*. Cologne, London and Tokyo: Taschen.

Hollander, Julia (2013) *Indian Folk Theatres*. London and New York: Routledge.

Jayasooria, Dension (ed.) (2013) *Developments in Solidarity Economy in Asia*. Kuala Lumpur: Centre for Social Entrepreneurship, Binary University.

Kasfir, Sidney Littlefield (1999) *Contemporary African Art*. London: Thames and Hudson.

Landy, Robert J. and David T. Montgomery (2012) *Theatre for Change: Education, Social Action and Therapy*. London: Palgrave Macmillan.

Lederach, John Paul (2005) *The Moral Imagination: The Art and Soul of Building Peace*. New York: Oxford University Press.

Lewis, Mike and Pat Conaty (2012) *The Resilience Imperative: Co-operative Transitions to a Steady State Economy*. Gabriola Island, BC: New Society Publishers.

Litvinoff, Miles and John Madeley (2007) *50 Reasons to Buy Fair Trade*. London and Ann Arbor, MI: Pluto Press.

Lucie-Smith, Edward (1995) *Movements in Art Since 1945*. London and New York: Thames and Hudson.

McKibben, Bill (2007) *Deep Economy: The Wealth of Communities and the Durable Future*. New York: Holt.

Miles, Malcolm (2000) *Art, Space and the City: Public Art and Urban Futures*. London and New York: Routledge.

Sachs, Jeffrey D. (2005) *The End of Poverty.* New York: Penguin Books.

Sachs, Jeffrey D. (2008) *Commonwealth: Economics for a Crowded Planet.* New York: Penguin Books.

Stoller, Paul (1997) *Sensuous Scholarship.* Philadelphia: University of Pennsylvania Press.

Thomas, Phillip L. (1986) *Like Tigers Around a Piece of Meat: The Baba style of Dondang Sayang.* Singapore: Institute of Southeast Asian Studies.

Tonkin, Elizabeth (1995) *Narrating Our Pasts: The Social Construction of Oral History.* Cambridge: Cambridge University Press.

Wickstrom, Maurya (2012) *Performance in the Blockades of Neoliberalism: Rethinking the Political Anew.* London and New York: Palgrave Macmillan.

Zukin, Sharon (1995) *The Cultures of Cities.* Oxford: Blackwell.

3

THE ARTS OF SUSTAINABILITY

Architecture, design and public art

The concept of sustainability has now entered the discourse of development in a very central way. Indeed, it is difficult to read anything in the field now that does not refer to the idea in some way or another – whether in relation to environment, resources, energy, cities, or just about anything else. The idea itself is not new – it has been in the vocabulary of development studies at least since the World Conservation Union began to use it in 1980 (IUCN 1980), and given even greater impetus by the World Commission on Environment and Development (WCED, often known as the "Brundtland Commission" after its chairwoman) which published its report *Our Common Future* in 1987 and which contained a definition of sustainability now known to just about everyone. That is, that "Sustainable development is development that meets the needs of the present without compromising the ability of future generations to meet their own needs" (WCED 1987). Many critics have argued that while this may be a good starting point, it leaves many questions unanswered: are development and sustainability compatible concepts at all? How can we know the needs of future generations? Is sustainability a process or an end goal? Is it too vague an idea to be of any real use? Or is it more of a moral principle than an actual guide to action? Clearly in the now huge literature on the subject, the notion is used in many different ways – as a steady state economy, as a mainly environmental concept, as an exhortation to reduce consumption and increase re-use and recycling or worse still, that it is so vague an idea that it can be easily co-opted by current established interests and used for purposes quite contradictory to its original intentions, which presumably were to ensure that there is a future at all, since logically an un-sustainable future is just that, and will be the end-point of civilization as we currently know it (for a good overview see Reid 1996).

In the last analysis (literally!) this point is really the issue to be addressed. An economy and its associated patterns of consumption, energy use and resource depletion that is using up and destroying its own natural capital (the biosphere on which all life ultimately depends) and which encourages lifestyles that are basically greed and self-interest at the individual level, and socially dysfunctional at the collective level: high levels of social inequality, hyper-urbanization and with it jammed 'freeways', serious atmospheric pollution, declining access to clean water, a mindlessly violent popular culture and indeed crime, conflict and violence both nationally and internationally. Few of us would agree that this is utopia or really the kind of society that we envisaged or ever really wanted to live in. Yet in many ways we tolerate it, and are consequently complicit in its perpetuation. It is all too easy to condemn the car as a highly dysfunctional form of urban transportation – inefficient, polluting, space-wasting, resource guzzling – while still wanting one for ourselves, or to desire to live in a large, detached and highly energy inefficient dwelling. This points us back to an idea discussed in the first chapter: that at root of our global problems are the values and practices of our civilization, and if we are to solve those problems, it is not enough to simply treat the symptoms, but to look at their roots. This is where culture enters the debate.

All of the core issues examined in *Our Common Future,* notably population, food security, species loss and ecosystem health, energy, industry, and urbanization, are all at base sociological and cultural rather than 'technical' in nature. Family size in human societies is not determined by food supply as it is in many animal communities, but by social and cultural (including of course religious) choices. What, when and how we eat is likewise a matter of cultural choice: bread or wheat? Vegetarian or meat eater? Kosher or who cares? Three big meals a day plus snacks, or just one and few snacks (ask any Buddhist monk in Southeast Asia)? Dairy or no dairy products in my diet? Likewise all of the pathways suggested to reach sustainability involve a social and cultural dimension. For the WCED these included a political system that ensures effective citizen participation (in other words, genuine democracy), a production system that respects and conserves the ecological base on which it is founded, and an international system that favours patterns of trade and finance that promote overall global sustainability. Other models of sustainability such as those proposed by the World Resources Institute two decades ago are similar: a stable or smaller population, abolition of mass poverty, environmentally benign technologies and environmentally honest pricing, sustainable consumption and education for sustainability (WRI 1992). But as many critics have again pointed out, while these are all good ideas, and despite all of these reports (and similarly the ones coming out of the UN "Earth Summit" – the 1992 UN Conference on Environment and Development and its 2012 successor, both held in Rio de Janeiro) would any national, let alone international, programme for genuinely sustainable development win political approval, and would the more radical implications of the idea of sustainability

> survive their mediation through the institutional machinery of mainstream development, staffed by an international desk-bound elite who have allowed bureaucracies to proliferate, but who have failed to arrest either the continuing degradation of the ecological systems of the planet or the deterioration of the welfare of many people throughout the world?
>
> *(Reid 1996: xviii)*

These are tough questions, and they take us not only into politics, but into an area curiously ignored in almost all development thinking – notably the psychology of change. While it is not difficult to suggest many practical strategies for practicing sustainability at the individual or social level (renewable energy resources, recycling, rainwater harvesting, localization and regionalization, low carbon economies and so forth), how to actually get people to adopt these is much more problematic. One thing is certain: propaganda rarely helps. Certainly there is a political context – where there is democracy and participation, empowerment follows. But as any student of social movements knows, even when such political conditions exist, it is still hard to mobilize people, keep them committed to a collective goal, and to encourage or demand the sacrifice of personal interests in pursuit of a long term and somewhat amorphous end point such as 'sustainability'. In a culture dominated by the idea of rights and entitlements, it is not easy to get people to think of their responsibilities. It is a great weakness of many social change and social movement theories that they do not address these motivational questions, or what Herbert Marcuse once called "the education of desire". Fundamental change comes from deep sources and the question then becomes: how to identify and tap those sources?

As long ago as 1975 people concerned with development were thinking about the direction and goals of that process. In 1975 the Dag Hammarskjöld Institute issued a report that, while it did not use the term sustainability, posed many of the questions that we are discussing here, and proposed approaching them from a rather different direction from the subsequent WCED report. That report, entitled *What Now? Another Development* (Dag Hammarskjöld Institute 1975) proposed another model not nearly so embedded in what was basically development/growth oriented thinking. This included the idea of the development of people, not just an increase in the number of things; that development, while certainly aimed at first meeting the basic needs of the poor, should also concern itself with the 'humanization' of people generally, by seeking to enhance their needs for expression, creativity and conviviality; that it should be endogenous and self-reliant and must be in harmony with the environment. Others have gone even further, such as the proposals of the Global Scenario Group that a new sustainability should be conceived as one in which society and individuals turn to non-material dimensions for fulfilment, and that these should include emphasis on the *quality* of life, the quality of human solidarity, and the quality of the Earth. The bottom line in this scenario is not more stuff, but rich quality of life, strong human ties and a resonant connection with nature, and these are the elements that will provide the foundation for any real sustainability (in addition no doubt to the more technical aspects of creating a 'green' economy, developing sources of non-polluting renewable energy and so forth). This kind of idea is now once again becoming popular – whether expressed as 'post-materialism', 'post-development', 'cultural alternatives to development' (this latter idea being the inspiration of the now sadly defunct Intercultural Institute of Montreal and its long running journal *INTERculture*), human security, or the life-styles being inspired by some of the environmental movements (low consumption, returning to organic farming and so forth). Of course one gets the impression that these are attractive alternatives in the already affluent West and Japan, but might be a little less so for those still living in situations of actual poverty and deprivation, where there is really no option but 'less consumption'. Nevertheless, as a shift in development discourse, such attempts to define alternatives are important. Many of them stand in the venerable tradition of utopian thinking and the many historical attempts to create ideal communities – communes, ashrams, housing associations, cooperatives and the many other experiments in alternative lifestyles, of which the now very visible 'transition' movement is a recent and significant expression, based on the rational planning of the major economic and social shifts that would necessarily accompany the shift to a post-petroleum world as oil resources dwindle and a lifestyle based on cheap and abundant energy resources recedes into history (Hopkins 2008).

This very real possibility has spawned not only serious analyses of a post-oil society (which would certainly solve a lot of our pollution problems) and the new forms of economy that it would entail (Urry 2012), but also new forms of literary utopias, of which a now modern classic example is Ernest Callenbach's *Ecotopia,* mentioned in chapter one, in which the author envisions an ecologically based society created when what is now California and Oregon secede from the United States to form a new democratic, environmentally based and simple-lifestyle experiment in living (Callenbach 2004). Others have turned to analyses of what a post-capitalist society might be like (Korten 1999, Kovel 2002, Theobald 1999), to trying to recover the ecological wisdom of pre-modern and pre-industrial peoples (Hartmann 2004, Kötke 1993), of attempting to define a spirituality for the massive shifts and disruptions that would inevitably accompany the collapse of our present form of civilization (Baker 2009), or of sketching the nature of contemporary civilization that the shifts in consciousness and social practice would need to accompany a shift to a sustainable, just and ecologically sound world (Korten 2006, Gershon 2009), and the new forms of leadership that would be necessary in a world in which old-style politics were no longer the paradigm for societal management (Parkin 2010), and of what a politics of the future might look like when positive values are at its basis, not the seeking for power and domination (Lerner 1996). We might be seeing here (especially when combined with the thinking and practices coming out of the environmental movement, particularly its more radical sectors) a genuine paradigm shift in development thinking. But yet there is a problem: none of them seriously discuss, or in most cases even mention, culture, let alone the arts. So we are left with a very peculiar lacuna: we are asked to envisage a new (post-oil) economy, a new political order beyond 'empire' (the old forms of domination, war, control and inequalities that marked the pre-transition political economy), and a new social order based on ecological responsibility, permaculture and sustainable agriculture and the use of renewable and environmentally benign non-extractive energy sources, but we are not asked at all to envisage what that post-capitalist, post-empire culture might be like. What forms might its arts, its film, its literature, its media, its theatre take? Would we expect to live in a culture of non-violent movies in which Rambo is considered not a hero but an extreme deviant, and in which gun fights, car chases, explosions, murders, crime, and war (the stuff of a very high proportion of Hollywood movies) would be considered aberrant expressions of a civilization now thankfully dead? What would we put in its place? What will we do in the evenings? We are told that a new civilizational story is necessary, but how do we create it? Where is the source of the new narratives that might lead us beyond our current dysfunctional civilization into the imaginative possibilities of a new one? The imagination has to be the source for it is out of the re-imagining that new forms of cultural practice compatible with a genuinely sustainable future will arise.

Art and sustainable futures

The architect James Wines has written that "without art, the whole idea of sustainability fails" (Wines 2008: 9). Let us now try to unpack this interesting and provocative idea, to show that it is not just an expression of the utopianism very common amongst architectural writers, but is a genuine basis for rethinking the relationship between art and sustainability. This we will pursue through an examination of the visual arts, and especially their expression in land art, ecological art, and the emerging theories of environmental aesthetics, through public art and the ideas of the re-enchantment of the world through art, through architecture, design and, briefly, through the ideas of ecological theatre and performance (not that they are not significant, but that is a theme to be developed at length in the subsequent chapter). The end point will be to establish very close connects indeed between the arts and sustainability, one that suggests their essential role in creating and sustaining such a viable future for both humanity and the rest of the biosphere.

Nature has of course always been a subject of art, in the East as much as in the West. Landscape painting for example has been a major tradition in the visual arts in China, Japan, Europe and a little later in the United States. The subjects of still lives have often been of material drawn from nature (vegetables, fruits and animals, even though the latter are often sadly dead). Particularly since awareness of the ecological crisis has grown and widely disseminated through the culture by way of the media, education, and observation, so the awareness of artists of the relationship between art and nature has crystallized and become an issue consciously addressed (Kastner 2012, Thomas 1999). In terms of expression and theory this has taken several forms. In terms of theory, an entirely new field of aesthetics has emerged – Environmental Aesthetics – concerned however less with the relationship of art to the environment than with the aesthetic qualities inherent *in* the environment (Carlson 2005). While the issues discussed in environmental aesthetics are largely phrased in terms of philosophical rather than environmentalist or developmentalist terms, it does have the useful role of drawing attention to the qualities of beauty, form, order and design in nature, and in so doing underlines the responsibility of anyone or any profession engaged with nature (not only environmentalists, but also architects, urban planners, designers, creators of public art and many other professions) to be acutely aware not only of the utility of nature for human goals, but also its intrinsic aesthetic qualities. In terms of practice the awareness of ecological issues has had many artistic effects – the emergence of 'environmental art' concerned directly with representing, documenting and incorporating nature into art; increasing interest in utilizing organic materials, recycling and situating art works in relation to their natural environment in harmonious ways (with sculpture in particular); and the emergence of what is now being termed 'land art'. Land art is the creation of art works not primarily for display in a gallery (although this may also be done), but intervening directly in nature to create art works. Actual examples have taken many forms – for example the well-known *Spiral Jetty* of the American artist Robert Smithson – a huge (450 metre long, 4–5 metre wide) coiled earth structure extending from the shore of the Great Salt Lake in Utah into the waters of the lake. The site is remote and actually visited (as with much land art) by very few (although much photographed) and is an intervention that while obviously manmade, appears almost to be an extension of nature itself, a natural feature of the rugged terrain surrounding the lake.

Other well documented examples include the earthworks of the former Bauhaus artist Herbert Bayer in King County, Washington, and in their harmony with the natural environments of which they are a part, the "Garden of Cosmic Speculation" by Charles Jencks in Scotland (built on the site of an old marsh) (Wines 2008: 97–101), and numerous minimalist interventions in natural environments (utilizing logs, stones, excavations or re-arranging natural features), often with the intention of enhancing perceptions of nature to which the art somehow draws attention, rather than to itself (the work of such artists as Patricia Johanson, Richard Long, Nancy Holt, Michael Heizer, Carl Andre and the ephemeral but beautiful work of the British land artist Andy Goldsmith, who amongst other things, creates sculptures out of ice, stones, flowers, leaves, bird feathers and sand), many of which, by the nature of their materials, last only a short time and have to be documented through photography (for an overview and many examples of these and other land artists, see Lailach 2007). In all cases these works illustrate the comment of the art critic John Anthony Thwaites who noted that "A new myth of nature has infected the fine arts" (Lailach 2007: 6). Not only has nature infected the arts, but land art is to be found *in* nature, not in the museum, and is consequently accessible to anyone who is prepared to make their way to the site. It is for the most part a form of 'open art' – free, visible, low cost and organic.

There are exceptions however. Many environmentalists, far from applauding all manifestations of artistic interventions in nature, have been highly critical of the disruption of natural processes caused by erecting structures or digging pits and removing and re-arranging rocks that is actually very interventionist. A paramount example of this has been the work of the artist couple Christo and Jeanne-Claude, whose forte is wrapping places, objects, buildings and even islands and whole coastlines, as they did in Sydney, wrapping a coastal area 2.4 kilometres long and from 46 to 244 metres wide, utilizing 92,900 square metres of fabric and 56 kilometres of polypropylene rope. Or in their even more controversial hanging of a giant orange curtain across the Grand Hogback valley in Colorado, utilizing 12,780 square metres of nylon fabric, ropes and cables, and necessitating blasting and anchoring in concrete at the edges, and which only lasted 28 hours (Lailach 2007: 32–35). Many critics have suggested that this is a prime example of totally non-sustainable art – expensive, damaging to the local environment, utilizing huge quantities of non-organic materials, and basically pointless, and certainly doing nothing to enhance nature or its appreciation on the part of the ill-informed culture vultures who swarm to see such installations. The problem is that a lot of contemporary art is really not sustainable – utilizing non-recyclable materials, often toxic substances or ones very hard to dispose of, and basically creating simply more stuff without it having many redeeming artistic qualities. This has been particularly true in the theatre, where sets are often made for one play, using large quantities of wood, paper, canvas, toxic paints and other materials which are simply disposed of at the end of a run, and are rarely recycled, an issue which is fortunately now being addressed by ecologically sensitive theatre directors and designers (Garrett 2012).

The links of land and environmental art to development are hopefully by now quite clear. They encourage appreciation of nature through sharpening or altering perceptions of the familiar or the often not-really-looked-at; they encourage the preservation and restoration of environment even when a not strictly activist stance is taken by the artist, who may operate through largely symbolic means, such as the activity of the North American artist Dominique Mazeaud which she called the "Great Cleansing of the Rio Grande River", which, while it did have the effect of objectively removing trash from the highly polluted river, was intended essentially as a symbolic gesture – drawing silent attention to pollution, waste dumping and the spoliation of the environment by the human species that inhabits its own fouled nest. It is this kind of process, and many other forms of visual and performance art, that have inspired the critic Suzi Gablik to formulate the idea of the 're-enchantment' of art through its discovery of its mythic, natural and spiritual roots, and through that re-enchantment to contribute to the re-enchantment of the world, especially through the recognition of what she calls the "Ecological Imperative", which she further footnotes as "a new cultural coding" (Gablik 2002: 76). Since the death of nature means the death of humankind, moving beyond the 'old mind' that has brought us to our present impasse, and which seems to offer few creative ways out, and the anthropocentrism inherent in modernist thinking, a re-engagement with nature is the fundamental premise of any survival or sustainability strategy for the future, and, certainly according to Gablik and others, it is art that is the most likely candidate to provide the imaginative energy, new story, and symbolic language to initiate that transition from the old world system into a radically new one (see also Gablik 2000). 'Development' in such a context applies not only to the 'developing' world, but also to the 'overdeveloped' one. For if the former needs more resources, material, intellectual and artistic, it may be that the latter has too much, and either needs less of almost everything, or at the least should be prepared to share the abundance that it has, not only to offset the effects of climate change generated by its own industrial and consumption activities, but to equally share its non-material heritage, and to accept into itself the non-material (i.e. cultural) heritage of the South, which may have much to teach in the ways of creativity, simpler living and local knowledge, not least in the form of its artistic and imaginative creations.

It is mostly in that 'developed' world that the notion of 'public art' has taken root. Public art is work, often in the form of sculpture or murals, displayed in public places such as parks, plazas or other accessible sites, and designed to enhance the aesthetic qualities of those sites. In much of the 'developing' world, much art is necessarily 'public' – the painted decorations on the outside of village houses in many parts of India, the cooperative painting of walls and buildings by Sirigu women of northern Ghana (Haverkort, Millar and Gonese 2003: 146–148), and the open street displays of art for sale, as with Indonesian batiks and the East African 'Tingatinga' paintings and textiles, visible on the streets of Kenya and Tanzania. In the West however (and elsewhere too – in Japan for example, where Tokyo abounds in examples of public art, usually in the form of sculptures and ceramic and mosaic wall decorations), the art is 'deliberate' – placed there with the intention of making areas more visually attractive, attracting tourists and making cityscapes more convivial by resisting 'urban blight'. Most public art, quite naturally, is found in urban settings where flows of people are greatest and where the visual environment tends to be the most degraded. As Henri Lefebvre has argued in his now classic book *The Production of Space* (Lefebvre 1991) no space is 'empty': all space is constructed by complex factors including memory, expectations, politics, nostalgia and gender. Space is furthermore *experiential* – it is not just 'there', but is felt as well as seen (Hiss 1991) and so is the site of emotions as well as representations. Art enters into these spaces with the intention of humanizing them: rendering anonymous space more intimate, or, as Malcolm Miles phrases it, following Ivan Illich, more convivial (Miles 2000).

And indeed, public art can very much enhance the quality of otherwise bleak urban spaces, both exteriors and interiors. Public art has taken the form not only of sculptures and monuments (a very common but often overlooked form of such art), but has also appeared as mosaics, posters and wall poems in London 'Tube' (subway) stations, and as mosaics, sculptures and ornamental railings in the New York subway (and of course in the form of 'unofficial' public art, notably graffiti); as mosaics, murals, paintings and stained glass in the public areas of UK hospitals and clinics; as posters and bus stop decorations addressing the issue of AIDS in New York and the UK; as public health announcements in Germany (poster art warning of the dangers of diabetes for instance) and public service announcements against littering, smoking, use of noisy radios and other electronic equipment, commonly seen in the Tokyo subways, these latter drawing often on the style of the ubiquitous Japanese *manga* or comics. While as Miles points out, many of the claims made for public art are not fully supported by the evidence – that it does attract more tourists, make bleak urban spaces really more attractive, and so on. This may be the case for several reasons – one being that

> What seems to have happened is that an enthusiastic visual arts lobby appropriated the case for the arts in regeneration and applied it to public art in development, despite that (modernist) art lacks the capacity for wide

participation provided by, say, street theatre, and is often opaque in meaning to non-art publics.

(Miles 2000: 109)

Another is that much public art is in fact corporate sponsored art, and as such represents corporate control over urban spaces rather than genuine participation on the part of the wider community. This kind of art (and the architecture with which it is associated) essentially glorifies the corporation, and is also often a means to the gentrification of the surrounding areas, and gentrification and the quasi or actual privatization of spaces (such as the atria of business buildings or malls) tends to exclude the poor and the scruffy. Any visitor to the more modernized cities such as Bangalore will have noted how well policed shopping malls are – not only metal detectors as the points of entry, but also swarms of security guards to ensure that 'undesirables' are excluded. The result is that such spaces become entirely middle-class enclaves, and no one from the working classes, except for those who actually work in the malls, will ever get to see the art works, sculptures and fountains which decorate their interior spaces.

Space furthermore (like the architecture that occupies and structures it) is political. This applies not only to the more obvious aspects – the presence of buildings of power such as parliaments, cathedrals, law-courts, barracks and so forth, but also to the ways in which these buildings are arranged in relation to one another. In the Japanese context William Coaldrake has shown how the 'architecture of power' has long worked in a non-Western society. He shows how the orientation of the Nijo Castle in Kyoto (the administrative headquarters of the Tokugawa Shoguns in the old imperial capital) as well as its interior decoration and layout were designed both to intimidate and reinforce the social and political hierarchies of pre-modern Japan, but also to show the Shogunal ascendency over the Emperor, the titular ruler of the country. The castle is placed to the north of the guest palace for use by the emperor when visiting the Shoguns; the north in Japanese Buddhist cosmology is the direction of danger; hence the Shogun is symbolically protecting the emperor, so we see at once where the real power lies (Coaldrake 1996: 138–162). This can be seen elsewhere too: the layout of New Delhi, specifically designed as the capital of the Raj, clearly demonstrates a similar understanding of space: vast boulevards linking massive colonial buildings, a geometrical layout, huge arches, monuments and large swathes of greenery, contrasting completely with neighbouring Old Delhi with its bazaars, crowded narrow streets, lack of any apparent town planning, small houses, proliferation of temples and mosques, and virtually no green spaces at all. Abidin Kusno has shown how Jakarta was re-made as the capital of independent Indonesia in which a modernist model of town planning, complete with wide boulevards, new monuments and public art, much of it quoting or referring to traditional Indonesian culture and architecture, was imposed on the old and 'chaotic' colonial city of Batavia (Kusno 2000). The Jakarta case is significant since while the basic motivation for its transformation was nationalistic, it nevertheless incorporated public art as an important part of its new urban plan. Other post-colonial cities in Southeast

Asia (Kuala Lumpur and Singapore for example) and in South Asia have followed a similar kind of plan: to remake the city is also to beautify it. The cities of the developing world are a major nexus of problems – crowding, pollution, poor infrastructure, water and energy shortages, unemployment or under-employment, street children and crime. Public art in such situations is perhaps even more important than it is in the cities of the developed world, since it carries with it the possibility of promoting civic pride, providing more convivial spaces, and contributing to the humanization of often ugly, aggressive and dirty urban spaces. In discussing the relationship between public art and sustainability, Miles concludes his book by suggesting that at least

> perhaps this is the point of departure for artists and craftspeople, their work either integrated into the design of cities, or intervening critically in the determination of what a city is, contributing to a way in which urban dwellers, too, might live lightly on an earth which they value and adorn.
>
> *(Miles 2000: 208)*

Scholars of course love definitional arguments, and there is clearly a huge overlap between 'public art' and what is usually called 'community art'. The major difference is that while public art is usually commissioned (by city authorities or planners or corporate interests), community art arises from the local community itself. While it may well be guided or supported by city authorities and professional artists, its well springs are local and indigenous. Good case studies of a number of community art projects can be found in Kate Crehan's book *Community Art* (Crehan 2011), which while it mainly focuses on the UK, has much wider implications for art and development in general. Concerned mostly with the story of a British community arts organization – the Free Form Arts Trust – and its genesis, history, development and activities, the book explores a range of community art projects in depressed and often socially and ethnically divided public housing estates in London and elsewhere. Projects developed by the FFAT included (eventually) mosaic murals, pathways and plantings to create and enhance desolate local spaces, play sculptures for children, street festivals and fire shows, collaborative activities with street theatre groups, hoardings for the former market area of Covent Garden incorporating the names of former market porters, a standing stone sculpture for a local copse, a carnival which also incorporated the collection and disposal of domestic and garden trash and environmental work. The outcome of these projects has not only been artistic: from the beginning it was conceived of as fundamentally political. As one earlier commentator on the community art movement has put it "Community arts proposes the use of art to effect social change and affect social policies and encompasses the expression of political action" (Kelly 1984: 2). By bringing art to deprived and often impoverished areas and by including as many as possible of the local inhabitants regardless of age, gender or race in the projects (often initially conceived by professional artists, but then planned in detail and executed by the community), multiple goals could be pursued simultaneously: beautification, incorporating excluded groups, promoting neighbourliness and cooperation between housing estate tenants, empowerment of local communities by giving them a sense of control over their habitat, positive environmental impacts and possibly more, including reduction of crime as neighbours got to know one another on a personal level and took an interest in the enhancement of their estates (and none of the community murals or gardens appears to have been defaced or vandalized, in areas where such anti-social activities are sadly rather common).

Community art does indeed underline the potential and actual socially transformative powers of art, and shows that art can have a positive impact on development – by promoting new models of sociability, overcoming the artistic deprivation of the working class (and to inspire some people to contemplate the possibility of a career in art), reducing racism through collaborative work on common art projects, and of course actually beautifying and in a sense taking control of a neighbourhood through participatory art. Some commentators have gone even further, such as the French philosopher and art writer Jacques Rancière and his concept of 'critical art': "a type of art that sets out to build awareness of the mechanisms of domination to turn the spectator into a conscious agent of world transformation" (Rancière 2009: 45). It is not difficult to see the many ways in which community art can be encouraged in the developing world, and we would assume that it would have similar effects, and perhaps even more radical ones, especially in situations where high levels of social injustice, deprivation, and caste and other forms of social inequality prevail.

Architecture and sustainability

Buildings are obviously one of the most visible aspects of all but the most rural landscapes. They are also huge consumers of energy when built, and the process of building them uses even more energy, materials and labour than practically any other human process in transforming the face of the earth (in the US buildings are responsible for 65% of all electricity consumption and 30% of total greenhouse gas emissions and generate 136 million tons per year of construction and demolition waste); and globally they account for 40% of all raw materials. And having used all that energy, steel, glass, concrete, rock, wood and plastic, the results are often ugly, inefficient, and do not resonate at all with those who have to live or work in them, or indeed with those who simply have to endure their presence as part of a more or less permanent landscape. Buildings affect light, airflow, traffic, pedestrian movements, and even health by way of their systems of lighting, heating and cooling, and their use of materials, some of which, such as asbestos, have turned out to be highly toxic. The impact of buildings on the environment – both natural and social – is thus enormous. It is response to this that within architecture movements have arisen variously named 'Green Architecture', 'Environmental Architecture', or 'Slow Architecture'. Whatever the name, all these movements are concerned with moving architecture in both the developed and developing world towards designing the human habitat in accord with ecological principles, and one should hopefully add, in accord with social and cultural principles too, and with considerable attention to aesthetic values.

If architecture at its best can be considered an art, then aesthetic factors should loom large in the design process, as well as considerations of functionality. Most of us can recognize buildings which combine these in a harmonious way – that are efficient, functional, attractive and pleasant to work in or visit, and have low carbon footprints. Some 'Green' architects such as James Wines relate this to the emerging field of eco-psychology, a field that deals with both the negative and positive aspects of our human relationship to nature. The negative is the treatment of the depressions, disturbances, and even illnesses that can result from prolonged separation from nature or the treating of nature as simply functional and from a purely mechanistic perspective. The positive is the recognition of the energy, affection, positive feelings towards one's self, others and animals, and the attraction to organic and natural forms in food, fashion, art and architecture. It follows fairly directly from this that a great deal of 'development', especially urban development, is highly destructive of this kind of 'biophilia' or close affinity with nature. Being forced to live in ugly, polluted, over-crowded environments is highly stressful and physically and psychologically damaging. Anyone who has spent time in most of the major cities of the developing world knows this to be true: traffic clogged with the pollution literally hanging in the air, thirty-minute journeys that take over two hours, inhuman crowding on the public transport, insecure and often insanitary housing and cooking spaces, water shortages and frequent power cuts and crime which comes from these factors as well as others such as high unemployment, all but make these cities uninhabitable. But inhabited they are, by millions (Drakakis-Smith 2000). It is suggested in this book that the idea of 'visual justice' is an important one – that it is unreasonable and unjust to assume that only the rich should have access to beauty, attractive living environments, and protection from pollution, waste and toxins. Also noted above was the fact that every list of human needs developed so far contains not only the fairly obvious ones of shelter, food, clothing and at least minimal energy resources for cooking and heating, but also the needs for leisure, nature and what might be termed 'aesthetic needs'. The consequences of the absence of these have become the subject matter of eco-psychology, and they are indeed serious with effects on health, both physical and mental, longevity, levels of violence and crime. This is where architecture (and its adjunct, urban planning) are deeply implicated, not only in such issues as the provision of housing, but in the provision of shelter that is also attractive, culturally appropriate, affordable and built on sound ecological principles.

Many architects and planners are evidently still addicted to the myth of the technological fix. Beijing is a very good example of this – traffic clogged and with appalling levels of atmospheric pollution, the solution to the incredible and unchecked rise in the number of cars and private vehicles has been to build more and more roads, not to address the car population problem at its roots, which is largely cultural. But fortunately many others have begun to turn to principles of ecological design: a concern with the carbon footprint of any building, particularly its energy consumption and waste production as well as its impact on its immediate environment, and designing so as to maximize natural sunlight for lighting and warmth and good insulation to minimize heat loss in winter, utilizing where possible natural or recycled materials with low embodied energy, employing water catchment systems, exclusion of ozone depleting or toxic substances in materials used or energy systems and low maintenance over the lifetime of the building (Wines 2008: 65–66). Others have attempted to learn from indigenous or vernacular architecture, which over centuries in many cases often in extreme climates, have developed very efficient building and heating/cooling solutions utilizing local materials, easy to build construction methods, longevity of the buildings and great aesthetic attractiveness (Chew 1998). Traditional Japanese buildings for example are constructed out of all-natural locally sourced materials – wood, rock, clay, straw and paper, all of which can be and traditionally were recycled in one form or another, usually in the construction of a new building, or alternatively used as compost (the straw *tatami* mats or the paper from the sliding doors and windows). Still others have looked to such factors as the 'bonding elements' that relate a building to its environment in the search for an integrated urban language, since one well-designed building that does not fit or relate at all to its surroundings is not really a success in total architectural terms. Further interesting initiatives include the incorporation of urban or 'vertical' gardens into buildings, to create greenery in the total environment without needing additional space for gardens or parks, to provide shade for the buildings themselves, and when edible plants are included, as an economic and dietary resource for the inhabitants.

But it is probably in the field of 'emergency architecture' that some of the most innovative initiatives have been made in the developing world. Emergency architecture refers primarily to buildings designed and constructed in such situations as post-earthquake reconstruction, tsunami hit areas, refugee camps and post-conflict situations. In all these cases architectural solutions have been sought that are cheap, fast to build, utilize as far as possible locally sourced materials, and which are culturally and socially appropriate. This is an important point, since people, while desperately in need of shelter, will still resist housing that is not culturally suitable in terms of such basic factors as sleeping arrangements, the location of toilets in relation to living and cooking areas, the location of the cooking area in relation to the rest of the dwelling, and so forth. In societies with significant gender segregation for example, the kitchens may be exclusively female domains, and in many South Indian societies toilet facilities should be well separated from other spaces in a house. Even in very modernized Asian societies like Singapore surveys discovered that, contrary to the expectations of architects employed by the Housing Development Board (HDB), a very significant institution in a society where over 80% of the population live in public or publically built housing, people did not want or use large kitchens, but preferred either an extra room or extended living room space, since many Singaporeans cook relatively little as prepared food is easily and universally available in the many "Hawkers Centres", food courts and restaurants that populate the city.

The realization of the responsibility of the architect in emergency situations has extended into other areas close to the concerns of development in a broader sense.

Much of the housing in the developing world is substandard: the huge death toll in the 2010 earthquake in Haiti can be attributed not only to the strength of the quake itself, but because of poor quality materials and construction. The same was true of the 2008 quake in Sichuan, China, where tragically 19,000 school children were buried when substandard school buildings collapsed. While natural disasters draw at least temporary attention to issues of design and building standards, the long-term chronic problems of poor quality housing and other buildings are often left unaddressed. It has been one of the positive effects of emergency architecture that there has been a spill-over of its concerns into much wider consideration of the relationships between architecture, planning and development. In the introduction to the excellent collection of case studies *Beyond Shelter: Architecture for Crisis,* the editor, Marie J. Aquilino, suggests three main ways in which architecture can contribute to development and emergency rehabilitation (Aquilino 2011). These are, firstly, capacity, since well-trained architects not only have design skills, but also expertise in project management, budgeting and materials. Secondly, what Aquilino calls "representation":

> Architects working in close collaboration with communities can help them act on their own behalf. Playing the roles of designer, historian, negotiator and advocate, architects develop site alternatives that help secure land tenure, reblock overcrowded slums, afford better access to water, sanitation, air, and light, introduce public spaces, and improve the relationship with the local ecology. They can then represent community consensus on viable projects to intransigent or indifferent governments, and this, in turn, promotes local independence.
>
> *(Aquilino 2011: 9)*

The third is what she terms "vision":

> In a state of emergency it is difficult for desperate individuals to imagine a better future. Architectural expertise can promote public health, encourage investing in new skills and environmental awareness, and advocate for mitigating risk, which together help ensure a sustainable and safe way of life.
>
> *(Aquilino 2011: 9)*

These in turn contribute to the preservation of both cultural integrity and community life (the latter in particular being often severely disrupted by both natural disasters and the effects of ill-planned development), and, in the best cases, promote active community participation in the conception and design of projects and involve local business and contractors in the execution of re-development plans.

Studies of post-disaster reconstruction (for example in Sri Lanka and in Indonesia after the 2004 Indian Ocean Tsunami) have also shown that both relief and development are ineffective unless NGOs and architects work closely together. NGOs may have the funds and the will, but not the expertise to build satisfactory shelters, with the sad result that the shelters they design and construct are often substandard. When all stakeholders in this context – local people, architects, NGOs and local government – work together, the results can be highly successful. The case studies presented in the Aquilino volume illustrate all these principles very well, and embody many of the aesthetic qualities that we have been advocating here. The studies include self and community built housing and community structures in tsunami destroyed Aceh in Indonesia, drawing on local wisdom and local expertise; post-earthquake reconstruction of schools and homes in the Solomon Islands, Gujarat (India), Pakistan and Peru; housing in post-tsunami Sri Lanka; re-development after Hurricane Katrina in New Orleans; slum re-development and improvement in Venezuela; the creation of sustainable communities through disaster prevention in the Philippines; the preservation of traditional housing in Tamil Nadu in South India; constructing new school buildings and a medical centre using traditional designs and local materials in the Sudan, Ladakh and India; and building for a sustainable peace in civil war–torn Sierra Leone.

In all the cases certain basic principles emerged. These include citizen participation in planning, design and execution; the need to train people in techniques of construction, stone masonry and basic engineering; preserving the cultural heritage; maintaining the unity of communities and their pre-existing mutual support networks; building with appropriate and locally sourced materials and placing new homes near sources of livelihood (many post-tsunami homes in Sri Lanka were never lived in as they were either built with corrugated iron roofs, making them into what, in a tropical climate, were locally referred to as 'microwave ovens', or were too far from the sea for fishing communities to be able to sustain their economic activities); drawing on vernacular styles and construction techniques; listening to surprising local demands and requests (what the teachers and children in a school for street children in Goa most wanted was a theatre!); and to prioritize what, in the context of the building of the Salam Centre for Cardiac Surgery in the Sudan, were the fundamental principles that the building appear hospitable, domestic and beautiful, since "The relationship of values to design, to beauty, is not tangential but essential", a concept that the leader of the design team calls "The ethics of beauty" (Pantaleo 2011: 216). In some cases, need and new aesthetic and design concepts have come together, as in the work of the Japanese architect Shigeru Ban who has pioneered light, cheap and easily assembled housing, mosques (in Sri Lanka), churches and concert halls in post-disaster situations utilizing not only wood, but, uniquely, paper tubes. He has recently come to some international fame through his paper-tube temporary cathedral in Christchurch, New Zealand, where the original cathedral was severely damaged by earthquake. As Ban himself has said "Out of conventional structural materials such as steel, concrete and wood, wood is the only material that is renewable" and out of this philosophy of materials he has designed some remarkable buildings including the Centre Pompidou-Metz in France, the Tamedia new office building in Switzerland, a paper-tube church in Takatori, Kobe, to replace the one destroyed in the fires that followed the great Kobe earthquake in 1995, paper-log housing in Kobe and in Turkey, a school utilizing the same techniques in Sichuan, and the Nomadic Museum, initially constructed in New York, moved in 1996 to Santa Monica in California and subsequently to Tokyo (Ban and Keio University SFC Ban Laboratory 2010).

The social power of architecture is this immense as it shapes our surroundings, movements, habitats, emotions and health. Sadly, few architects appear to see themselves as agents of such profound social change, or when they do, have very utopian expectations about the beneficial effects of their buildings on the wider society. But others, as we have seen, have acknowledged the profound social role of the architect, and have accepted responsibility for positive development interventions, not only in the setting of emergencies and disasters, but as a long-lasting contribution to constructive social change and improvement of life and living conditions. In some cases this challenge is grasped directly. In her study of four major architectural projects each designed to contribute to both social change and cultural preservation, Lisa Findley discusses four such projects. These are the Tijabaou Cultural Centre, designed by Renzo Piano in highly distinctive but culturally appropriate form to showcase and preserve the culture of the Kanak people of New Caledonia; the Uluru Kata-Tjuta Cultural Centre at the base of the great red sandstone protuberance known in English as Ayers Rock in central Australia, or as Uluru in Aboriginal languages, designed by Greg Burgess, blending in both with the local ecology and expressing the culture of the local Anangu people; the Museum of Struggle in Port Elizabeth in the Mandela Municipality of South Africa designed by Noero Wolff Architects; and the Southern Poverty Law Center in Montgomery, Alabama, an organization devoted to the litigation of civil rights cases and crimes of hatred, eventually completed by a consortium of Erdy McHenry Architecture and the local Montgomery firm of Goodwyn, Mills and Cawood (Findley 2005). Placing her discussion in the context of the relationship of architecture to power, Findley organizes her book around four themes: building the future, building visibility, building memory and building presence. Each of these themes illustrates the relationship between art, society and development from a different perspective. Development is clearly not just to do with economic growth, but equally with cultural preservation, human dignity, recognition (especially of occluded or excluded minorities), preserving memory (especially of events or times of massive suffering and injustice such as Apartheid in South Africa or the Holocaust), and intervening in society to promote change, reduce injustice and to ensure that rights are not just recognized, but enforced and respected. What Findley shows is the ability of buildings and what they contain to contribute to these goals. Art has power, and architecture is one of the most socially influential of the arts, its effects inescapable and consequently its responsibilities great and its possibilities enormous (Bell 2003).

Design for sustainability

Design and architecture are clearly closely related (as are art and architecture since buildings often incorporate art in the form of murals, sculpture, stained glass, mosaics or other forms, or may be themselves designed to showcase some art form, as with a gallery, museum or theatre). Design however is often left out of discussions of art, or at the best included together with crafts or the 'applied arts' (as distinct presumably from the 'fine' ones). As should be apparent by now, this is a distinction that is ignored in this book for many reasons. Crafts are frequently superior aesthetically and in the skill levels required to create them than much that passes for art, and most of the art work that we are likely to come into contact with in our everyday lives is of course of the 'applied' variety: furniture, appliances, tableware, clothes, carpets, and the endless gadgets with which we surround and entertain ourselves. Hostility to such an unnecessary distinction is not new: it can be found at least as far back as the pioneering work of the nineteenth-century English designer William Morris whose work in many media including tapestry, wall papers, furniture, stained glass, book design and upholstery (and dabbling in socialism) were inspired by a firm belief in the unity of art and craft, the transforming effects of good art on society and the making available to wider classes of society beauty in the form of well-designed everyday objects (Burdick 2006). It has had more recent expression in the work of the highly influential Bauhaus school and movement in inter-war Germany with its strong emphasis on the "total work of art" – the unity of art and craft, and the accessibility of good design to everybody, including, especially, the working classes (Droste 2006). Design, far from being of luxury products for the well-heeled, becomes a potentially significant contribution of the arts to development, especially through the medium of what is now being called 'social design'.

Social design is sometimes also called 'eco-design' because it is clearly linked to sustainability (Reynolds, Blackmore and Smith 2009: 128). The importance of the idea of social/sustainable/ecological design is now recognized in a rapidly growing literature (Walker 2014, Fleming 2013, DeKay 2011, Parr and Zaretsky 2010, Sparke 2012). A slightly earlier generation of development thinkers liked to talk about the idea of 'appropriate technology' suitable for Third World conditions and activities: perhaps the time has now come to talk about 'appropriate design'. Many of these ideas found their first coherent formulation in Cynthia Smith's seminal *Design for the Other 90%* (Smith 2007). The *Social Design Atlas* by Yamazaki Ryo (2012) – unfortunately only available in Japanese – lists over fifty examples drawn from right across most of the world – Africa, Asia, Europe, the United States and Latin America – that range across examples as diverse as ecologically constructed primary school buildings utilizing local materials, straw bale housing, furniture made from wood from destroyed houses after Hurricane Katrina in New Orleans, the use of adobe to construct contemporary buildings, simple solar powered laptops for use in schools in the developing world, mural painting on the walls of *favela* dwellings in Brazil, rainwater harvesting, calm and aesthetically pleasing cancer centres, urban gardening, a 'play pump' through which children playing on the equipment are also pumping up ground water, water rollers (plastic roll-along containers that enable village women in Africa to transport water easily from well and pumps to their dwellings), wheel chairs designed for the rough and uneven road and sidewalk conditions of many cities in the developing world and the now famous 'life straw' – a simple device that is both a straw and a water filter combined, enabling people to safely drink unpurified water without complex procedures of boiling and straining. These concerns have had a profound effect on the world of design itself – moving many designers beyond its "public reputation as the (superficial) aesthetic styling of lifestyles products" to addressing real issues in the under-privileged parts of the world. While part of this is driven by bottom-line thinking on the part of the market, ever alert to new profit-making opportunities, it is also true that "design seems to have taken a shortcut: it works, changes and operates in real life with the apparent aim not of transforming art into life but providing life itself with the potential to change through the objects it creates" (Mazanti 2011: 68–9). Symptomatic of this was the inauguration in 2005 of the biannual world design event called *Index* in Copenhagen, with the title "Design to Improve Life".

Design for sustainability has emerged as an important contribution both to sustainability itself, and to the dialogue between the arts and development. Designing *with* nature, not against it has been expressed in a number of important guiding documents. Even as the Earth Charter has helped crystallize and focus human attitudes to responsible relations with nature, so these documents help to do the same for the relationship between design, ecology and sustainability. They include the Hannover Principles that recognize that human design interacts with and depends on the natural world, the need to create safe objects of long-term value rather than carelessly designed things that will cause burdens of maintenance or disposal in the future, eliminating the concept of waste, relying on natural energy flows and being humble in recognizing the limitations of design (Edwards 2005: 99–101). Many of these ideas, formulated for the Hannover Expo 2000 by William McDonaugh Architects, were embodied in a later book by McDonaugh and Michael Braungart *Cradle to Cradle: Remaking the Way We Make Things* (2002) redefining how products are designed and how they should be integrated into a regenerative cycle. Other important statements or manifestos include Sim Van der Ryn and Stuart Cowen's "Five principles of Ecological Design" (Van der Ryn and Cowen 1995), John and Nancy Jack Todd's "Principles of Ecological Design" (Todd and Todd 1994) involving work with energy, architecture, waste management and food production, and such valuable technological innovations as working to improve the design of local fishermen's vessels through their Ocean Arks International and Living Technologies organizations; the Sanborn Principles stressing ecologically responsive, healthy, socially just, culturally creative and beautiful design for human habitats (Edwards 2005: 106–7) and the LEED (Leadership in Energy and Environmental Design) Green Building Rating System created by the US Green Building Council (Edwards 2005: 109–111). In all cases the underlying principles are the same: that design, to contribute to sustainability, must be ecological in nature and must be directed towards not just lifestyle products for the affluent, but towards addressing real problems that are encountered daily by the majority of the world's population: dirty drinking water, polluting and unhealthy cooking devices, sub-standard dwellings, inadequate water harvesting or transportation systems, bad sanitary conditions, lack of energy sources, poorly made utensils and containers and so on.

The pioneering work of William Morris, the Bauhaus and others have shown that such conditions are not inevitable. Far from it: beautiful design is embodied in craft traditions worldwide and if these are nurtured their products become integrated into everyday life and its beautification. This is not only true of architecture and long lasting artefacts such as pottery and household utensils, but also of, in the context of development, the important field of fashion. Fashion (since most of us wear clothes a lot of the time) is a highly significant aspect of culture, supports many productive and retail enterprises, cooperatives, weavers, designers and sewers, and is a very important part of identity (ethnic and national costumes) and status (class, caste, rank, wealth), self-presentation and identity and relation to modernity and globalization (for a wonderful case study from the Congo, see Friedman 1996). Fashion systems, as they are integrated into other cultural systems of display and consumption, are often not very sustainable at all, but involve frequent discarding or destruction of perfectly wearable items, the purchase of often unnecessary new ones, the constant addition of accessories, jewellery, cosmetics, shoes, bags and other paraphernalia, and the endless consumption of "information", often in the form of expensively printed magazines, to allow one to keep up with the very latest trends. Seen both from a sustainability point of view, and in the light of the non-availability and un-affordability of many such items in much of the developing world, from a social justice point of view, the whole fashion system needs also to be placed in a sustainability framework (Fletcher and Tham 2014), and at the same time seen as a significant art form with many cultural dimensions and embodying local and historical notions of style, beauty and status.

All of the problems listed immediately above can in fact be addressed by good and appropriate design that is culturally sensitive and takes the time to find out what people actually want and need, and this should be the calling of politically and socially sensitive designers as much as of architects. Yet this is still so often not the case. The environmentalist and educator David Orr for example points out that "It is paradoxical that buildings on college and university campuses, places of intellect, characteristically show so little thought, imagination, sense of place, ecological awareness, and relation to any larger pedagogical intent", but have more affinities to shopping malls than to their supposed role in transforming the world through knowledge. They in a sense often work in subliminal ways to contradict the very messages being taught in their laboratories and classrooms (Orr 1994: 112.) If this is true of our educational buildings, including the places where art is taught, then it is no wonder that we have created a very schizophrenic civilization.

All this points us back to the critical questions of the sustainability of our civilizational path, and hence, to culture. The Global Sustainability Alliance has initiated a project called MAHB: the Millennium Assessment of Human Behaviour, to explore how cultures change "which underlines the desperate need for global society to focus its attention on the need for a cultural revolution", a project that "will invite people from literature and the arts to develop narratives and visual materials as signposts to guide civilization towards sustainability" (World Watch Institute 2010: 81 For details of the MAHB initiative see Ehrlich and Ehrlich 2004 and Ehrlich and

Kennedy 2005). These are not simply aesthetic matters, but very much ethical ones as well (Rolston 2012). Others have argued that aesthetics and ethics are actually facets of each other and reflect each other: a lot can be told about the ethics of a society from its art and architecture, and how access to these is distributed across the social spectrum. In the same way, the arts and sustainability go together, and sustaining the beauty of the world, and of the objects that we use to navigate in it, are at the core of any desirable future society.

Key readings

On architecture a good place to begin is with James Wines (2008) *Green Architecture,* Cologne, London and Tokyo: Taschen. On the idea of culturally appropriate emergency architecture, the collected volume edited by Marie J. Aquilino (2011) *Beyond Shelter: Architecture for Crisis,* London: Thames and Hudson, is an excellent starting point and includes many case studies from around the developing world. On culturally appropriate architecture Lisa Findley's *Building Change: Architecture, Politics and Cultural Agency* (London and New York: Routledge, 2005) has both a good theoretical discussion and excellent case studies. Possibly the best sourcebook for the idea of design for sustainability is Cynthia E. Smith's 2007 book *Design for the Other 90%,* New York: Cooper-Hewitt National Design Museum. Amongst the other key sources consult William McDonaugh and Michael Braumgart (2002) *Cradle to Cradle: Remaking the Way We Make Things,* New York: North Point Press. There is now a rapidly expanding literature on "Green" or ecological architecture and design. Good source books that contain large numbers of examples are Alex Sánchez Vidiella (2010) *Atlas of Eco Architecture,* Barcelona: LOFT Publications, and Sergi Costa Duran and Julio Fajardo (2010) *The Sourcebook of Contemporary Green Architecture,* New York: Collins Design.

Specifically on Asia see Nirmal Kishnani (2012) *Greening Asia: Emerging Principles for Sustainable Architecture,* Singapore: BCI Asia.

Resources

If you are interested in architecture and design, there are many online resources that you can consult. The Buckminster Fuller Institute is devoted to design for a sustainable future based on the pioneering ideas of the visionary architect Buckminster Fuller, and can be found at www.bfi.org. One of the leading sustainability design institutes in the world is the Rocky Mountain Institute, originally focused on energy issues, it now works across a whole range of design solutions, and is accessible at www.rmi.org. The International Society for Ecology and Culture which is concerned with the protection of both biological and cultural diversity, and which grew out of the work of the anthropologist Helena Norberg-Hodge and her now classic book *Ancient Futures: Learning from Ladakh* (San Francisco: Sierra Club Books, 2009). Specifically related to architecture are a number of groups. Consult the sites of Architects/Designers/Planners for Social Responsibility at www.adpsr.org,

Builders Without Borders who focus on ecological design at www.builderswith outborders.org, the Ecological Design Collaborative at www.ecodesign.org and Cradle2Cradle, a site managed by the non-profit Earth Care International. A major coordinating body is the World Green Building Council at www.worldgbc.org. For a useful reference site that provides Internet links throughout the world that relate to environmental ethics and philosophy (which includes of course aesthetics) look at the site of the Center for Environmental Philosophy at www.cep.unt.edu/default.html. The appendix to Andres Edwards *The Sustainability Revolution: Portrait of a Paradigm Shift* (Gabriola Island, BC: New Society Publishers, 2010) provides an extensive listing of many other organizations, publications and sites all connected in some way to sustainability. For work of the Architecture for Humanity project go to www.nathanielcorum.com and its Open Architecture Network view http://www.designthatmatters.org/impact/#ourwork; for the project of decorating *favelas* (slum communities) with imaginative murals and wall decorations, see www.favelapainting.com and www.jr-art.net and for design for development go to iDE (International Development Enterprise) at www.ideorg.org/OurTechnologies. Between them these sites cover many of the issues raised in this chapter.

DISCUSSION QUESTIONS

1. The architect James Wines has argued that there can be no sustainability without art. What do you understand by this statement and how might it be applied in practice?
2. What do you understand by the much used term 'sustainability' and how is it related to culture?
3. Take a particular art form (for instance theatre, painting, architecture, fashion) and show how it can contribute to creating and maintaining sustainability.

References

Aquilino, Marie J. (ed.) (2011) *Beyond Shelter: Architecture for Crisis*. London: Thames and Hudson.

Baker, Carolyn (2009) *Sacred Demise: Walking the Spiritual Path of Industrial Civilization's Collapse*. New York and Bloomington: iUniverse.

Ban, Shigeru and Keio University SFC Ban Laboratory (2010) *Voluntary Architects' Network: Making Architecture, Nurturing People: From Rwanda to Haiti*. Tokyo: INAX Publishing.

Bell, Bryan (2003) *Good Deeds, Good Design: Community Service Through Architecture*. Princeton, NJ: Princeton Architectural Press.

Burdick, John (2006) *William Morris: Redesigning the World*. New York: New Line Books.

Callenbach, Ernest (2004) *Ecotopia*. Berkeley: Banyan Tree Books.

Carlson, Allen (2005) "Environmental Aesthetics". In Berys Gaut and Dominic McIver Lopes (eds.) *The Routledge Companion to Aesthetics*. 2nd edition. London and New York: Routledge, pp. 541–555.

Chew, Christopher Chee Wai (1998) *Contemporary Vernacular: Conceptions and Perceptions.* Singapore: AA Asia.

Coaldrake, William H. (1996) *Architecture and Authority in Japan.* London and New York: Routledge.

Crehan, Kate (2011) *Community Art: An Anthropological Perspective.* London and New York: Berg.

Dag Hammarskjöld Institute (1975) *What Now? Another Development.* Uppsala: Dag Hammarskjold Institute.

DeKay, Mark (2011) *Integral Sustainable Design: Transformative Perspectives.* London and New York: Routledge.

Drakakis-Smith, David (2000) *Third World Cities.* 2nd edition. London and New York: Routledge.

Droste, Magdalena (2006) *Bauhaus 1919–1933.* Cologne, London and Tokyo: Taschen.

Duran, Sergi Costa and Julio Fajardo (2010) *The Sourcebook of Contemporary Green Architecture.* New York: Collins Design.

Edwards, Andres R. (2010) *The Sustainability Revolution: Portrait of a Paradigm Shift.* Gabriola Island, BC: New Society Publishers.

Erhlich, Paul R and Anne H. Erhlich (2004) *One With Nineveh: Politics, Consumption and the Human Future.* Washington, DC: Island Press.

Erhlich, Paul R. and Donald Kennedy (2005) "Millennium Assessment of Human Behaviour: A Challenge for Scientists". *Science,* July, 76, 562–63.

Findley, Lisa (2005) *Building Change: Architecture, Politics and Cultural Agency.* London and New York: Routledge.

Fleming, Rob (2013) *Design Education for a Sustainable Future.* New York and London: Routledge.

Fletcher, Kate and Mathilda Tham (eds.) (2014) *Routledge Reader of Sustainability and Fashion.* London and New York: Routledge.

Friedman, Jonathan (1996) "The Political Economy of Elegance". In *Cultural Identity and Global Process.* London and Thousand Oaks, CA: Sage, pp. 147–166.

Gablik, Suzi (2000) *Conversations Before the End of Time.* New York and London: Thames and Hudson.

Gablik, Suzi (2002) *The Reenchantment of Art.* New York and London: Thames and Hudson.

Garrett, Ian (2012) "Theatrical Production's Carbon Footprint". In Wendy Arons and Theresa J. May (eds.) *Readings in Performance and Ecology.* London and New York: Palgrave Macmillan, pp. 201–209.

Gershon, David (2009) *Social Change 2.0: A Blueprint for Reinventing Our World.* West Hurley, NY: High Point/Chelsea Green.

Hartmann, Thom (2004) *The Last Hours of Ancient Sunlight: The Fate of the World and What We Can Do Before It's Too Late.* New York: Three Rivers Press.

Haverkort, Bertus, David Millar and Cosmas Gonese (2003) "Knowledge and Belief Systems in Sub-Saharan Africa". In Bertus Haverkort, Katrien van't Hooft and Wim Hiemstra (eds.) *Ancient Roots, New Shoots: Endogenous Development in Practice.* Leusden, The Netherlands: ETC/Compas and London: Zed Books, pp. 137–152.

Hiss, Tony (1991) *The Experience of Place.* New York: Vintage Books.

Hopkins, Bob (2008) *The Transition Handbook: From Oil Dependency to Local Resilience.* White River Junction, VT: Chelsea Green.

IUCN (1980) *World Conservation Strategy: Living Resources for Sustainable Development.* Gland, Switzerland: International Union for Conservation of Nature.

Kastner, Jeffrey (ed.) (2012) *Nature.* Cambridge, MA: MIT Press.

Kelly, Owen (1984) *Community, Art and the State: Storming the Citadels.* London: Comedia.

Kishnani, Nirmal (2012) *Greening Asia: Emerging Principles for Sustainable Architecture.* Singapore: BCI Asia.

Korten, David C. (1999) *The Post-Corporate World: Life After Capitalism.* West Hartford, CT and New York: Kumarian Press.

Korten, David C. (2006) *The Great Turning: From Empire to Earth Community.* San Francisco: Berrett-Koehler Publishers and New York: Kumarian Press.

Kötke, William H. (1993) *The Final Empire: The Collapse of Civilization and the Seed of the Future.* Portland, OR: Arrow Point Press.

Kovel, Joel (2002) *The Enemy of Nature: The End of Capitalism or the End of the World?* London and New York: Zed Books.

Kusno, Abidin (2000) *Behind the Postcolonial: Architecture, Urban Space and Political Cultures in Indonesia.* London and New York: Routledge.

Lailach, Michael (2007) *Land Art.* Cologne, London and Tokyo: Taschen.

Lefebvre, Henri (1991) *The Production of Space.* Trans. D. Nicholson-Smith. Oxford: Basil Blackwell.

Lerner. Michael (1996) *The Politics of Meaning: Restoring Hope and Possibility in an Age of Cynicism.* New York: Addison-Wesley.

Mazanti, Louise (2011) "Super-Objects: Craft as an Aesthetic Position". In Maria Elena Buszek (ed.) *Extra-Ordinary: Craft and Contemporary Art.* Durham, NC and London: Duke University Press, pp. 59–82.

McDonaugh, William and Michael Braungart (2002) *Cradle to Cradle: Remaking the Way We Make Things.* New York: North Point Press.

Miles, Malcolm (2000) *Art, Space and the City: Public Art and Urban Futures.* London and New York: Routledge.

Orr, David W. (1994) "Architecture as Pedagogy". In his *Earth In Mind: On Education, Environment, and the Human Prospect.* Washington, DC: Island Press, pp. 112–16.

Pantaleo, Raul (2011) "On Beauty, Architecture and Crisis: The Salam Centre for Cardiac Surgery in Sudan". In Marie J. Aquilino (ed.) *Beyond Shelter: Architecture for Crisis.* London: Thames and Hudson, pp. 210–19.

Parkin, Sara (2010) *The Positive Deviant: Sustainability Leadership in a Perverse World.* London and Washington, DC: Earthscan.

Parr, Adrian and Michael Zaretsky (eds.) (2010) *New Directions in Sustainable Design.* London and New York: Routledge.

Rancière, Jacques (2009) *Aesthetics and Its Discontents.* Cambridge: Polity Press.

Reid, David (1996) *Sustainable Development: An Introductory Guide.* London: Earthscan.

Reynolds, Martin, Chris Blackmore and Mark J. Smith (eds.) (2009) *The Environmental Responsibility Reader.* London and New York: Zed Books.

Rolston, Holmes III (2012) *A New Environmental Ethics: The Next Millennium for Life on Earth.* London and New York: Routledge.

Smith, Cynthia E. (2007) *Design for the Other 90%.* New York: Cooper-Hewitt National Design Museum.

Sparke, Penny (2012) *An Introduction to Design and Culture.* 3rd edition. London and New York: Routledge.

Theobald, Robert (1999) *We DO Have Future Choices: Strategies for Fundamentally Changing the 21st Century.* Lismore, NSW: Southern Cross University Press.

Thomas, Martin (1999) *Uncertain Ground: Essays Between Art + Nature.* Sydney: Art Gallery of New South Wales.

Todd, John and Nancy Jack Todd (1994) *From Eco-Cities to Living Machines: Principles of Ecological Design.* New York: North Atlantic Books.

Urry, John (2012) *Societies Beyond Oil: Oil Dregs and Social Futures.* London and New York: Zed Books.

Van de Ryn, Sim and Stuart Cowen (1995) *Ecological Design.* New York: Island Press.

Vidiella, Alex Sánchez (2010) *Atlas of Eco Architecture.* Barcelona: LOFT Publications.

Walker, Stuart (2014) *Designing Sustainability: Making Radical Changes in a Material World.* London and New York: Routledge.

WCED (World Commission on Environment and Development) (1987) *Our Common Future.* Oxford: Oxford University Press.

Wines, James (2008) *Green Architecture.* Cologne, London and Tokyo: Taschen.

World Resources Institute (WRI) (1992) *World Resources 1992–3: A Guide to the Global Environment.* Washington, DC: WRI.

World Watch Institute (2010) *State of the World 2010: Transforming Culture from Consumerism to Sustainability.* London and Washington. DC: Earthscan.

Yamazaki, Ryo (2012) *Social Design Atlas.* Tokyo: Kajima Publishing (in Japanese).

4

PERFORMING DEVELOPMENT

Theatre of the oppressed and beyond

Of all the branches of the arts most engaged with development, it is the performing arts, and amongst them theatre, that leads the way. There are a number of reasons for this: a long history of engagement with political and social issues, the fact that theatre is an almost universal art form with deep roots in many cultures, and theatre's entertaining and effective way of conveying social and developmental ideas and practices to a wide range of audiences. Activist theatre has a long history: in Europe for example it was an expression of the Dada movement (a precursor of Surrealism) amongst German speaking exiles in Zurich during the First World War, and in the politically and socially tumultuous years following that war it took the form of (often satirical and critical) cabaret in Germany (Jelavich 1996) and 'Agitprop' theatre in the streets and factories of revolutionary and immediately post-revolutionary Russia and Weimar-era Germany. Many other expressions have appeared throughout modern history: Verdi's operas subtly protesting against Austrian domination of Italy, the 'revolutionary operas' of Cultural Revolution–period China and the political and socially critical plays of the acclaimed German playwright and director Bertolt Brecht, to name some conspicuous examples. But in relation to what we would now call 'development' (as opposed to general political critique, promoting revolution, or simply satire) it is probably in the work of the Brazilian theatre director and theorist Augusto Boal that the clearest statement of the role of the performing arts is to be found, and particularly in his seminal book *Theatre of the Oppressed* (Boal 2008). It is largely from his work that a whole new vocabulary has emerged – 'applied theatre', activist theatre, social theatre, theatre for social change, and various concepts of the therapeutic possibilities of drama and dance for whole communities as well as individuals. And of course, we must not forget music, a universal 'language' of protest and celebration, and an inherent part of opera, dance and many forms of drama.

In his book, first published in Buenos Aires in 1973 when Boal was in exile from Brazil, then under military dictatorship, a number of important ideas found their first expression, and which were later developed into the notions of the 'aesthetics of the oppressed' and the 'poetics of the oppressed'. These ideas included the perception that the study of theatre is actually the study of human beings and the history of humanity, that through theatre "We are discovering ourselves. Above all: we are discovering that we can change ourselves, and change the world" (Boal 2008: ix). In encouraging (as did his predecessor Brecht) participative forms of theatre in which the audience is not just a passive spectator, but is drawn into the play and its characters, and becomes what Boal calls a "Spect-Actor" thereby democratizing the whole concept of drama for this 'trespass' is actually a responsible act since it is the internalizing of the fiction of the play into a truth, a truth that can only be grasped when the spectator can actively transform the fiction of the play into a social reality by 'invading' the theatrical representation and changing it into a mode of relating to the world:

> This invasion is a symbolic trespass. It symbolizes all the acts of trespass we have to commit in order to free ourselves from what oppresses us. If we do not trespass (not necessarily violently), if we do not go beyond our cultural norms, our state of oppression, the limits imposed upon us, even the law itself (which should be transformed) – if we do not trespass in this we can never be free. To free ourselves is to trespass, and to transform. It is through the creation of the new that that which has not yet existed begins to exist. To free yourself is to trespass. To trespass is to exist. To free ourselves is to exist. To free yourself is to exist.
>
> *(Boal 2008: xxi–xxii)*

By this means of symbolic trespass, fiction (the play) is transformed into a reality: it subverts the normalizing functions of the 'system' in which we live much of our lives unconsciously embedded.

The theatre then is both an agent of and a rehearsal for what Boal calls the "transition" – the movement from our current unjust society and its often puerile and destructive culture to one transformed. The role of theatre is not to reflect or celebrate the status quo, but to show the way beyond it, by, amongst other means, taking theatre into the streets. It is a de-stabilizing medium.

> Brecht contends that the popular artist must abandon the downtown stages and go to the neighbourhoods, because only there will he find people who are truly interested in changing society: in the neighbourhoods he should show his images of social life to the workers who are interested in changing that social life since they are its victims. A theatre that attempts to change the changers of society cannot lead to repose, cannot re-establish equilibrium.
>
> *(Boal 2008: 86–7)*

Art is a form of knowledge, but this knowledge cannot be neutral: it must be activist if it is to have any impact on social reality. If Boal builds on Brecht, Brecht himself built on ideas of other experimental and socially engaged dramatists, and particularly on the work of Erwin Piscator. In his essay *Experimental Theatre* Brecht says of him that

> Piscator saw the theatre as a parliament, the audience as a legislative body. To this parliament were submitted in plastic form all the great public questions that needed an answer. Instead of a deputy speaking about certain intolerable social conditions there was an artistic copy of these conditions. It was the stage's ambition to supply images, statistics, slogans which would enable its parliament, the audience, to reach political decisions. Piscator's stage was not indifferent to applause, but it preferred a discussion. It didn't want only to provide its spectator with an experience but also to squeeze from him a practical decision to intervene actively in life.
>
> *(Brecht 1959 in Bentley 1992: 98)*

Summarizing his discussion of (European and Russian) experimental theatre Brecht concludes with a number of questions very pertinent to the study of the relationship between the performing arts and development.

> How can theatre be both instructive and entertaining? How can it be divorced from spiritual dope traffic and turned from a home of illusions to a home of experience? How can the unfree, ignorant man of our century, with his thirst for freedom and his hunger for knowledge, how can the tortured and heroic, abused and ingenious, changeable and world-changing man of this great and ghastly century obtain his own theatre which will help him to master the world and himself?
>
> *(ibid.: 104)*

These are the (still totally relevant) questions that we will now try to answer.

It is out of this fertile soil that a whole group of movements, largely united in basic practice even if going by different names: theatre of the oppressed, social theatre, applied theatre, theatre for development, and no doubt yet other labels, have emerged. Such forms of theatre have been utilized not only in development contexts, but in prisons, as forms of the community arts discussed in the previous chapter, as 'theatre of faith' – i.e. religious theatre, and as an extension of educational drama in schools and drama therapy (for an overview of all these forms see Landy and Montgomery 2012). Underlying all these varieties is a strong belief in the transformative power of performance. This has long been visible in religion and in ritual studies and amongst anthropologists such as Victor Turner who have devoted much of their work to studying these processes and the interfaces between ritual and theatre (Turner 1982), and the study of performance (including dance, sport, trance, ceremonies secular and religious) has now burgeoned into an extensive field of study in its own right (Schechner 2013). And it is important to remember that the idea of transformation is the key. The rather ugly term 'applied theatre' implies drama as a rather mechanical process, as a kind of (socially positive) advertising. But as Landy and Montgomery point out at the very beginning of their book ". . . art, and perhaps most of all the drama, is essentially anarchic and volatile. In the unpredictable medium of theatre it is not always possible to anticipate the directions in which any desired change may occur" (Landy and Montgomery 2012: ix). Throughout our discussion of theatre for development, this should be kept firmly in mind: the intentions of a writer or director may not be mirrored in the reception of an audience, since all perceptions will be passed through filters of culture, ideology, class, age and gender. But recognizing this fact in reality gives us a firmer basis for discussing performance and development, recognizing that both are uncertain, ad hoc and fluid processes.

Transformative performance

Development itself is in a sense 'performance' – the carrying out of certain actions conventionally included under that label. These actions – applying a new kind of fertilizer, supplying a certain kind of aid or technical advice, moving into industrial wage-labour from a previously nomadic or agricultural background, and so on – constitute actions, and actions of a recognizable type: those that will be listed and discussed in any standard textbook of 'development'. But then two questions arise – how to bring about such new performative actions on the part of the subjects of a putative development process (they may after all resist or ignore the invitation to act in a new way), and whether actions that we normally regard as constituting the field of culture 'count' as development-related actions. In the context of this chapter we will suggest that theatre for development is important in both respects: in the former as a culturally appropriate and entertaining vehicle for conveying social messages, and in the latter as the preservation, deepening and extension of the local cultural repertoire itself. In other words, theatre can make life richer, and that richness is the key part of what we should regard as legitimate or holistic development. Performance itself (here understood as drama, dance and music) both elucidates – it assists in the perception and understanding of life circumstances – and potentially transforms – by suggesting new courses of action to change those life circumstances. It may do this in many ways – through education, through the revelation of structures of oppression (caste, class, gender) that are largely un-thought aspects of the daily 'reality' of the subjects' lives, through satire and humour, through quite openly suggesting courses of social action leading to higher levels of social justice or ecological responsibility, or, as much good fiction does, encouraging visions of a better world. Or as Bertolt Brecht rightly put it: "Change the world: it needs it" (Brecht 1977: 1).

A major role of the arts is to promote such changes of perspective. Many people would probably agree that in relation to promoting social change, it is drama that is the most effective of the arts in that it has an immediacy and an engagement with its audience that the visual arts for example rarely have. It potentially engages the emotions in ways that no other art form can, and it actually represents these emotions, roles and conflicts, in front of or with the participation of, the live audience, and so the barriers between the real and the make-believe are dissolved. It is for this reason that drama has proved useful (although sensitive and potentially even explosive) in conflict resolution, where role playing, seeing the situation from the perspective of the other and finding ways to manage emotions of anger, hurt and resentment, can be literally acted out, and as such, if not fully resolved, at least experienced by the participants (Landy and Montgomery 2012: 32–6). The same can be true of role playing drama (and the actual writing of plays by participants in applied theatre workshops) addressing many other issues than conflict, including the disabled, the elderly, migrants, refugees, school truants, the homeless, shut-ins (not all of them elderly), prostitutes, petty criminals and other socially or culturally excluded or marginal groups. When presented *as* plays (rather than as experimenting with roles in a workshop setting), they collectively constitute what Brecht called *Lehrstucke* or "learning plays", often intended for audiences of children, and designed precisely to educate, raise awareness and inspire to action.

These principles can be seen most closely at work if we look at some actual case studies of theatre in relation to development.

a.   *El Teatro Campesino.* Latin America has long had a vibrant theatrical tradition. A city like Buenos Aires for example abounds in small theatres and the playwrights who constantly produce new work to fill them. But it is also a continent that has experienced huge social inequalities, oppressive political regimes, and the migration of large numbers of its citizens to North America. These latter, although many have successfully integrated, often remain marginalized as illegal and exploited workers, seasonal farm labourers, domestics and other low-income, low-respect jobs. El Teatro Campesino and its director Luiz Valdez, during the 1960–80s, initiated forms of social and political theatre that had several functions: to highlight the situation and injustices of the Chicano (Mexican-American) community in the US, to represent through drama what was and is a large but often theatrically 'invisible' community, and to create a forum through which the work of Hispanic playwrights could be produced and presented. El Teatro Campesino in turn inspired such major Hispanic playwrights and theatre scholars as Jose Cruz Gonzalez, Cecilia Aragon, Nilo Cruz and many others, the creation of Chicano youth theatres and the inclusion in their repertoires of plays by Hispanic playwrights and about Hispanic issues in an increasing number of 'mainstream' US-based theatre companies. Development of course is not only about the 'Third World', it is also about the situation of 'Third World' communities embedded in the societies and economies of the 'First' world – in the US, in Western Europe, in Japan, Hong Kong, Singapore and other 'developed' situations. Migrant workers, the displaced, refugees, asylum seekers, are now a significant part of the population of the over-developed world, and are often essential to its functioning as a cheap, non-unionized and usually compliant labour force. Bringing the stories of such people to light is an important part of drama (including film) and of the work of art critics, such as John Berger, known not only for his work on the visual arts (on both TV and in books), but also as a novelist of peasant society in Europe, and as an essayist and co-author of an important study of migrant workers (Berger and Mohr 1975). El Teatro Campesino is an important model for high quality theatre (not just didactic educational plays) that throws light on these topics (for more information see Landy and Montgomery 2012: 96–98, and El Teatro Campesino 2010).

b. *Theatre for Life*. Theatre for Life is one of the many theatre companies that have emerged in South Africa since the collapse of the violent and oppressive apartheid regime. South Africa since its 'liberation', not from external colonialism, but from the extraordinary internal colonialism and racism of its former white-controlled regime, has developed a vibrant arts scene, in both the visual arts and in drama, and a city like Cape Town now abounds in galleries and museums. But at the same time, poverty is widespread, large numbers of black South Africans still live in shanty towns and slums, levels of crime and violence are high, corruption is rife amongst the political class and access to good educational and health services for much of the population are highly restricted. It is not surprising that in this situation, all the more tragic given the post-apartheid euphoria of the new regime under the inaugural presidency of the late-lamented Nelson Mandela, that while much work in the visual arts and textiles rightly celebrates the rich and diverse African cultural heritage, a great deal of work in theatre addresses the questions of inequality, poverty and violence that are part of everyday experience, especially in the townships or slum settlements. Amongst these is Theatre for Life which bills itself as 'applied theatre', addressing mainly young people both to express their experiences and to help them and others analyse and manage these experiences and to work towards reconciliation in what was a deeply divided society (arepp:Theatre for Life 2011). Other similar work such as that of the anthropologist and drama facilitator Efua Prah involves working with township children to develop their own plays and then to present them to audiences, encapsulating their own daily experience of violence and insecurity. Other major initiatives have occurred in Kenya, Ghana, Uganda, in Rwanda in the aftermath of the genocide there, in Senegal and elsewhere. A very good and well documented example of this is the work of the Kenyan scholar and theatre for development promoter Christopher Odhiambo Joseph, who has drawn on both Western mentors such as Boal and Paulo Freire and on local post-colonial theorists such as the novelist and critic Ngugi wa Thiong'o and Opiyo Mumma, and has directed the attention of theatre for development not only to the classical problems of underdevelopment, but also to the newly emerged ones, and in particular the epidemic of HIV/AIDS that afflicts much of Africa (Odhiambo 2008, Byam 1999).

c. *Jana Sanskriti* and *Kala Jatha*. India has a very rich theatrical tradition, much of it expressive of or intimately linked to the various religious traditions, and in particular the myths, stories and deities of Hinduism. Jana Sanskriti is a northern Indian theatre group that has organized its praxis around Boal's *Theatre of the Oppressed* work, and translated it into an Indian idiom, which it brings to rural communities as an educational, consciousness raising and entertaining tool of development (Ganguly 2010). Much of the Indian theatrical tradition is rooted in folk drama, often toured around the villages by itinerant companies and linked to the cycles of religious celebrations. While these draw mostly on Hindu folk tales, it has also been found that they can be utilized to very effectively convey social and development messages. India is an extraordinarily diverse society, with many languages, castes, tribal communities, and with an equally large variety of folk theatre reflecting this diversity. Jacob Srampickal in his book *Voice to the Voiceless: The Power of People's Theatre in India* identifies more that seventy such forms, and there are no doubt many others (Srampickal 1994). Julia Hollander for example in her study of Indian folk theatres (Hollander 2008) includes such examples as *Loknatya Tamasha* or 'people's theatre', a form of performance principally found in the state of Maharashtra and which is traditionally vulgar and risqué, which has been adapted and utilized to educate villagers, promote family planning, gender equality and rural health schemes, to criticize untouchability, and to encourage the use of new agricultural technologies and procedures under the prodding of central government (Hollander 2008: 87, 120) in ways that are both stylistically familiar to villagers, and reach audiences without electricity or television and are so untouched by the messages reaching other sectors of the poor through the mass media.

Most of these forms of folk theatre are street shows, or are held in the open air on temporarily erected stages, and combine both entertainment and education. In the Kala Jatha form, traditional folk theatre is used to promote gender equality. In discussing attempts to do this, Joy Deshmukh-Ranadive explains that

> The intervention is an attempt to involve entire households in villages, in witnessing plays that question traditional socio-cultural norms within the family. Folk theatre groups perform plays that are scripted around these questions. Social conditioning and social norms are depicted by a character, which instigates people into behaving in a non-equitous manner. Another character, depicting human rights, confronts the former through members of the household.
>
> *(Deshmukh-Ranadive 2003: 1674)*

The goal here is empowerment through the revelation of traditional roles and the possibility of changing them in more equitable ways. The plots are based on domestic situations that the audience would easily recognize and empathize with (for example gendered division of labour within the household, conflicts over the wife attending literacy classes and as a result 'neglecting' her domestic duties and relationships between mothers-in-law and daughters-in-law), and in each case question accepted social norms, roles and values. There is plenty of evidence to suggest that these dramas do indeed promote questioning, behavioural modification and restructuring of roles, and as a result have both domestic and larger political and sociological consequences. In the case of Kala Jatha, not only are the plays performed, but then discussions are held between the actors and the audiences to elicit comments, debate and suggestions for action. The format then combines the elements of drama and education in a way that most certainly encourages consciousness-raising about gender issues in often remote Indian villages with high levels of illiteracy and little access to formal education or the mass media.

In India these and similar issues have long been part of popular theatre. The wrenching experiences of colonization, independence and decolonization, industrialization, urbanization, and struggles over caste and religion, have been a large part of the Indian scene for generations, even centuries, and have often found their expression in popular drama. Examples of this can be found in the south-western state of Kerala, a state with the highest literacy levels in India, governed by a succession of Communist governments, with a large Christian population (unique in India), and with a past history of a highly oppressive caste system and associated landlordism and of struggles to overcome it. Many of these issues were encapsulated in the highly popular play *Rent Arrears* written in 1937, banned at one time by the colonial government, and dealing with struggles for land reform, poverty and resulting starvation and prostitution. The plays of the prominent Kerala playwright Toppil Bhasi, including his play about landlordism and the struggle of agricultural labourers and poor peasants, in conjunction with a widespread progressive literary movement, are now credited with transforming local consciousness in ways that spilled over into the subsequent transformation of Kerala politics and society, and beyond the state borders as they were translated and performed in Tamil and other languages. Part of the effect of the plays was derived from their use of songs and music, which linked these overtly political plays seamlessly with popular local music dramas in South India (Zarrilli 1996, 2000).

d.   *Philippine Educational Theatre Association (PETA).* PETA was founded in 1967 as a way of bringing culturally and socially appropriate alternative theatre to facilitate social change and works with rural and urban audiences, usually of the poor, other acting groups, children and teachers. It is based on an interactive and dialectical methodology through which it constantly revises its own productions and approaches in response to dialogue with its audiences. Uniquely amongst major theatre for development groups, the actors are themselves children, including street children, child labourers in plantations and homeless and abused children. While presenting their stories to others (where possible in schools, to local government bureaucrats, landowners and parents), the acting also provides a kind of therapy and security for the child-actors themselves, and a strong sense of community and belonging as they identify with PETA. The plays concern such issues as poverty, health and lack of access to affordable health care, labour conditions, lack of schooling, hunger and the deprivation of play. The Philippines is a classic case of uneven development: extensive urban and rural poverty coexisting with pockets of the rich, an oligarchic and semi-feudal rural social structure and political system, high levels of corruption, an identity problem resulting from its former status as a semi-colony first of Spain and then of the US and an economy based on export of low-value-added agricultural products, and its own people – as construction workers in the Gulf and Middle East, as entertainers and embassy servants and drivers and as domestic maids in places like Singapore and Hong Kong. Social problems are as a result wide and deep, but two of the cultural resources that have helped people deal with these are religion (in the form principally of Roman Catholicism in most of the country, and Islam in parts of the south) and an extensive NGO culture, including theatre. In a society where music and performance are popular, there is a strong convergence between popular culture and theatre, and PETA, amongst other groups, has been able to tap into this cultural energy to effectively address social issues, and to provide a profession and security to its small actors.

These examples show something of the range and types of theatre for development. There are of course issues: not all such theatre is straightforward. There are questions of ethics: who are the performances for? Is it legitimate for outsiders, however well intentioned, to show up and effectively criticize the social organization and practices of some other group or community? When the theatre troupe has moved on, what are the consequences for the villagers left behind who have to wrestle with the issues raised or portrayed during the performances? There are aesthetic issues too: is the work of applied theatre of the standard of mainstream theatre, or are people being presented with low quality performances that are thought to be appropriate to their artistic and social 'level' (and who decides what that level is?). In her study of Indian folk theatre, Julia Hollander found that some theatre people were very critical of attempts to adapt traditional forms to the illumination of social issues, feeling that the integrity of the original artistic styles and content were thereby compromised and watered down, and the bawdy and risqué elements removed, leaving a bowdlerized and inauthentic (and politically manipulated) shell of the original behind (Hollander 2008: 175). These are questions that will have to be addressed by people working with this medium, since they point to deeper connections between performance and development that we will now go on to explore.

Performance, culture and development

As an interesting and effective intervention in development, and in the delivery of development 'goods', we can certainly argue that theatre is an excellent tool; and as a contribution to sustaining and preserving local cultures it is a vital element in sustainability and maintaining cultural diversity. But it can be more than this: in fact an effective way into exploring deeper issues of the relationship between culture and development in general. A generation ago Johan Huizinga convincingly documented in his now classic book *Homo Ludens* (Huizinga 1970) that play, far from being simply something that children engage in, is a fundamental part of culture. Art, and especially its performative forms, can be seen as adult play, or as 'deep play' – a form of expressive behaviour necessary for healthy human functioning (see also Turner 1982 for a more anthropological approach). It is also a form of communication, and an important way in which identity, individual and collective, is formed: we recognize cultures by their characteristic forms of dance, theatre and sport. For this reason they are an important element in intercultural communication: a means of bridging cultures through performance.

But this subject – sometimes called 'interculturalism' in theatre studies, is also a fraught one, for it raises the spectre of cultural imperialism – notably borrowing (or stealing) elements from the indigenous performative repertoire of one culture (dances, rituals, ceremonies, theatrical practices) and incorporating them (often without acknowledgement) into the performances of another (usually Western) one. While quite rightly substantial debate has swirled around the question of the legitimacy of theatrical interculturalism, it must also be acknowledged that, when handled sensitively and in full awareness of the dangers of illegitimate cultural appropriation, theatre can be a powerful tool for addressing a whole range of intercultural issues, including migration and diasporas, human rights, environment, gender and many other issues (for an overview of the main issues and literature in theatre and interculturalism see Knowles 2010). In these contexts, theatre can take many forms, including a means of establishing cultural exchange and greeting rituals between locals and outsiders, as with the Maori *marae* or meeting house, which is a place of convocation, greeting, peace-making and theatre, all rolled into one (Balme 1996), in which what the scholar of Maori culture Eric Schwimmer has called "semiospheres" are negotiated, and where the boundaries between ritual, politics, religion and theatre are eroded and where different meaning-systems are brought into dialogue with one another and new subjectivities formed (Schwimmer 2004).

Theatre across cultures has of course meant extensive borrowing and adaptation – Shakespeare in India for example, or Brecht in China, Africa and Japan. In a globalized world this is hardly surprising and oddly the issue of globalization is one that intercultural theatre theorists have not much addressed. This is especially strange in that studies of popular cultures – for example of Japanese popular culture – have shown clearly how it spreads and is assimilated into other cultures and not only adjacent ones (China, Taiwan, Hong Kong and Southeast Asia), but worldwide (e.g. Iwabuchi 2002, Iwabuchi, Muecke and Thomas 2004). Globalization has brought with it numerous problems, including new diasporas and major environmental problems as pollution and resource destruction are 'exported' across national boundaries. Theatre has been able to address many of these problems. An excellent example would be the play *Wild Man* by the Nobel Prize–winning Chinese writer Gao Xingjian, an appropriation of Brecht using a large cast of actors, singers and musicians to address the ecological consequences of industrialization. Similarly, theatre has been used as an important part of the process of decolonizing of cultures: in addressing and redressing the impact of (mostly Western) colonialism and its injustices, economic exploitation, cultural, religious and linguistic suppression, racism, sexism and the erosion of indigenous identities, value systems, kinship systems and political practices. Theatre then becomes a significant part of the postcolonial project, even as imperialism itself was a deeply cultural as well as economic and political project (Said 1993). For "decolonizing the mind", to use the Kenyan novelist Ngugi wa Thiong'o's celebrated phrase (Thiong'o 1986), is the first step towards cultural freedom. New models of intercultural performance are possible that specifically address the issues that have arisen both from the colonial experience and from the forms of what are effectively neo-colonialism carried by globalization. A number of major theatre scholars have addressed these issues, amongst them Christopher Balme in his *Decolonizing the Stage* (Balme 1999) and Rustom Bharucha in the second part of his *Theatre and the World* (Bharucha 1993). These works are important because they bring together the aesthetic and the political. Bharucha provides many examples of what he calls not *inter*-culturalism, but rather *intra*-culturalism within India, where the many diverse and linguistically distinct cultures interact with each other, contradicting the notion of 'India' as a mono-culture and de-stabilizing the ideas coming from the centre of a common identity and an essentialized notion of the 'nation' equated with the state. Balme's range of examples is even more extensive, and he draws on a wide range of indigenous performances (although mostly in English and many of them drawing on scripts and ideas of theatre from the Western world) from Africa, India, the Caribbean, New Zealand, Australia and North America including such instances as Yoruba travelling theatre in Nigeria and South Indian *kathakali* dance-drama. These examples not only show the vitality and range of indigenous theatre in formerly colonized societies, but which by adapting, subverting and questioning many of the commonly accepted forms of Western theatre aesthetics, quite literally 'decolonize' the stage.

Such examples of these (and others such as Julie Holledge and Joanne Tompkins' important *Women's Intercultural Performance* [2000] which foregrounds gender) point up a number of significant aspects of intercultural theatre as it pertains to development. These include the political possibilities of theatre, its role in not simply the critique of colonialism and neo-colonialism, but in more subtle ways exploring the issues of post-colonial identity and subjectivities, the body (and its frequent exploitation or abuse in new conditions of globalized labour and migration), negotiations of meaning between cultures now increasingly brought into contact with one another, the possibilities and practice of artistic South-South cooperation, and new forms of (non-imperialistic) representations that do not simply reverse Orientalism, but transcend it through the invention of new codes, images and modes of intercultural conversations. Interculturalism is a two-way process, and has long been so, and many forms of 'traditional' drama and dance actually have their roots in earlier situations of culture contact and borrowing. The "invention of tradition" to use Eric Hobsbawn's celebrated phrase (Hobsbawn and Ranger 1992) is as apparent in the theatre, including its putative indigenous expressions, as it is in other spheres of social and cultural life (Lo and Gilbert 2002).

Performance then has been shown to have many potentialities in addressing not only 'development' in a narrow sense, but also the context in which development takes place (notably globalization, and the forms of neo-colonialism, cultural and otherwise, that it promotes), and many of the issues that are highly important, but which often do not appear in a conventional development studies textbook. These latter include issues which have been the subject of indigenous and intercultural theatre such as diasporas and diasporic identities and all that they entail – separation from the homeland; encapsulation within alien societies and cultures; a sense of exile; developing new methods of coping with extended sojourns abroad, often under less than desirable conditions of employment and pay (Yan 2005); new forms of cosmopolitan identity that are emerging as a consequence of or response to globalization (Gilbert and Lo 2007) and with them new identities, subjectivities, linguistic competences (or lack of competence); and the experience of living in large urban settlements, themselves multi-racial, multi-cultural and both the subject of and generators of, forms of globalization. Ric Knowles, in his book on intercultural theatre for example discusses the large range of intercultural theatre that exists in the single city in which he lives – Toronto in Canada – which he describes as "the intersection of hundreds of diasporas" (Knowles 2010: 61). Toronto can boast one theatre company focused on the Filipino diasporic community and experience (the Filipino Carlos Bulosan Theatre), others such as the AfriCan Theatre Ensemble, Theatre Archipelago and Rasik Arts concerned respectively with the African, Caribbean and Indian experiences and situation, and yet others representing the Native Canadian, Latino, 'Asian Canadian' and women of colour communities (the latter being represented by the feminist Nightwood Theatre company) (Knowles 2010: 62–39) and which collectively utilize such theatrical tactics "as strategic reappropriation, diasporic transnationalism or transindigeneity and urban interculturalism in their work" (Knowles 2010: 63, Knowles 2009).

Significant here too have been debates about the relationships between theatre and human rights. Theatre has proved to be a very effective tool in drawing attention to rights abuses and to representing and giving voice to the victims of social and political violence in situations as diverse as South Africa, Cambodia, Rwanda; to torture victims and as a quite literally dramatic way of staging mock tribunals relating to war crimes, abuses of power, failure of the police to take action in the case of racially motivated crimes and similar examples encouraging the formal judicial process to act responsibly and justly. As with intercultural theatre, there are of course problems: of how effective theatre can be in documenting and highlighting such cases, of whose voices it represents, of how an idea both as important and as fuzzy and contested as human rights (let alone animal rights) can be represented fairly in a staged setting (for a good overview see Rae 2009). Nevertheless, activist theatre has huge potential in drawing attention to another of the factors that accompanies and often undermines development processes – not the expansion of human rights (although sometimes this does happen), but sadly, their continuing abuse, and abuse often triggered by the very nature of 'development' itself – forced displacement, loss of land, very bad working and safety conditions (as in the Bangladeshi textile factories much exploited by Western clothing chain stores, on plantations supplying affluent Western coffee shops or amongst migrant labourers from India and the Philippines in the Gulf). A Human Rights group as prominent as the internationally respected Amnesty International has institutionalized this by creating its Freedom of Expression award as a competition amongst theatre groups for plays addressing human rights issues.

In many cases, given the complexity of the issues involved (rights, war, genocide, racism, all combined into a single situation), theatrical responses have also developed multimedia approaches acknowledging that no single story can possibly represent the horror and tragedy of situations where massive rights abuses occur. An example is the Belgian-Rwandan collaboration *Rwanda 94* by the Groupov troupe, which combined theatre, documentary footage, eye-witness reports, songs, music and statistics into a six-hour presentation. Other plays have dealt with discrimination, state violence, political oppression, truth and reconciliation tribunals and war crimes (for examples see Rae 2009: 20). These theatrical experiments have in turn given rise to explorations in methodology, such as the 'tactical handbook' of the Bangladeshi activist Motahar Akand, which outlines not only the steps through which a local situation might be analysed and turned into a drama, but also the very much neglected issue of follow-up: what is to be done when the performance is over and the theatre troupe has departed? He recommends not only the research and performance, but also an extended process of helping the target community to find means of resolving the issues that are confronting them, taking steps to avoid their recurrence, and ideally establishing a long-term base in or with the community to ensure that sustainable development and local rights regimes will continue (Akand 2007). Theatre can be particularly effective in preserving and promoting the *cultural* rights of indigenous peoples by allowing a form of expression that is not only dramatic, but is not so easily commodified or co-opted as can be the case with the visual arts, that can be so readily assimilated into the 'art world' and its market-based values. Theatre is almost always communal (except in the case of one-person performances or monologues, but even they require technical support, lighting and so forth) – it requires a troupe of actors, people to direct, write, design and paint scenery, sew costumes and of course an audience. It is inherently a communicative medium, again in ways in which the visual arts are not necessarily so effective.

It is here that the elusive quality of creativity enters the picture. The arts of all stripes rarely succeed in changing anything by being didactic, as the 'Socialist Realism' of the former Soviet Union, China and other state Communist societies so clearly demonstrated. Their ability to effect change often lies in more subtle directions: in influencing the emotions, creating new images, in making one think or see differently. In relation to the question of theatre and human rights, Paul Rae summarized this point very effectively:

> For its part, de-linking theatre from the assumption that it must either promote or reactively 'problematise' human rights frees it up to pursue a parallel enquiry whose outcomes may be productively at odds with some of the basic assumptions behind the modern idea of human rights. The status of the body; the nature of subjectivity and intersubjectivity; the relationship between the individual and the state; the psychologically complex and sometimes self-destructive dynamics of suffering, oppression, need and desire; cultural memory, especially as an embodied practice; human relationships, especially as they emerge through dialogue and social participation; our continuing dependency on the non-human world; that crazy little thing called love – these are some of the central problems of the human condition that theatrical processes and

performances of all kinds tussle with. 'Human rights' offers one noble and rather ingenious response: the strength of the theatre lies in the opportunities it affords to interrogate the basic conditions within which those rights must be anchored and, where they do not, to envision alternatives.

(Rae 2009: 40–1)

The many examples of activist theatre that exist and which constantly come into existence as situations of rights, regimes, development, gender relations, abuse and hope change and emerge, show the continuing vitality of theatre as an art form that very directly addresses these key existential issues and the social contexts in which they are situated. It is not likely to fade away.

If interculturalism and human rights provide us with two exemplary interfaces between theatre and development, another one of increasing importance is the relationship between theatre and the environment, and the question of in what ways performance can address and illuminate the ever-growing ecological crisis that now besets us. Nature itself has of course always been both the subject of art and its inspiration. The difference today is that nature itself is threatened, and with it human life and civilization which is dependent on it. This recognition of ecological crisis has led many artists and theatre people to begin to specifically address the environment, and to foreground issues of pollution, loss of biodiversity, diminishing resources and the destruction of natural beauty in the name of 'development'. In the theatre this concern has been expressed in a number of forms, including the legitimacy of using animals in performance, anti-nuclear dramas, 'ecoactivist performance' as a form of environmental protest movement, 'greening' canonical or traditional plays by producing and directing them in ways that draw attention to ecological themes, devising educational dramas that highlight environmental problems, and concern with the carbon footprint of theatrical production (its use not only of energy, but also of non-reusable sets and costumes, often made with or painted with toxic materials) (Arons and May 2012). Both directors and theatre scholars have increasingly recognized the environment as a key element in responsible contemporary performance, as a growing literature attests (see for example Chaudhuri 1994, Giannachi and Stewart 2005) and which is closely aligned with the emerging field of ecocriticism in literature and the arts generally (Love 2003).

It follows from these initiatives that theatre has an ethical as well as educational dimension: not only to be responsible in its own practices, but also to address the most pressing contemporary issues, which now absolutely must include the ecological. This may be done by playwrights and directors deliberately devising plays that address environmental issues, or may be a spontaneous response by communities to natural disasters or other forms of ecological catastrophe. An example of the former is the play *Green Piece*: a collaborative effort emerging from a workshop on theatre and ecology, strongly intercultural utilizing elements from West African dance, Australian Aboriginal 'dream time' conceptions of creation, an Iroquois myth and the story of the Bishnoi people of Rajasthan who were martyred for their attempt to protect their native forests, and designed to use recycled materials for sets and props. The play itself was contextualized in a learning situation involving discussions, lectures, fieldtrips and research, and was basically the final outcome and expression of those activities (D'Zmura 2012). An example of the latter is found in the performative responses to the 1997 volcanic eruption that destroyed two thirds of the Caribbean island of Montserrat, where local dance and drama became an important way to come to terms with the disaster and to begin to rebuild a sense of community amongst the survivors, including, very significantly, the preservation of cultural memory (Gough 2012).

Theatre, used in these ways, can become a form of environmental activism in its own right, may embody and illustrate sustainability, question normative values and suggest alternatives, and provide new themes for playwrights, actors and directors. These possibilities can be seen not only in theatre, but also in its close cousin film, as signalled by the success of the blockbuster movie *Avatar* with its interlocking themes of ecological preservation, the integrity of native peoples, and the hubris and violence of ever-expanding technological civilization – in this case one now engaged in the colonization of other planets, having successfully pillaged and ruined the Earth. In practice, the issues of human (and animal) rights, interculturalism, and the many other themes that activist theatre has addressed are of one piece. The problems, mostly induced by humans themselves, are of a holistic nature, and as such can only be fully grasped by an equally holistic methodology. While this certainly requires intellectual tools, it also very much requires imaginative ones: one that can reveal the shortcomings of the 'old story' and suggest the elements of a new one, including new myths and symbols with which to grasp and understand the emerging world. This it can be argued is the essential role of the arts, theatre and other forms of performance amongst them.

Bertolt Brecht, whose name we have invoked a number of times in these pages, was convinced that the theatre must be political. In one sense it always is: to question values or to suggest or critique forms of behaviour is itself a political act, and one that theatre has long been engaged in. Expression is always 'political' in the widest sense of that term. Theatre is consequently connected with development through many links: even as development is always political so is performance. As we have seen this can take many forms: theatre as a form of community art, for, by or with local societies and cultures; it can heighten awareness of inequalities, gender issues, health problems and forms of violence, and can illuminate in ways that perhaps no other art form can, the basic and universal existential issues of human existence. It furthermore has an active and participatory character: even as many aspects of our identity such as gender are constituted through performance, so 'development' is also constituted through performance, in which case alternative forms of performance become a vital way of creating and establishing other realities and other possibilities. The future in other words is not determined: it must be brought into existence, it must be 'performed'. Theatre can contest power, censorship, accepted modes of bodily presentation, given identities, and language itself. Cultures to a great extent express themselves through performance: through rituals, dance, ceremonies, and theatre itself. Theatre, as we have seen, has been a major part of the critique of the cultural politics of colonialism, and the creation of post-colonial cultures and the huge complexities that such a project entails (including rethinking 'tradition', and searching for new forms of cultural integrity in situations where cultural memory itself and the languages in which it is embodied, may have been distorted, colonized or even invented by the colonial power).

All of these issues are implicated in contemporary development and globalization. This is true in two ways in specific relation to theatre. The first of these is instrumental: theatre as a tool of education, of political critique, of consciousness raising. But the second directly addresses the much discussed question of whether cultural practices can initiate social change (for example Reinelt 1996). The argument here is that indeed they can for several reasons. These include the fact that art movements are also social movements: cultural change is itself a profound form of social change that deeply modifies our patterns of entertainment and leisure, our subjectivities, our modes of communication, our fashions and forms of everyday behaviour and our emotions. Cultural change *is* social change, and it is only our fixation on the economic, the technological and existing political institutions as largely constituting 'society' that prevents us from seeing this. Cultural politics' is just that – *politics* – and no discussions of culture can ever exclude questions of ideology, power and hegemony (Goodman and de Gay 2000). The challenge is to apply these insights from theatre, theatre studies and performance studies and cultural studies, specifically to development. Much of the debate in cultural studies has gone on in the context of the rich industrialized countries, including, rather paradoxically, much of the writing in post-colonial studies, a field that seems to have become something of a sub-speciality in the English departments of many Western universities. In this chapter we have suggested some of the ways in which this might be done, and specifically how theatre in its 'applied' forms plays an important role, not only in a purely didactic way, but also through the more subtle mechanisms of raising awareness, changing perception, modifying emotions and presenting potentially transformative alternatives. Theatre, because it involves real people actually acting out roles and telling a story, impacts the consciousness in ways that no other art form except possibly film can do. Its transformative and alternative posing potentialities are consequently huge, and with that potential also comes responsibility: to identify and present key contemporary issues, to do so in ethical and sensitive ways and to not only present democracy, but to be democracy – a medium with unique potential to be collaborative, participatory and engaging.

It is also of course the case that forms of performance – dance and ritual as well as theatre – are part of other fundamental cultural expressions. Dance is a form of performance almost universal and deeply tied in with cultural identity. There is now an interesting literature emerging that relates dance to the question of cultural identity – for example in Senegal, where dance is a major form of cultural expression, performed by both professionals and amateurs on almost any occasion (Kringelbach 2013) – and to issues of human rights, racism, slavery and refugees (Jackson and Shapiro-Phim 2008). Dance, seemingly the least political of all the performing arts because it does not require spoken language, in fact historically has been deeply tied to politics, national identity, conceptions of ethics, concepts of the body, notions of freedom and many other issues that tie it closely to politics, both conventional and cultural, in both developed and developing countries, and this is even the case with forms of dance such as ballet, which are seemingly far from any concern with protest or representing cultural alternatives (for examples of which see Homans 2010, Nicholas 2007).

Celebration, life-cycle events, trance, exorcism, rites of passage, healing, religious services, play, political rallies, sporting events and legal proceedings are all accompanied by or are themselves performances (Schechner 2013). So too are the large-scale expressive events known as Carnivals, especially those associated with Brazil (DaMatta 2005), Trinidad (Aching 2002, TDR Fall 1998), and the West Indian communities of London, in the famous Notting Hill Carnival, in which display, gender and class inversion, play, music and the temporary abandonment of abstract values are publically manifested. Performance is an important element in what Kevin Hetherington calls "expressive organization" and its accompanying creation of emotional communities (Hetherington 1998: 83–100) and in so doing points to its role in social movement formation, the formation of 'tribes' or expressive communities in post-modern society, its role in identity expression and formation, and its place in the imagination of utopias. Identity in other words is enacted, not only in the context of theatre in the more formal sense, but persistently in everyday life. Development too is enacted, and the critical questions then become: by whom? For whom? By whose authority? By what means and to what ends? At what costs, environmental and human? These are all questions that applied theatre is able to address, in ways that take them out of abstract debate and present them in concrete terms to, with, and by the very people concerned with these life-changing issues.

Key readings

The place to begin is undoubtedly Augusto Boal's seminal work *Theatre of the Oppressed,* trans. Charles A. and Maria-Odilia Leal McBride and Emily Fryer, London: Pluto Press, 2008. Many subsequent works have built on his insights and practices, and the best guide to the literature on action theatre, and theatre as applied to education and therapy is Robert J. Landy and David T. Montgomery (2012) *Theatre for Change: Education, Social Action and Therapy,* London and New York: Palgrave Macmillan. For the general theory of performance, including many case studies and illustrations go to Richard Schechner (2013) *Performance Studies: An Introduction.* 3rd edition, Abingdon and New York: Routledge. For studies of performance and the environment, good guides are Wendy Arons and Theresa J. May (eds.) (2012) *Readings in Performance and Ecology,* New York and London: Palgrave Macmillan, and Richard D. Besel and Jnan A. Blau (eds.) (2013) *Performance on Behalf of the Environment,* Lanham, MD: Rowman and Littlefield. Two very accessible guides to the issues of human rights and theatre and intercultural performance respectively are two of the volumes in Palgrave Macmillan's *Theatre and . . .* series, notably respectively Paul Rae, *Theatre and Human Rights* (2009), and Ric Knowles (2010) *Theatre and Interculturalism,* both London and New York: Palgrave Macmillan. These will lead you to the wider literature, including case studies and extensive bibliographies. On the broader subject of culture and human rights consult the collections edited by Jane K. Cowan, Marie-Bénédicte Dembour, and Richard A. Wilson (eds.) 2001 *Culture and Rights: Anthropological Perspectives,* Cambridge: Cambridge University Press, and specifically on Asia, Michael Jacobsen and Ole Bruun (eds.) 2003, *Human Rights and Asian Values: Contesting National Identities and Cultural Representations in Asia.* London: Curzon Press for the Nordic Institute of Asian Studies.

Resources

Many of the groups listed in this chapter have their own websites and can easily be located via Google, Facebook or Wikipedia. Dedicated sites that are very relevant however include those of the Center for Victims of Torture, the publishers of Motahar Akand's *Action Theatre* at https://www.newtactics.org/resource/action-theatre-initiating-changes In Place of War at www.inplaceofwar.net and the Theatre of the Oppressed international network at www.theatreoftheoppressed.org. Other groups and individuals involved in action theatre include The Atlas Group at www.theatlasgroup.org and the activist performance artist Coco Fusco who maintains her site at www.cocofusco.com. For activities relating to theatre and ecology consult the Center for Sustainable Practice in the Arts at www.sustainablepractice.org. The Centre for Applied Theatre Research at Manchester University can be accessed from www.arts.manchester.ac.uk/catr/about. El Teatro Campesino maintains a site at www.elteatrocampesino.com. The third and most recent edition of Richard Schechner's foundational volume on performance studies contains numerous links to related sites, videos and organizations.

DISCUSSION QUESTIONS

1. What do you understand by the concept of 'performance' and in what ways can development itself be seen as performance?
2. What is 'action theatre'? How has it been utilized in different cultural contexts to promote development and/or social justice?
3. How is the issue of interculturalism in the performing arts related to questions of development?

References

Aching, Gerard (2002) *Masking and Power: Carnival and Popular Culture in the Caribbean.* Minneapolis: University of Minnesota Press.

Akand, Motahar (2007) *Action Theatre: Initiating Change.* Minneapolis: Center for Victims of Torture/New Tactics for Human Rights Project (https://www.newtactics.org/resource/action-theatre-initiating-changes).

arepp:Theatre for Life (2011) http://www.arepp.org.za

Arons, Wendy and Theresa J. May (eds.) (2012) *Readings in Performance and Ecology.* London and New York: Palgrave Macmillan.

Balme, Christopher (1996) "Between Separation and Integration: Intercultural Strategies in Contemporary Maori Theatre". In Patrice Pavis (ed.) *The Intercultural Performance Reader.* London and New York: Routledge, pp. 179–87.

Balme, Christopher (1999) *Decolonizing the Stage: Theatrical Syncretism and Post-Colonial Drama.* Oxford: Clarendon Press.

Berger, John and Jean Mohr (1975) *A Seventh Man.* Harmondsworth: Penguin Books.

Besel, Richard D. and Jnan A. Blau (eds.) (2013) *Performance on Behalf of the Environment.* Lanham, MD: Rowman and Littlefield.

Bharucha, Rustom (1993) *Theatre and the World: Performance and the Politics of Culture.* London: Routledge.

Boal, Augusto (2008) *Theatre of the Oppressed.* Trans. Charles A. and Maria-Odilia Leal McBride and Emily Fryer. London: Pluto Press.

Brecht, Bertolt (1959) "Über experimentelles Theater". In *Theater de Zeit,* 4. Quoted in English as "On experimental theatre", trans. John Willett, in Eric Bentley (1992) *The Theory of the Modern Stage,* London: Penguin Books, pp. 97–104.

Brecht, Bertolt (1977) *The Measures Taken and Other Lehrstucke.* London: Eyre Methuen.

Byam, L. Dale (1999) *Community in Motion: Theatre for Development in Africa.* London: Bergin and Garvey.

Chaudhuri, Una (1994) "'There Must Be a Lot of Fish in That Lake': Toward an Ecological Theatre". *Theatre,* 25, 1 (Spring/Summer), 23–31.

Cowan, Jane K., Marie-Bénédicte Dembour and Richard A. Wilson (eds.) (2001) *Culture and Rights: Anthropological Perspectives.* Cambridge: Cambridge University Press.

DeMatta, Roberto (2005) "A Concise Reflection on the Brazilian Carnival". In Angela Hobart and Bruce Kapferer (eds.) *Aesthetics in Performance: Formations of Symbolic Construction and Experience.* New York and Oxford: Berghahn Books, pp. 182–195.

Deshmukh-Ranadive, Joy (2003) "Placing Gender Equity Centre Stage: Uses of 'Kala Jatha' Theatre". *Economic and Political Weekly,* April 26, 1674–1679.

D'Zmura, Anne Justine (2012) "Devising *Green Piece:* A Holistic Pedagogy for Artists and Educators". In Wendy Arons and Theresa J. May (eds.) *Readings in Performance and Ecology.* London and New York: Palgrave Macmillan, pp. 169–79.

El Teatro Campesino (2010) www.elteatrocampesino.com

Ganguly, Sanjoy (2010) *Jana Sanskriti: Forum Theatre and Democracy in India.* New York: Routledge.

Giannachi, Gabriella and Nigel Stewart (eds.) (2005) *Performing Nature: Explorations in Ecology and the Arts.* Oxford: Peter Lang.

Gilbert, Helen and Jacqueline Lo (2007) *Performance and Cosmopolitics: Cross-Cultural Transactions in Australia.* Basingstoke: Palgrave Macmillan.

Goodman, Lizbeth and Jane de Gay (eds.) (2000) *The Routledge Reader in Politics and Performance.* London and New York: Routledge.

Gough, Kathleen M. (2012) "Natural Disaster, Cultural Memory: Montserrat Adrift in the Black and Green Atlantic". In Wendy Arons and Theresa J. May (eds.) *Readings in Performance and Ecology.* London and New York: Palgrave Macmillan, pp. 101–112.

Hetherington, Kevin (1998) *Expressions of Identity: Space, Performance, Politics.* London and Thousand Oaks, CA: Sage.

Hobsbawn, Eric and Terrance Ranger (eds.) (1992) *The Invention of Tradition.* Cambridge: Cambridge University Press.

Hollander, Julia (2008) *Indian Folk Theatres.* London and New York: Routledge.

Holledge, Julie and Joanne Tompkins (2000) *Women's Intercultural Performance.* London and New York: Routledge.

Homans, Jennifer (2010) *Apollo's Angels: A History of Ballet.* London: Granta.

Huizinga, Johan (1970) *Homo Ludens: A Study of the Play Element in Culture.* London: Paladin.

Iwabuchi, Koichi (2002) *Recentering Globalization: Popular Culture and Japanese Transnationalism.* Durham, NC and London, Duke University Press.

Iwabuchi, Koichi, Srephen Muecke and Mandy Thomas (eds.) (2004) *Rogue Flows: Trans-Asian Cultural Traffic.* Hong Kong: Hong Kong University Press.

Jackson, Naomi and Toni Shapiro-Phim (eds.) (2008) *Dance, Human Rights, and Social Justice: Dignity in Motion.* Lanham, MD: Scarecrow Press.

Jacobsen, Michael and Ole Bruun (eds.) (2003) *Human Rights and Asian Values: Contesting National Identities and Cultural Representations in Asia.* London: Curzon Press for the Nordic Institute of Asian Studies.

Jelavich, Peter (1996) *Berlin Cabaret.* Cambridge, MA and London: Harvard University Press.

Knowles, Ric (2009) "Multicultural Text, Intercultural Performance". In D. J. Hopkins, Shelley Orr and Kim Solga (eds.) *Performance and the City.* Basingstoke: Palgrave Macmillan, pp. 73–91.

Knowles, Ric (2010) *Theatre and Interculturalism.* London and New York: Palgrave Macmillan.

Kringelbach, Helene Neveu (2013) *Dance Circles: Movement, Morality and Self-fashioning in Urban Senegal.* New York and Oxford: Berghahn.

Landy, Robert J. and David T. Montgomery (2012) *Theatre for Change: Education, Social Action and Therapy.* London and New York: Palgrave Macmillan.

Lo, Jacqueline and Helen Gilbert (2002) "Towards a Topography of Cross-Cultural Theatre Praxis". *The Drama Review,* 46, 3, 31–53.

Love, Glen A. (2003) *Practical Ecocriticism: Literature, Biology, and the Environment.* Charlottesville: University of Virginia Press.

Nicholas, Larraine (2007) *Dancing in Utopia.* Alton: Dance Books.

Odhiambo, Christopher Joseph (2008) *Theatre for Development in Kenya: In Search of an Effective Procedure and Methodology.* Eckersdorf: Pia Thielman and Eckhard Breitinger.

Rae, Paul (2009) *Theatre and Human Rights.* Basingstoke: Palgrave Macmillan.

Reinelt, Janelle G. (ed.) (1996) *Crucible of Crisis: Performing Social Change.* Ann Arbor: University of Michigan Press.

Said, Edward W. (1993) *Culture and Imperialism.* London: Chatto and Windus.

Schechner, Richard (2013) *Performance Studies: An Introduction.* 3rd edition. Abingdon and New York: Routledge.

Schwimmer, Eric (2004) "Making a World: The Maori of Aotearoa/New Zealand". In John Clammer, Sylvie Poirier and Eric Schwimmer (eds.) *Figured Worlds: Ontological Obstacles in Intercultural Relations.* Toronto and London: University of Toronto Press, pp. 241–274.

Srampickal, Jacob (1994) *Voice to the Voiceless: The Power of People's Theatre in India.* New Delhi: Manohar.

TDR: The Journal of Performance Studies. (1998), 42, 3 (Fall). Special number on Trinidad Carnival.

Thiong'o, Ngugi wa (1986) *Decolonizing the Mind: The Politics of Language in African Literature.* London: James Curry.

Turner, Victor (1982) *From Ritual to Theatre: The Human Seriousness of Play.* New York: PAJ Publications.

Yan, Haiping (ed.) (2005) *Other Transnationals: Asian Diasporas in Performance.* Special issue of *Modern Drama,* 48, 2.

Zarrilli, Phillip B. (1996) "Introduction". In Toppil Bhasi, *Memories in Hiding.* Calcutta: Seagull Press, pp. 1–10.

Zarrilli, Phillip B. (2000) "Introduction to Part Seven". In Lizbeth Goodman and Jane de Gay (eds.) *The Routledge Reader in Politics and Performance.* London and New York: Routledge, pp. 223–25.

5

VISUALIZING DEVELOPMENT

Film, photography, representation

A great deal (indeed the greatest bulk) of development studies is textual: reports, books, essays, policy proposals, resolutions, and the way in which a great deal of information about development issues reaches a broader public beyond the 'development professionals' is in the form of written documents. All these texts of course have their effects: they are a primary means by which we learn about the world. But at the same time, culture is becoming in many a way more 'visual': our knowledge (and opinions) about the world are more and more often mediated through visual media: film, television, YouTube, and the material posted on the social media such as Facebook and Twitter. But here we must also introduce a distinction: between *representing* development – that is showing images or depictions *of* it, and using visual media as a means of actually *creating* development. The first is of course important as it shapes our perceptions of what is happening around us, and especially in the 'Third World' which many in the over-developed countries may have little contact with or information about (or even interest in). The question of representations of development have been dealt with in at least one full-length study (Lewis, Rodgers and Woolcock 2013) and will not be the main concern here. Rather, the focus of this chapter will be on the relatively unexplored area of the use of visual media, and in particular film, as a means of critiquing underdevelopment and suggesting alternatives. Film, not *about* development, but as the voice and perceptions of the 'underdeveloped' and those going through the experience of rapid and often disruptive social change, is an important way of linking the arts and development. Film, sometimes called the 'seventh art', is now one of the dominant and most accessed forms of expressive culture in the world. Its role in relation to development is then well overdue for investigation.

The absence of film from every development textbook known to me, and very surprisingly, also from those that purport to deal with the issue of 'culture and development', is remarkable. So too is the fact that in the classical studies of imperialism, colonization and post-colonialism, even though other forms of visual art, and especially the painting style that became known as 'Orientalism', as well as literature are discussed in detail, film is entirely absent (e.g. Said 1985, 1993, Lemaire 2008). Of course the excuse can be made that even in the 1980s, film was not so prominent a medium as it now is, but that is hardly the case whether one is thinking of the West, or of the rapidly emerging cinemas of countries such as India. Rather the over-textuality of development thinking has led to the neglect of other media very relevant to the study of social change. Possibly the one exception to this is not cinema, but still photography, where a number of studies have explored the relationship between the camera and colonialism, and representations of the body and of the 'Other' that emerged during the period of high imperialism (Thomas 1994, Lalvani 1996). Still photography has a long and honourable tradition of representing poverty, peasant struggles, the situation of share-croppers, industrial labour, famine, war and other products of mal-development – one thinks of the work of such photographers, photo-activists and photo-journalists as Tina Modetti, Weegee (Arthur H. Fellig), David Seymour, Marc Riboud, Gordon Parks, Dorothea Lange, Lewis W. Hine, Werner Bischof and Evans Walker, to name just a few of the prominent ones of the twentieth century (Museum Ludwig 1996). Part of the problem of course has been the sheer expense and technical requirements of producing films, but as we will see, many exceptional movies have been produced nevertheless, and an examination of these is a valuable route into exploring the ways in which ideas of development and underdevelopment are mirrored and expressed.

In some respects of course film shares many of the characteristics of theatre discussed in the last chapter, but it is also different in important respects. It is for example portable, storable, reproducible and transmittable. Theatre in an important sense *is* the performance: no two shows will ever be exactly alike, and unless it is filmed, the event is over once it reaches its conclusion. And even a filmed version is not the same as a live performance. To repeat it is to do the whole thing over again. This ephemerality of theatre and dance (and indeed of music) is the bane of theatre historians, or of directors or choreographers who wish to reconstruct a show: often the only evidence is the script, perhaps some sketches or paintings of the scenery or costumes, and in the case of ballet, possibly notations of the movements which give some indication of the organization of the dance. But otherwise the performance is the event, whereas in film precisely the same material can be shown over and over again: its utility as both a form of entertainment and for practical development education is consequently immense. For again like theatre, film can be 'applied' or activist, or of course can be escapist. Film can take the form of critique, of documentary reportage (which often has an implicit critical agenda), it can record – for example vanishing indigenous forms of dance, song or crafts, or even a whole society in the case of the genre usually called ethnographic film, it can stimulate new perceptions of the world by exploring situations or relationships that may be outside the experience of the average viewer and of course it can entertain. As we noted before, in every list of basic 'human needs' generated by those who have attempted to classify such things, leisure and aesthetic needs ranked prominently, and for many of us the world over it is now through film (whether delivered via cinema, television, CD, DVD, or streamed through our personal computers) that we gain a huge portion of our entertainment. The expansion of such spaces of relaxation, fantasy and fun should be an important part of any sound and humane development policy.

The power of film has of course been recognized since its early days and has often taken the form of propaganda – whether in wartime, or in support of a particular ideology and its supportive culture – as seen widely in Soviet cinema, in China in the recent past, in Cuban cinema and in the not such distant past in the famous or infamous ideological documentaries of the Nazi-era director Leni Riefenstahl such as her 1934 work *The Triumph of the Will*. Cinema is also quite a useful indicator of the themes that are penetrating popular culture. To take two quite different examples of this: some have argued that the large number of fantasy films appearing in the West in recent years (*Lord of the Rings, Narnia, Harry Potter* and many others) is a response to the disenchantment of the modern world and reflects a desire to re-enchant it, at least in the imagination. Similarly the last decade has seen a number of major Hollywood films about natural disasters (*Ice Age, The Perfect Storm, 2012*), or reflecting directly ecological themes (*Avatar*), all signalling the fact that environmental concerns are now reaching the popular consciousness (and maybe influencing that consciousness in environmentally positive directions). If the developing world faces one set of typical problems, it may be that the over-developed world now faces another, and that film is one of the ways in which a critique of that late modernity is emerging, and an important one, because of its huge popularity and impact. Increasingly teachers are using film as a teaching medium – movies such as *The Eleventh Hour* about the impact of climate change and human-induced destruction of the natural environment, *Hard Rain* that discusses energy issues and in particular the dangers of nuclear power, *A Quiet Revolution* that documents local initiatives to address environmental problems and *Trafficking* that addresses, as its title suggests, the widespread problem of human trafficking especially for the purpose of prostitution are good examples. Because film engages the senses and attention in ways that probably no other medium does, its educational role is profound, and consequently its application to development issues potentially very wide-ranging. Film in fact provides one of the most significant and creative interfaces between culture and development and it is very important to include it in any discussion of the arts in relation to those world-transforming processes. It is also the medium in which the developing world expresses many of its opinions about the forces working on it, and how identities, lifestyles and material conditions are transformed. We will accordingly examine film along two main dimensions:'applied film' or film as an educational and consciousness raising tool in development; and 'art film' or films that reflect from within the very conditions of underdevelopment, and how these constitute an important art form in their own right and one that deserves to be better known.

Cinema and the aesthetics of development

'Third World Cinema' has in fact a long and distinguished history and vibrant local cinema cultures have flourished in Cuba, Egypt, Senegal, Brazil, and very much in India. Many of these cinemas have drawn on Western modernism, but in ways that have transformed it into authentic indigenous statements. The Senegalese director Djibril Diop Mamete (*Touki-Bouki*), the Mauritanian Med Hondo (*Soleil O*), and the world-famous Indian director Satyajit Ray (*Pather Panchali, Aparajito, The World of Apu*) have all entered to some degree world cinema, while an active cinematic 'underground' of small budget, local language and non-commercial films has flourished in Brazil, Argentina, the Philippines and many other developing world contexts. The aesthetics of these films is often rather different from that of mainstream Western ones: as Ella Shohat and Robert Stam put it:

> These aesthetics bypass the formal conventions of dramatic realism in favor of such modes and strategies as the carnivalesque, the anthropophagic, the magic realist, the reflexive modernist, and the resistant postmodernist. The aesthetics are often rooted in non-realist, often non-Western or para-Western cultural traditions featuring other historical rhythms, other narrative structures, other views of the body, sexuality, spirituality, and the collective life. Many incorporate non-modern traditions into clearly modernizing or postmodernizing aesthetics, and thus problematize facile dichotomies such as traditional/modern, realist/modernist, and modernist/postmodernist.
>
> *(Shohat and Stam 2002: 41)*

This is important, for while many 'Bollywood' films (Indian dramas produced in Mumbai, usually incorporating singing, dancing and romance) are certainly escapist, many serious Third World films are certainly not, but address significant problems in the local society: caste, oppressive marriage customs, inequalities and so forth; and in the context of that society: colonialism, migration, the effects of globalization and the penetration of the world economy into previously insulated or isolated communities. 'Social dramas' of one kind or another (and we will look at some examples below) consequently comprise a significant percentage of films produced in the developing world, and at the same time the aesthetics expressed in such films may be significantly different from those found in typically Western-style productions.

The Nigerian filmmaker Ola Balogun for example suggests that it is more appropriate to see African film less as an example of the performing arts than as ritual or ceremonies into which magical and spiritual elements are quite naturally incorporated. The 1991 film *Kasarmu* ("This Land is Ours") for example involves playful spirits that do not require the same kind of suspension of belief that they would in a Western film (probably categorized as a 'fantasy' one), but reflect cultural conventions and forms of causality quite acceptable to their intended audiences. This should come as no surprise to anthropologists: issues of non-linear and magical causality have been the subject of many studies of what usually gets to be called 'witchcraft' in the African context, such as in E. E. Evans-Pritchard's classic study of the Azande of the Sudan (Evans-Pritchard 1968). As Shohat and

Stam go on to argue, this is also true of films influenced by the diaspora of African cultures:

> The values of African religious culture inform not only African cinema, but also a good deal of Afro-diasporic cinema, for example Brazilian films like Rocha's *Barravento* (1962) and Cavalcanti's *A Forca de Xango* (The Force of Xango, 1977), *Amuleto de Ogum* (Ogum's Amulet, 1975), Cuban films like *Patakin* and *Ogum,* and African-American films like Julie Dash's *Daughters Of the Dust,* all of which inscribe African (usually Yoruba) religious symbolism and practice. Indeed, the preference for Yoruba symbolism is itself significant, since the performing arts are at the very kernel of the Yoruba religions themselves, unlike other religions where the performing arts are grafted on to a theological/textual core. The arts inform the religions in multifaceted ways. The arts – costume, dance, poetry, music – create the appropriate atmosphere for worship. The arts also inform cosmogony and theology.
>
> *(Shohat and Stam 2002: 43)*

Much the same can be said about a great deal of Indian cinema, especially that of Tamil Nadu in the south, where the cross-over and interplay between religion and the secular is very marked, and where a well-trod path to political power is via film: actors and actresses having played gods and goddesses, find it not too difficult to translate that aura into the realm of politics, where their appeal may not be so much their policies as their on-screen personas. While the theory of secularization is largely a European invention, it has much less application to Asia, Africa and Latin America, and to the huge diasporas of peoples rooted in those cultures to North America, Australia and elsewhere, where they very much take their religious cultures with them (Yoo 1999, Clammer 2009) and in doing so often influence the local religious cultures of their new host societies, as has happened with the Japanese 'new religions' of Buddhist or Shinto origin that have penetrated European, Latin American, other Asian, and North American religious cultures in quite substantial ways (Clarke and Somers 1994, Ben-Ari and Clammer 2000). If religion and broader and popular culture go closely together, then this nexus is an important and neglected theme in studies of culture and development.

Religion of course is not the only theme of film produced in developing countries, and in any case rarely is it the direct subject matter – rather it is the magical elements that pervade culture and are then inserted into film – as in Jean-Pierre Bekolo's 1992 film *Quartier Mozart* depicting a typical Cameroon local neighbourhood, and one pervaded with the magical, which is deployed however in a distinctively post-modern fashion, quoting international popular culture, making references to the films of Spike Lee and questioning in subtle ways social roles and categories, such as gender. The magical and the post-modern coexist comfortably, transcending the tired categories of 'tradition and modernity' that pervade so much thinking and writing about the developing world. What these examples point to of course is the fact that culturally speaking the 'developing' world is already highly developed, with complex and intricate systems of symbolism, humour, lateral thinking and assumptions, both difficult for the non-native to fully access, and often for that very reason containing clever and indirect critiques of modernity, development, social hierarchies and 'tradition' itself. The 'magical realism' of a great deal of Latin American literature also pervades the worlds of film and theatre. A deep hybridity is the result, one expressed not only in film and popular culture, but also in events such as carnivals, which are not simply occasions of display, but are also frequently transgressive (of gender roles, sexuality, social roles, mainstream politics, presentation of the body and fashion), and are ways of possessing the streets and transforming them – removing traffic, restoring a legitimate form of disorder, dissolving the boundaries between spectator and performer – and of working through the many cultural tensions that can be tense, even violent, in ethnically, religiously and class-divided societies.

An expression of this is that while direct social critique does cinematically occur (and we will explore some examples shortly), it is often irony that is the main tool situation in which an apparently serious issue becomes a kind of subtle and extended joke, humour being one of the most subversive possible social solvents, in which themes as apparently serious as cannibalism (Nelson Pereira dos Santos' *How Tasty Was My Frenchman* [1971]) or the experience of return migration to a developing country after an extended sojourn in a 'developed' one (Artur Omar: *Triste Tropico,* 1974), the latter being also a kind of extended visual pun on Claude Lévi-Strauss' well-known anthropological travelogue *Tristes Tropiques,* can be expressed. So too is the 'aesthetics of garbage' (*estetica do lixo*) in which trash – the very by-products and throw-aways of consumer capitalist societies, becomes not only a subject of film, but a metaphor for the marginality of those who are forced to live by scavenging the rubbish of the rich (for example the Brazilian director Sganzerla's 1968 *Red Light Bandit,* or the collage-like movie of Jorge Furtado's *Island of Flowers* [1989], which takes its very title from a Brazilian garbage dump on which women and children scavenge) and which uses humour to point to very significant issues – trash itself and its ecological and socio-political meanings, inequality, health issues, gender, and the web of connections linking consumers, producers and the poor 'recyclers' at the end of the food-chain, who are paradoxically eating worse than the pigs that are the source of the sausages that feed the rich.

Other examples address the issues of development equally directly, without necessarily ever naming it, or its cousin, globalization. Similarly the subjects of colonization and post-colonialism have been natural subjects for cinema in the developing world, as have such subjects as racism, poverty and forced marriage and the abuse and exploitation of brides. And given that exploitation and poor work conditions also occur widely in 'developed' countries, many of these themes appear in the critical and ethnographic cinemas of the 'First World' too. For example as far back as the 1920s, the American director Oscar Micheaux made films with exclusively black casts (*Body and Soul,* 1928, *The Exile,* 1931, and *God's Step Children,* 1938) that were very popular both with black audiences in the United States and in Latin America, while in the then new Soviet Union Sergei Eisenstein made the subject of Czarist oppression leading to the revolution his theme, as famously expressed in his 1925 classic *The Battleship Potemkin*. The stupidity of war itself was the theme of the equally classic film Lewis Milestone's 1930 *All Quiet on the Western Front*, and Joris Ivens' indictment of fascist war atrocities during the Spanish Civil War in his 1937 *The Spanish Earth*. In the same period the UK developed a tradition of socially sensitive documentary filmmaking, expressed in such movies as John Grierson's *Drifters* (1929), a study of the North Sea fishing fleet and its crews, and Edgar Anstey and Arthur Elton's 1935 *Housing Problems*. Post-war film in Europe maintained much of this tradition, as in Vittorio De Sica's 1948 *Bicycle Thieves*, depicting the everyday life of the urban poor as Italy struggled to reconstruct in the aftermath of defeat and ruination.

This tradition of critical cinema, often taking as its subject matter (as with *Bicycle Thieves*) everyday life, has continued in the developing world. Even films now widely regarded as 'art films' such as the aforementioned Apu Trilogy by the Indian filmmaker Satyajit Ray (1955–8) in fact depict poverty (the theme of the films is the growing up of a poor Bengali boy), the existential realities of suffering and death, the penetration of Western values into traditional Indian society and human frailty and greed. In some cases underdevelopment itself becomes the primary theme as in the Cuban Tomas Gutierrez Alea's 1968 *Memories of Underdevelopment,* or the Turkish *Yol,* written by Yilmaz Guney and directed by Serif Goren, which is an extended allegory on Turkish underdevelopment. Africa has been particularly rich in films of this nature, including Egyptian depictions of urban and rural poverty (Youssef Chahine's *Cairo Station* and Shadi Abdel-Salam's *The Night of Counting the Years),* critiques of colonialism (the Senegalese director Ousmane Sembene's satire *Xala,* and the Mauritanian Med Hondo's *Soleil O, Sarraounia*), and many others from Nigeria, Ethiopia, Burkino Faso and Tunisia. India too, as might be expected, has contributed many insightful films to the specific analysis of the social problems of underdevelopment, such as those of Mrinal Sen many of whose films are searing attacks on exploitation (of the poor in *Akaler Sandhaney/In Search of Famine,* 1980, and of women in *Ek Din Pratidin/And Quiet Rolls the Day,* 1979); Mira Nair's *Salaam Bombay!* (1988) which addresses the large issue of street children in urban India and her more recent films *Fire* which deals with the taboo subject of lesbianism in India and the cinematically beautiful *Water* which explores the subject of child widows and Indian widowhood in general. Latin American film has likewise addressed parallel problems in that continent, such as Nelson Pereira dos Santos' powerful *Vidas secas,* a movie examining the extreme poverty of a family of homeless 'Nordestinos', rural peasants from north-eastern Brazil, or the political documentary *The Hour of the Furnaces: Notes and Testimonies on Neo-Colonialism, Violence and Liberation* (Fernando Solanas and Octavio Getino) examining dictatorship, political brutality, and globalization in Argentina. Numerous other examples can be found from Mexico, Cuba and elsewhere on the continent. (For a good summary which locates these films in the context of world cinema see Mast 1992).

While Third World film covers a huge range of subjects – including of course plenty of soap operas, Bollywood romances, fantasy, horror, crime, and romantic comedies, those films that relate to development issues naturally fall into the kinds of categories enumerated above, and also address the questions of nationalism and identity that inevitably arise in situations of colonialism and globalization, situations in which traditional identities are threatened, sovereignty eroded and linguistic and cultural autonomy undermined or destroyed. Cinema is an important and powerful cultural practice with profound political and sociological implications. Its multiple ways of addressing the world – through comedy, realism, tragedy, escapism, fantasy, humour, irony, direct critique – and its immense popularity as a medium (especially when intensified and multiplied by television and easily and cheaply available videos and DVDs) impacts subjectivities in many ways paralleling the multifaceted nature of cinema itself: fashion, modes of language, self-images, knowledge about the world, new ways of perceiving or representing that world – all are formed and influenced by film. It follows from this that so are social attitudes, hence the importance of film as propaganda and as critique. The idea of 'national cinema' is consequently both important and contentious: important because it can become a voice of autonomy, indigenous aesthetics and identity; contentious because it can become a tool of narrow nationalism, tribalism and the views of a particular elite, not necessarily shared throughout the rest of the society in question. Nevertheless, national cinemas have been powerful tools in the critique of colonialism in particular, and similar modes of engagement now carry over into the critique of neo-colonialism and globalization.

Nationalism is quite naturally a primary tool in any anti-colonial struggle, and is still evident as a means of identity mobilization in many societies across the world – national day celebrations, flags, national anthems, coronations, and even elections, still for many retain their power to stoke nationalistic sentiments. Inevitably nationalism requires a symbolic vocabulary, and while in the initial phases of nationalism and 'nation-building' (as the phrase once commonly used in post-colonial Singapore used to put it) it is, as Benedict Anderson so cogently illustrated in his now classic study of nation-formation, the print media that play that role (Anderson 1993), it is now to a great extent the electronic media that have taken over those functions. Cinema has also been an important medium for undermining the hegemonic ideology of the centralized nation-state by showing that slogans such as "unity in diversity" actually act as mechanisms for the marginalization of minorities who do not have a voice in the discourses and power structures of the supposedly unitary state. Two good filmic examples of this are the Indian filmmaker Saeed Akhtar Mirza's *Salim Langde Pe Mat Ro/Don't Cry for Salim the Lame,* which explores the situation of the Muslim minority in largely Hindu India, and the Chinese director Zhang Nuanxin's *Qungchun Ji/Sacrificed Youth* that deals in a sensitive way with the situation of ethnic minorities in primarily Han Chinese (and Communist) China. Film is thus also a way of both preserving history (and often recounting it for nationalistic purposes), and a form of counter-memory, allowing the voices of those submerged in a hegemonic historical discourse to emerge and be heard and their protagonists seen, the very people now referred to in post-colonial language as the 'subalterns' (for good African examples see Niang 2014). The representation of suffering and its psychic economies can take a much more concrete form in the medium of the cinema than it can in the grand narratives of historians.

Frederic Jameson, speaking of literature, but in a passage that can equally well be applied to film has argued that in the context of Third World writing

> Those texts, even those narratives which are seemingly private and invested with a properly libidinal dynamic, necessarily project a political dimension in the form of national allegory: the story of the private individual destiny is always an allegory of the embattled situation of the public Third World culture and society.
>
> *(Jameson 1987: 142)*

While this is certainly something of an overstatement, it does contain an important large element of truth: that Third World cinema is to a very high degree concerned with the same issues as literature from the same regions. It is in other words (or certainly contains) a cinema of decolonization and liberation, while also reworking images of the body, gender, the self and identity. This can be seen very clearly in Asian film – the surfacing of liberationist themes emerging from Korean *Minjung* philosophies and theologies, and a concern with realism and the depiction of the conditions of the working class as intensive and rapid industrialization started to take place in the wake of the Korean War. Also reflected in Asian cinema are new ways of imagining the future; war films in Vietnam and now films about the struggle to make sense of the emerging new order of what is actually capitalist development and tourism taking place in the context of what is still a Communist state; tensions between the city and the countryside in Thai film; proletarian dramas in Indonesian film and theatre (Peacock 1987); representations of colonialism in Indian film; nationalism and pluralistic cultural discourses in Sri Lanka, Malaysia, Indonesia and Singapore; the problems of minorities, of gender relations and of urban youth across the region (for an extensive overview with many examples see Dissanayake 1994). It is important to point out that cinema is also an *industry* – a significant economic actor at both the production and consumption ends, and a major source of cultural productivity in any society with a film industry. This industry is of note too for the fact that it is itself pluralistic, ranging from large studios to small independent filmmakers, usually involving governments at some level (as producers, censors, patrons), and extruding work of a large range of styles – popular, escapist, critical, surrealist: 'art' films as well as box-office hits, documentaries as well as features and documentaries that deal more with nature than with social critique, educational films and pure entertainment, films that keep alive painful memories and those that occlude them. The power of cinema lies both in its popularity and in its ability to encompass all these genres and more: its protean nature and easy accessibility give it influence that no other medium shares. After all, you don't even have to be literate to enjoy a movie.

As formal colonialism recedes, new forms of international structuring appear, including as we have suggested, neo-colonialism, often expressed in the idiom of globalization, and its close cousin, cultural imperialism (on the latter and its connections with economic globalization see Hamm and Smandych 2005), and on the new social forms that accompany it, and especially urbanization, not least the kinds of hyper-urbanization experienced by many Third World societies: think of Lagos, Calcutta, Bombay, Mexico City and Sao Paulo as primary examples. Cities in a sense 'condense' globalization: they intensify its effects through their density of population, architecture, consumption, cultural production, entertainment, transportation and industry. For this reason they have become the focus of film in and about the developing world, since there the effects of globalization are magnified and more easily visible, and where uneven development is most conspicuous – the familiar scenes of slums and gleaming high-rises, of shanty towns and mega-malls, of affluent shoppers and beggars, of protected gated communities and make-shift housing, all cheek-by-jowl. Cinema has long used the city as its stage: Los Angeles, London, Berlin. But in the developing world the issue is not the city as backdrop, but the city as in a sense the actor: as encapsulating the very forces that work their impersonal way out on the humans who inhabit them (or at least the less privileged ones): poverty, displacement, violence, crime, inadequate housing, lack of work or poor working conditions, racism and minimal access to education and health services. Cinema has consequently come to be a barometer of social changes (for Latin American examples see Burton 1986). At the same time, the power of the international (largely US) film industry prevents many of the films made in these contexts from ever being seen outside (or even inside) their countries of origin: monopolies of distribution and ownership of cinemas greatly restricts the circulation of some of the most socially important films (Armes 1987, Wasko 1994) so that many Western audiences for example may never have seen an African film unless at a film club, specialized (probably NGO operated) small cinema or at a film festival (Diawara 1992), or be able to find any examples in their local video rental store. Yet South Africa, Nigeria and other major African countries have significant film industries, both formal and informal, the latter represented by the proliferation of low budget video films produced and widely viewed in Lagos and throughout Nigeria (Oha 2001). Brazilian film is probably better known, and some, such as the internationally distributed drama of violence, drugs, gangs and redemption in the *favelas, Cidade de Deus/City of God,* being available in many countries. The cinema of the Third World city is then a very valuable route into understanding the reality of life in those places in ways that even the most sensitive urban sociology would find it hard to depict. It is also the case that it is often the visual that incites people to act: in this case to address the problems and injustices that the films, even if fictional, reveal. Or as the prize–winning British novelist Julian Barnes has nicely put it (speaking of the novel, but equally of film): "It tells beautiful shapely lies which enclose hard, exact truths" (Barnes 2009: 78).

Theorizing film and development

In her book on Chinese cinema, Rey Chow poses the interesting and challenging suggestion that

What is needed, after the ethical polemic of Said's *Orientalism* is understood, is the much more difficult task of investigating how visuality operates in the postcolonial politics of non-Western cultures besides the subjection to passive spectacle that critics of orientalism argue. How do we deal with the fact that non-Westerners also gaze, are voyeurs and spectators? What does it mean for non-Western intellectuals to live as 'subjects' and 'agents' in the age of 'the world as exhibition'? After demonstrating the bloodiness of the Western instruments of vision and visuality, how do we discuss what happens when the 'East' uses these instruments to fantasize itself and the world?

(Chow 1995: 13)

In a way, this whole book is an attempt to take up Chow's challenge. For the issues are evidently manifold. For example in the past it was mainly writing that influenced film (novels being turned into screenplays, plays filmed, and many of the conventions of literary fiction – plot, clear characterization, a satisfactory and unambiguous ending – carried over into movies). Now the situation is often reversed and filmic conventions – flashbacks, montage, lack of a clear plot and so forth – now influence writing. Films, despite the expense and technology involved in producing them, are a remarkably democratic medium that is much less mediated by language than any form of literature. Furthermore, given the social and spatial plurality of large societies like India, China or Indonesia, many viewers may be seeing aspects of their 'own' society, geography and culture which they were previously completely unacquainted with. That is obviously one reason why we watch documentaries. In film, something can be used as a metaphor for something else, as for example when the Chinese director Xie Jin employed the metaphor of theatre to examine lives traversing the turbulent years of war, Japanese occupation, Nationalist occupation and the transition to Communism in the film *Wutai jiemei/Two Stage Sisters,* without the film itself being overtly 'political'. As Gina Marchetti puts it in her essay on the film

Two Stage Sisters of Shaoxing [a genre of Chinese folk opera] as a metaphor for political and social change. The film also represents a search for a Chinese cinema aesthetic based on these traditions as well as on Hollywood and socialist realist forms.

(Marchetti 1997: 59)

If issues of identity and nationhood come together in film so do issues of aesthetics and geopolitics: the definition and independence of the state, the political economy of the international film distribution system and of film festivals (Stringer 2001), the distribution of cultural power in the world system and the increasing move by states to promote themselves internationally through 'soft power' (contemporary Japan being a very good case in point with its popular culture, especially in the form of *manga* [comics], *anime* [cartoon films] and the costumes of the characters depicted in them now being actively exported and used as a basis for attracting tourists to the country). Indeed, Japan is a particularly interesting case: a country with a large film industry, with most productions being for the domestic market (few except for *anime* are shown abroad except for what are now regarded as classic art films) and which, while never formally colonized was once itself a colonizer of Korea, Taiwan, Manchuria, parts of China and parts of the Pacific, not including its brief and disastrous attempt to occupy Southeast Asia (Goodman 1991), now turned into a war-renouncing nation of huge economic power, and one which places its cultural productions, both traditional and modern, at the heart of its self-perceived cultural identity. This is particularly pertinent now as new developmental challenges arise: not just globalization in the abstract, but entirely new challenges such as climate change, new conflicts and geopolitical struggles in Asia and the Middle East, political transitions in Myanmar and North Africa, resource struggles, new and unexpected forms of infectious disease, increasing global shortages of water, pollution and loss of biodiversity and no doubt many more. While the older issues of colonialism and the patterns of underdevelopment that it gave rise to have not gone away, the challenge is for Third World filmmakers to identify and respond to these new issues, even as some filmmakers in the West are slowly beginning to do. The other and classical problem is that of signalling these concerns to the wider world. Given the political economy of the world film distribution system it remains hard for Third World filmmakers' products to be seen internationally. As Gayatri Chakravorty Spivak put it in an interview

> For me, the question 'Who should speak?' is less crucial than 'Who will listen?'. 'I will speak for myself as a Third World person' is an important position for political mobilization today. But the real demand is that, when I speak from that position, I should be listened to seriously; not with that kind of benevolent imperialism, really, which simply says that because I happen to be an Indian or whatever . . .
>
> *(Spivak and Gunew 1994: 194)*

This is as true of film as it is of any other media or form of expression.

Third cinema and third-world cinema

One of the main theoretical debates in film studies as it relates to development, is discussion about the distinction between 'Third World Cinema' and 'Third Cinema'. At first sight they appear to be basically the same idea, but a little analysis shows this to be not the case. 'Third World Cinema' refers to works produced in the developing world by indigenous filmmakers. 'Third Cinema' on the other hand refers to film that attempts social critique and ideological deconstruction and demystification, and as such can and does occur in the context of First World Cinema. Some prominent examples blur the line between the two concepts, a much analysed example being the famous 1966 film *The Battle of Algiers,* made by the Italian Communist and anti-fascist director Gillo Pontecorvo, with the script co-written with Franco Solinas, and music by Ennio Morricone, also both Italians. The film, made shortly after Algeria finally gained independence from the French, depicts the colonial military's brutal suppression of the FLN, the Algerian National Liberation Front, the main guerrilla force opposing the French occupation. So while made by First Cinema people, the film, made with the support of the new independent Algerian government, is entirely about the anti-colonial struggle of a Third World people. So while Third World Cinema relates primarily to a geographical concept (and also to attendant aesthetics and cultural politics), Third Cinema refers to a set of cinematic strategies designed to promote a genuinely transformative and social justice promoting form of cultural production, that invariably involves explicitly or implicitly a rejection of the globalization practices of neo-liberal capitalism, and of the liberal multiculturalist socio-political positions that accompany it. It is then a site of symbolic resistance, and as we have suggested before, the power of symbolism to inspire, activate and promote practical interventions and action should not be under-estimated. The Latin American filmmaker Glauber Rocha, seeking a cinema that would seriously address issues of social justice, coined the telling phrase "a cinema of hunger" (Rocher 1997: 59) perhaps to be compared with Boal's notion of the 'theatre of the oppressed' (for a discussion of these issues and a detailed examination of *The Battle of Algiers,* see Wayne 2002).

The nature (at least in its ideal types) of Third Cinema is to transform both First and Second Cinema by pushing them in the direction of social engagement and ideological critique, and of course with the intention of changing society itself. This may in some cases lead it in the direction of becoming 'Utopian Cinema' – cinema depicting what might be rather than what is, and should ideally engage the audience and shift them from being simply passive observers, to participants – to having a distinct consciousness-raising quality. As Julia Garcia Espinosa puts it:

> A new poetics for the cinema will, above all, be a 'partisan' and 'committed' poetics, a 'committed' art, a consciously and resolutely 'committed' cinema – that is to say an 'imperfect' cinema. An 'impartial' or 'uncommitted' one as a complete aesthetic activity, will only be possible when it is the people who make art.
>
> *(Espinosa 1997: 79)*

Another way to phrase this might be to talk of a 'cinema of the oppressed', or simply of authentic cinema – one that is rooted in culture, sensitive to issues of gender, race and class, grasps the socio-historical context that it represents and which is intended to help the exploited understand the conditions that have brought about their subjection, and suggest tools, practical and imaginative, for them to act to change this. All this may seem to be a tall order, but these themes are expressed in whole or in part in all the examples that we have mentioned, and in many more found around the developing world, and being made by First World directors to address the emerging problems of globalization, environment, and social justice, including such everyday issues of where our clothes come from, and how their relatively cheap price can be traced back to their origin in the sweated labour factories of Bangladesh and China. Much the same kind of analysis has been made by documentary filmmakers of food (including fish), coffee, tea, sugar, flowers and many of the other taken-for-granted products that make life so pleasant in the developed countries, but which have their roots in exploitation, ecological damage and continuing underdevelopment elsewhere. Here in fact we see the re-emergence of something like the old 'dependency theory' paradigm of underdevelopment: that the rich world by its actions, consumption, aid and trade patterns actually underdevelops the developing world and keeps it in a permanently subordinate position from which it alone benefits (for more on Third Cinema see Solanas and Getino 1976, and Gabriel 1982, the latter an important book on the 'aesthetics of liberation').

Amongst the arts that relate to the subject of development, cinema has a paramount role. This we have suggested is for several reasons. Cinema is now perhaps the most popular of all the media and its apparent decline in the 1960–70s because of the widespread availability of television has been reversed by the advent first of video and then of the DVD, which may have led in some countries to decline in cinema attendance, but have at the same time promoted the watching of the actual films – at home, at social gatherings, on one's PC, while travelling in a plane. Made-for-TV films now constitute a substantial part of television programming. Video games have extended the viewing of (and interaction with) film in unexpected new directions. The animated film has extended film viewing and socialization into the habit of the very youngest children. The 'social media' now often includes homemade films streamed as part of personal postings, and more. Twitter has become a significant outlet for posting photos, videos and information on endangered species and environmental issues and the site called Wild Me is attempting to become an animal's equivalent of Facebook amongst other attempts to use social media in an ecologically activist way (for more details see the Resources section). Precisely because of its huge appeal, cinema has huge potential as a means of consciousness raising, social critique, documentation, education and resistance. We have examined some of the ways in which this has been done by actual Third World directors who have indeed explored issues of colonialism, poverty, gender, child labour, revolution, globalization, environment and work as being amongst the major issues that should concern a socially committed cinema. While this has often been done through documentary or quasi-documentary methods, it has also very successfully been achieved through humour, satire, drama, adventure and other cinematic techniques familiar from 'First Cinema', making the resulting movies both attractive and enjoyable viewing experiences, as well as containing deeper social messages.

As the world enters deeper into the crises that the development path so far followed (industrialization, resource depletion, hyper-urbanization and consumerism) has brought upon us (or we have brought upon ourselves), cinema in general is likely to begin to respond more adequately to these issues. As society becomes more and more of a "Risk Society" to use Ulrich Beck's celebrated phrase (Beck 1992) of unknown dangers, unmanageable crises, and unprecedented conflation of issues (climate, resources, population, pollution, new diseases), so popular culture will at least to some degree respond. After all, even Hollywood has begun to depict ecological and geo-tectonic shifts in movies such as *2012,* even if wrapped up in the usual romance and happy-ending (at least for the survivors) typical of the most paradigmatic of all First Cinemas. Given the huge social significance of cinema (far more people globally attend cinemas or watch movies in other contexts than ever go to live theatre for example) its study should be at the forefront of any discussion of 'culture and development'. For here we see culture in one of its most widely accessed forms, and one that directly interfaces with key development issues. This also provides a unique opportunity for cultural studies, often wrapped up in trivial and ephemeral issues, to relate itself very directly to the very real world. As the media sociologist and cinema scholar Norman Denzin has put it, this is a chance to create "a cultural studies that makes a difference" (Denzin 1994). Although writing about post-modernism, and utilizing examples drawn from First Cinema, Denzin's analyses converge closely with Third Cinema issues, or as he puts it

> I seek not a theory of cultural indifference, but a theory of resistance. Such a theory examines how the basic existential experiences with self, other, gender, race, nationality, family, love, intimacy, violence, death, and freedom are produced and given mythical meaning in everyday life. This must be a feminist, post-colonial cultural studies theory of micro-politics which sees networks of power-relations subsisting at every point in a society.
>
> *(Denzin 1994: xi)*

Third Cinema issues then can be examined in the context of First Cinema productions, even if not so explicitly: they are fundamentally universal. Cinema as a whole then must be seen as a major cultural force and social actor, not only as an industry and through the familiar mechanisms of the 'star system', but as a tool of critique, a major means of consciousness raising, and as such as a potentially powerful leader in re-shaping our civilization in more socially just, convivial and ecologically sustainable directions, whether in the Third World or the First.

Key readings

A good general history of film that unlike many others also discusses 'Third World' film is Gerald Mast's 1992 *A Short History of the Movies,* 5th edition, New York: Macmillan. For studies of the relationship between nationalism and cinema in the developing world see, for Asia, Wimal Dissanayake (ed.) (1994) *Colonialism and Nationalism in Asian Cinema,* Bloomington: Indiana University Press, and for Africa, Sada Niang (2014) *Nationalist African Cinema: Legacy and Transformations,* Lanham, MD: Lexington Books. Slightly dated but still very fundamental is Roy Armes' 1987 book *Third World Filmmaking and the West,* Berkeley and London: University of California Press. A good collection of readings that contextualizes cinema and many other cultural expressions in the light of both colonialism and globalization is the book of readings edited by Rasheed Areen, Sean Cubitt and Ziauddin Sardar (2002)

The Third Text Reader on Art, Culture and Theory, London and New York: Continuum, and on visual cultures including film see Nicholas Mirzoeff (ed.) (2002) *The Visual Culture Reader,* London and New York: Routledge.

Resources

The best thing to do is to actually locate and watch some of the movies mentioned in this chapter. A good list is provided in Gerald Mast's book mentioned above (pp. 602–604, 614–615, 617). A number of NGOs make and distribute films on development issues such as the Tokyo-based Pacific Asia Resource Centre (PARC) at http://parc-jp.org/english/index.html and in the UK Purple Field Productions, which has devised a portable pedal-powered cinema for use in Malawi and elsewhere (www.purplefieldproductions.org). Many good documentary films as well as feature films are available and these include films on water issues, development in general, nuclear power (for example the documentary *Hard Rain*), and others on refugee issues, asylum seekers, human trafficking and other pressing questions. A good example of a feature film, in this case addressing the conflicts in Bolivia over water privatization is the 2010 movie *Even the Rain (Tambien la lluvia* in its Spanish original), directed by Icíar Bollaín, and which incidentally has much to say, or show, about the arrival of Columbus and subsequent Spanish colonization of Latin America. The United Nations High Commission for Refugees (UNHCR) sponsors local film festivals through its regional offices, such as the annual Refugee Film Festival in Tokyo and is a rich source of information on documentary and feature films addressing refugee issues (www.UNHCR.org).

DISCUSSION QUESTIONS

1. How can film be utilized to promote development goals, whether through documentary or feature film formats?
2. Activist photographers and photo-journalists have made significant contributions to documenting and representing situations of underdevelopment, inequality and social violence. Examine in detail the work of one or more such photographers.
3. How has 'Third World Cinema' taken up issues of development, colonialism, or post-colonial problems? Explore in relation to either a particular film or films, or the work of a specific director from the developing world.

References

Anderson, Benedict (1993) *Imagined Communities: Reflections on the Origin and Spread of Nationalism.* London and New York: Verso.

Areen, Rasheed, Sean Cubitt and Ziauddin Sardar (eds.) (2002) *The Third Text Reader on Art, Culture and Theory.* London and New York: Continuum.

Armes, Roy (1987) *Third World Filmmaking and the West*. Berkeley and London: University of California Press.

Barnes, Julian (2009) *Nothing to Be Frightened Of*. London: Vintage Books.

Beck, Ulrich (1992) *Risk Society: Towards a New Modernity*. London and Thousand Oaks, CA: Sage.

Ben-Ari, Eyal and John Clammer (eds.) (2000) *Japan in Singapore: Cultural Occurrences and Cultural Flows*. Richmond: Curzon Press.

Burton, Julianne (ed.) (1986) *Cinema and Social Change in Latin America*. Austin: University of Texas Press.

Chow, Rey (1995) *Primitive Passions: Visuality, Sexuality, Ethnography, and Contemporary Chinese Cinema*. New York: Columbia University Press.

Clammer, John (2009) *Diaspora and Belief: Globalization, Religion and Identity in Postcolonial Asia*. New Delhi: Shipra.

Clarke, Peter B. and Jeffrey Somers (eds.) (1994) *Japanese New Religions in the West*. Folkstone: Japan Library.

Denzin, Norman (1994) *Images of Postmodern Society: Social Theory and Contemporary Cinema*. London and Thousand Oaks, CA: Sage.

Diawara, Manthia (1992) *African Cinema: Politics and Culture*. Bloomington and Indianapolis: Indiana University Press.

Dissanayake, Wimal (ed.) (1994) *Colonialism and Nationalism in Asian Cinema*. Bloomington and Indianapolis: Indiana University Press.

Espinosa, Julia Garcia (1997) "For an imperfect cinema". In Michael T. Martin (ed.) *New Latin American Cinemas: Theory, Practices and Transcontinental Articulations*. Detroit: Wayne State University Press, pp. 71–82.

Evans-Pritchard, E. E. (1968) *Witchcraft, Oracles and Magic Among the Azande*. Oxford: Clarendon Press.

Gabriel, Teshome (1982) *Third Cinema in the Third World: The Aesthetics of Liberation*. Ann Arbor: University of Michigan Press.

Goodman, Grant K. (ed.) (1991) *Japanese Cultural Policies in Southeast Asia During World War 2*. Basingstoke: Macmillan.

Hamm, Bernd and Russell Smandych (eds.) (2005) *Cultural Imperialism: Essays on the Political Economy of Cultural Domination*. Peterborough: Broadview Press.

Jameson, Frederic (1987) "World Literature in an Age of Multinational Capitalism". In Clayton Koelb and Virgil Locke (eds.) *The Current in Criticism: Essays on the Present and Future of Literary Theory*. West Lafayette, IN: Purdue University Press, pp. 141–158.

Lalvani, Suren (1996) *Photography, Vision, and the Production of Modern Bodies*. Albany: State University of New York Press.

Lemaire, Gerard-Georges (2008) *The Orient in Western Art*. Berlin: h.f.ullmann.

Lewis, David, Dennis Rodgers and Michael Woodcock (eds.) (2013) *Popular Representations of Development: Insights from Novels, Films, Television and Social Media*. London and New York: Routledge.

Marchetti, Gina (1997) "*Two Stage Sisters:* The Blossoming of a Revolutionary Aesthetic". In Sheldon Hsiao-peng Lu (ed.) *Transnational Chinese Cinema: Identity, Nationhood, Gender*. Honolulu: University of Hawai'i Press.

Mast, Gerald (1992) *A Short History of the Movies*. 5th edition, revised by Bruce F. Kawin. New York: Macmillan.

Mirzoeff, Nicholas (ed.) (2002) *The Visual Culture Reader*. London and New York: Routledge.

Museum Ludwig Cologne (1996) *20th Century Photography*. Cologne, London and Tokyo: Taschen.

Niang, Sada (2014) *Nationalist African Cinema: Legacy and Transformations*. Lanham, MD: Lexington Books.

Oha, Obododimma (2001) "The Visual Rhetoric of the Ambivalent City in Nigerian Video Films". In Mark Shiel and Tony Fitzmaurice (eds.) *Cinema and the City: Film and Urban Studies in a Global Context*. Oxford and Malden, MA: Blackwell, pp. 195–205.

Peacock, James L. (1987) *Rites of Modernization: Symbolic and Social Aspects of Indonesian Proletarian Drama*. Chicago: University of Chicago Press.

Rocher, Glauber (1997) "An esthetic of hunger". In Michael T. Martin (ed.) *New Latin American Cinema: Theory, Practices and Transcontinental Articulations*. Detroit: Wayne State University Press, pp. 59–61.

Said, Edward W. (1985) *Orientalism*. London: Penguin Books.

Said, Edward W. (1993) *Culture and Imperialism*. London: Chatto and Windus.

Shohat, Ella and Robert Stam (2002) "Narrativizing Visual Culture: Towards a polycentric visual culture". In Nicholas Mirzoeff (ed.) *The Visual Culture Reader*. London and New York: Routledge, pp. 37–59.

Solanas, Fernando and Octavio Getino (1976) "Towards a Third Cinema". In Bill Nichols (ed.) *Movies and Methods*. Vol. 1. Berkeley and London: University of California Press, pp. 44–64.

Spivak, Gayatri Chakravorty and Sneja Gunew (1994) "Questions of Multiculturalism". In Simon During (ed.) *The Cultural Studies Reader*. London and New York: Routledge, pp. 193–202.

Stringer, Julian (2001) "Global Cities and the International Film Festival Economy". In Mark Shiel and Tony Fitzmaurice (eds.) *Cinema and the City: Film and Urban Societies in a Global Context*. Oxford and Malden, MA: Blackwell, pp. 134–144.

Thomas, Nicholas (1994) *Colonialism's Culture: Anthropology, Travel and Government*. Cambridge: Polity Press.

Wasko, Janet (1994) *Hollywood in the Information Age*. Cambridge: Polity Press.

Wayne, Michael (2002) "The Critical Practice and Dialectics of Third Cinema". In Rasheed Araeen, Sean Cubitt and Ziauddin Sardar (eds.) *The Third Text Reader on Art, Culture and Theory*. London and New York: Continuum, pp. 211–25.

Yoo, David K. (ed.) (1999) *New Spiritual Homes: Religion and Asian Americans*. Honolulu: University of Hawai'i Press.

6
WRITING DEVELOPMENT
Literatures of critique and transformation

Writing *about* colonialism and imperialism, seen by many as the precursors of contemporary globalization, and as, depending on your ideological viewpoint, either
the beginning of 'development' as we now understand it, or as the beginning of the
very process of continuing underdevelopment and dependency that still plagues the
planet, has been a long tradition. Writing from *within* those same processes however
is a somewhat different matter. The former approach has given rise to a large schol-
arly literature, much of it contained within the rubric of 'Post-Colonial Theory/
Studies' that has not only examined the whole colonial process historically and
economically, but has also drawn attention to the fact that colonized peoples also
possessed a literature, and that much of that literature is in the form of a critique of
the very colonial conditions imposed on non-metropolitan writers that has in many
cases produced a distinctive form of writing. So whereas writing about colonialism
has been largely the territory of First World academics and intellectuals, many of
whom have probably never even been to the Third World, writing from within it
has been the province of indigenous writers, playwrights, critics and intellectuals. In
this chapter we will focus on the literary writings of the latter group, but necessarily
against the background of academic debates emanating from the West, and from
local academics heavily influenced by theoretical writing coming from outside of
their own societies.

Probably the grandfather of all these debates is the late Edward Said whose two
key books *Orientalism* (Said 1985) originally published in 1978, and *Culture and
Imperialism* (Said 1993) set many of the terms for the subsequent debates. In the
former Said was concerned with the representations of the Orient (understood
as what today we would call the Middle East) in the writings of Western travel-
lers (mostly French and British) and novelists, in such a way that, in line with
nineteenth-century ideas of racial hierarchies, the relationship between the West

and the Orient was always an unequal one, one structured by power and giving rise to the what Said calls the "Theses of Oriental backwardness, degeneracy, and inequality with the West" (Said 1985: 206). The result, quite naturally, was the denigration of the cultures of the Orient, their art, mores, sexual customs, and of course religions (in particular Islam) and the depiction of the Oriental as somehow less than human, or at best, as inferior to her or his Western counterpart. Literature, in the forms of travel writing (immensely popular in the nineteenth century), fiction and academic or quasi-academic writings thus had according to Said, immense power in forming images of the East that had the effect of justifying Western imperial ambitions in the Middle East. And although Said does not discuss the visual arts, other scholars have shown how similar images were generated in painting in particular (Lemaire 2008). Paradoxically of course, the very same space was also the site of the origin of Christianity, the very religion that almost all Orientalist writers would have publically espoused.

In his *Culture and Imperialism,* Said turned directly to the study of literature of a later period and admits in the introduction that "What I left out of *Orientalism* was that response to Western dominance which culminated in the great movement of decolonization all across the Third World" (Said 1993: xii), an absence that he intends to make up for by exploring in much more detail the broad connections between culture and the colonial project. The importance of the literary in this is expressed through the power of narratives:

> The power to narrate, or to block other narratives from forming and emerging, is very important to culture and imperialism, and constitutes one of the main connections between them. Most important, the grand narratives of emancipation and enlightenment mobilized people in the colonial world to rise up and throw off imperial subjection; in the process, many Europeans and Americans were also stirred by these stories and their protagonists, and they too fought for new narratives of equality and human community.
>
> *(Said 1993: xiii)*

In 'First World' literature the issue of empire was increasingly expressed in the writings of novelists such as Conrad, Kipling writing in English and Gide and Loti writing in French. Anthropologists too, while benefitting from the access that their status as imperial citizens gave them to the colonies, were in many cases highly critical of the colonialist policies and practices that they observed on the ground (Asad 1975). As a result a complex dialectic has arisen between history, geography, anthropology, comparative religion and literature in one sphere, and between First World writers and imperialism, between Third World writers and that same imperialism experienced as a victim (or in some cases as a beneficiary) of its institutions and practices and between Third and First World writers, the former often drawing on the work of social theorists, philosophers, social activists, artists and artistic movements and political thinkers from amongst the latter, and First World thinkers and artists gaining inspiration from the arts and religions of the Third World – Europe in very real sense needing the 'Others' as its point of contrast, source of inspiration outside of the tired themes and motifs of the 'old' local cultures (one thinks of Picasso and the German Expressionist painters discovering African sculpture in the ethnographic museums of Paris, Munich and Berlin), and even as a kind of representation of a simpler and more natural past of the metropolitan country, as the Japanese discovered in their colony of Korea (Atkins 2010). But if the absence of the narratives of decolonization was the big gap in *Orientalism,* the big gap in *Culture and Imperialism* is the absence of genuine Third World voices – of the many writers whose fiction, poetry, and literary criticism actually expresses the indigenous viewpoint, initially of colonialism, and now of its latter day clones, neo-colonialism (including very much of the cultural type) and globalization.

In Said's large book, these voices are not entirely absent, but are very much occluded by those of the major Western writers whose work has addressed or at least touched on the subject of imperialism, a subject so big and so world-forming that as Said himself notes, it is quite amazing that so many major writers and critics could manage *not* to address it in their often voluminous works. Nevertheless many did, in novels, travelogues, works of history, sociology, racial studies and through photography. Representations are important: they create not only images of the Other, but also hierarchies through which inequalities are expressed. And amongst those who did, in the metropolitan centres many wrote against injustice. But while critique of colonialism from within is important, and had, like earlier critiques of slavery, political results, the voices from within are even more worthy of attention. An important exponent of that point of view is the Kenyan writer and organic intellectual Ngugi wa Thiong'o whose book *Decolonising the Mind* (1986) both debates the role of literature in furthering African liberation, cultural as well as political, and marks its author's determination to thereafter write in the vernacular, and not in English. Cultures of resistance arise from many sources, and amongst these Said argues is the recovery of a sense of the land: to resist the mapping and hence conceptual appropriation of the very spaces inhabited by the native peoples. This was true in Ireland (Said 1993: 273), in Southeast Asia, even in the parts such as Thailand not directly colonized by the Western powers (Winichakul 1994), Fiji (Clammer 1975), and across the globe where the 'East', 'Africa', and other zones and regions ('The Middle East', 'Southeast Asia') were formed not out of natural geographical areas (if such exist) as from the colonial imagination (Lewis and Wigen 1997). Maps themselves are a form of art, and mapping becomes a place where conceptions of space, its visual representation, politics, power and identity converge like no other.

It is for this reason that a preoccupation with the land is so central to much resistance literature, for example in Palestine where the loss of ancestral land during the formation of the new state of Israel continues to be the basis of conflict, trauma and a sense of existential loss, as depicted in for example the novel *On the Hills of God* by Ibrahim Fawal (2002). Said, himself of Palestinian origin, comments on this phenomenon as follows:

> One of the first tasks of the culture of resistance was to reclaim, rename, and reinhabit the land. And with that came a whole set of further assertions, recoveries, and identifications, all of them quite literally grounded on this poetically projected base. The search for authenticity, for a more congenial national origin than that provided by colonial history, for a new pantheon of heroes and (occasionally) heroines, myths, and religions – these too are made possible by the sense of the land reappropriated by its people. And along with these nationalistic adumbrations of the decolonized identity, there always goes an almost magically inspired, quasi-alchemical redevelopment of the native language.
>
> *(Said 1993: 273)*

Development discourse itself can have a major effect on these processes, by insinuating a certain language of 'modernization', 'progress', 'growth', and 'change', by denigrating by implication or directly, tradition, and by undermining cultural integrity by holding up a foreign model as the goal to be aimed for by all right-thinking people. Now of course it is not only such developmentalist discourses, but equally the news media and the corporations behind them that set 'values', fashions, cuisines, images of the world and political models before huge and globalized audiences, and influence them subliminally if not overtly by such methods. In other words, advertising on a world scale.

One major consequence of this has been the rise of 'cultural politics': politics concerned not so much with the older issues of work, class, wages, and economic entitlements, as with identities, multiculturalism, religions and the right (or not) to wear religious dress in public places. Anthony Giddens has argued that one of the major shifts in 'late modernity' (i.e. now and the recent past) has been a shift from 'emancipatory politics' concerned with the classic issues of the French Revolution – Liberty, Equality and Fraternity, to what he terms "life-style politics" – politics concerned with identity, self-protection and self-promotion and a consequent loss of a sense of community or solidarity in society as a whole (Giddens 1991). This may be true of the West, or at least of Britain, from where Giddens writes, but it is far from true of much of the rest of the world where cultural politics is the struggle not necessarily any longer for freedom from formal colonialism, but for its successors. 'Development' is built to a great extent on the ruins of colonialism, and the expanding cultural and environmental depredations of globalization set the themes for post-colonial literature, especially in the societies most deeply affected by its inroads.

Post-colonial literatures

A great number of critics have spent a great deal of energy and ink in arguing over exactly what constitutes the 'post-colonial' (Childs and Williams 1997): is it just literally after colonialism? Or do continuing forms of oppression and foreign interference also constitute the field of post-colonialism? Here I want to bypass this extensive debate by regarding the post-colonial along three main axes: yes, as literally after the end of formal colonialism; as engaging with neo-colonialism (including globaliza-tion); as continuing forms of largely one-sided interaction between the 'developed' and the 'developing' world largely fuelled by economic interests including resource competition; and as forms of literary and artistic response to the emerging problems and experience of development and the new issues such as climate change that are falling disproportionately on the developing world.

One of the first systematic efforts to survey post-colonial literature was the 1989 seminal volume *The Empire Writes Back* (Ashcroft, Griffiths and Tiffin 1989), in which it is recognized that imperialism does not necessarily end when the colonizers withdraw: forms of hegemony deriving from economic power, control of multilat-eral institutions such as the World Trade Organization, and the immense influence of the metropolitan languages on subsequent cultural production in the Third World, to say nothing of forms of intervention such as aid, the arms trade and tourism continue and may even grow. A paradoxical example of this is the fact that most of the literature surveyed in *The Empire Writes Back* and similar analyses is written in English (or indeed in French and Spanish and to some extent in Portuguese in the smaller literature on post-colonialism that has emerged from those other old colonial powers). Most of the Western scholars who have made post-colonialism their rather trendy and radical chic speciality evidently do not read the languages in which much of actual post-colonial literature is produced – Swahili, Hindi, Bengali, Malayalam, Fijian and many others. This is a problem that we will return to in a while. But nevertheless, much literary production in the developing world has two key charac-teristics: it believes that culture has a major role in resistance and in the defining of alternatives to conventional development paths, and much of it has ideological roots in the works of two key post-colonial theorists who articulated workable models of opposition to cultural hegemony – notably Frantz Fanon and Amilcar Cabral and whose active cultural work (centred on North Africa and Guinea-Bissau respectively) continues to inspire the contemporary generation of Third World writers, especially in Africa (for a detailed discussion see Childs and Williams 1997: 49–59). While less concerned with liberation struggles, the aforementioned Kenyan writer Thiong'o raises similar concerns about the domination through culture of the colonizers over the colonized, and the need not only to resist this (in part through the encouragement of writing and drama in the indigenous languages), but also through encouraging a paradoxical process of universalism (all cultures are equal in dignity and potentiality), and of decentring, moving away from the centralized structures of cultural power represented by the metropolitan countries towards a pluralism of many centres in which autonomous cultures can flourish without appearing as somehow second class or inferior to the 'high cultures' of the internationally dominant societies (Thiong'o 1993). *Mental decolonization* is just as important as political decolonization, and in fact the latter can never be complete if the former is ignored. So by now hopefully this general position is established: that culture is a vital component in interrogat-ing 'development' in all its forms – colonial, post-colonial, neo-colonial, nationalism (including post-colonial forms of nationalism and nativism), globalization, aid and the operations of both multilateral institutions (the World Bank, the United Nations, the WTO, the International Monetary Fund) and multinational corporations, many of which are devoted precisely to the spread of particular forms of culture (the major film companies, satellite TV companies, music producers and international publishers.) It is implicated in issues of identity, language, autonomy and self-determination. And it may, in the last analysis, be the point of development: to produce a civilization in the true sense of the word, one rich in its symbolic, performative and expressive modes and one committed to social justice and a harmonious relationship to the natural environment. If this is so, then literature, (and the arts in general), have a major role to play in promoting genuine and rounded development. The place now to turn is to literature itself, to see how these ideas have played out in practice.

Literatures of protest, affirmation and identity

The range of possible examples is vast. The Caribbean for example has produced a plethora of distinguished poets (Lorna Goodison, Louise Bennett and the Nobel Prize–winning Derek Walcott, to name a few), novelists (V. S. Naipaul is a major example, as is the much more radical Wilson Harris), essayists, critics and writers such as Edouard Glissant who combine many of these categories – in his case as poet, novelist, historian and cultural theorist. Most touch in one way or another on issues of race, identity, underdevelopment and post-colonialism. Cuba alone has produced a large literature on these themes, and naturally on the questions of revolution, socialism, and the continuing impact of the US embargo on relations with the country. Examples available in English include Antonio Benítez-Rojo's *A View from the Mangrove* (1998), G. Cabrera Infante's *A View of Dawn in the Tropics* (1990) and Alejo Carpentier's *Explosion in a Cathedral* (1971). Two cases from Africa and the African diaspora stand out as both poets intensely involved in politics and in the development paths of their respective nations are undoubtedly the Senegalese poet, politician and promoter of local theatre and performance forms Leopold Sedar Senghor, and Aimé Cesairé from Martinique, who was responsible for coining the term "Negritude", an important concept referring to the production of a literature by Black people of both Africa and the Caribbean, much of it seen as a literature of liberation and resistance, in a sense by its very nature, for here was a literature of quality being produced not in the metropolis, but at the very margins of former Empires, and asserting the dignity and unity (even to the extent of a kind of pan-Africanism) of the Black peoples (Irele 1981). Edouard Glissant mentioned above, has produced a variant of Negritude with his own theory of *Antillanité* or "Caribbeanness" (now available in an English translation: Glissant 1989). The Black experience in North America has of course also produced a large and distinguished literature, much of it congruent with the concerns of Third World literature revolving around race, inequality, gender, violence and uneven development, and much of it also contesting imposed identities and representations (for two examples from a large critical literature see bell hooks 1992 and Davis 1994).

Contemporary Africa continues to produce writers addressing the ongoing issues of underdevelopment, violence, the problems of the post-apartheid society in

South Africa, dictatorship, urbanization, civil war and religious conflict. Prominent examples whose works are available in English or French include the Nigerians Chinua Achebe and Uzodinwa Iweala, the Senegalese Cheikh Hamidou Kane, the Cameroonian writer Mongo Beti, the Ghanaian novelist Kojo Laing, the Kenyan Binyavanga Wainaina and many more, some of whom are represented in the accessible literary magazine *Granta* which in 2005 devoted a special issue to new African writing (Granta 92, 2005). India produces perhaps even more, with a very lively literary culture in both English and the many vernaculars, with active publication of novels, poetry and short stories, many of them addressing questions of caste, gender, poverty, the rural-urban divide and the situation of migrants to the crowded and polluted cities (for example Ratan 2003). Neighbouring Sri Lanka has generated a parallel literature dealing with the same issues, plus those of decolonization, cultural erosion and the tragedies of the long internal war between the Sinhalese majority and the Tamil minority. The major Sri Lankan writer and novelist Martin Wick-ramasinghe has touched on many of these issues in his essays and short stories (for example Wickramasinghe n.d.). Indonesia likewise has a strong tradition of novels addressing colonialism, underdevelopment, oppression both internal and external, and the problems experienced by a traditional and even feudal society in adjusting to modernization, a classical example being the novels of Pramoedya Ananta Toer, who spent over a decade as a political prisoner in one of independent Indonesia's most notorious concentration camps, and two years in a Dutch colonial prison. His experiences were distilled into a cycle of novels, critical writings and essays, many of which, including his major work *This Earth of Mankind* are available in English translations (Toer 1981).

It might be fruitful, having now hopefully established the existence of a large and vibrant literature addressing the problems of post-colonialism, underdevelopment, and the displacements and disruptions that accompany modernization, development and urbanization, to examine a small number of cases in more detail. Here I will take four: an Indian exemplar, a Palestinian novel, a Latin American poet, and some contemporary African short stories. These will help us see in greater depth the ways in which the broad themes of the interaction of literature and development interrelate and illuminate each other. I will start with the Indian case for here we have an instance of someone writing largely in the vernacular – in Oriya, the language spoken in the western Indian state of Orissa, a state with a large tribal population (that term is still used in India), serious problems of poverty, rural underdevelopment, encroachment of mining companies onto tribal lands, inter-religious violence, and also a vibrant literary culture, folk theatre and folk art tradition – the latter represented by the Orissan *Patta* paintings in particular. One of the prominent indigenous intellectuals was the recently deceased writer Chitta Ranjan Das, whose work helps us to see the dynamics of Third World literature and criticism at play.

Das was a writer whose work spanned many genres – fiction, literary criticism, sociology, diaries, collections of his letters, essays on current political and social topics and treatises on education (for a representative sampling see Das 2011, and for commentary see Giri 2012), mostly in Oriya or in English. His work raises many interesting issues, quite apart from its intrinsic literary merit, including, in a post-colonial society, the role of the writer in that society, the place of 'indigenous' or vernacular literature in the wider (including universal) literary canon, and the place of the imaginative life in the wider economy and ecology of culture as a whole. Do the arts have a role in society other than that of entertainment and distraction? This was a question to which much of Das's literary output was designed to answer, in the positive.

He recognized early in his work, and partly informed by his work in sociology, that a simply functionalist approach was completely inadequate. Rather, the writer should ask what constitutes a society's self-understanding, and its modes of self-representation (whether or not these are 'accurate'). To discover this internal hermeneutics it is necessary to discover the deep cultural grammar of a society. Das began his career as a rural sociologist, and soon came to the conclusion that such a grammar could not be discovered through questionnaires, but requires an understanding of the arts of a society as these constitute its way of structuring its expressivity and its relationship to the spiritual, and form its vehicle for exploring its largely unconscious emotional dynamics. The arts in Das's view are not then separate from life, but are both its means of expression and its means of self-exploration. As such they are both analytical and prophetic: they can both expose and critique existing patterns of society, psychology and culture, and can provide guidelines to future possibilities by nurturing the imagination, the most powerful in his view of all the human faculties. The role of the literary critic is to act as a kind of bridge between the creative artist and the wider society: to help both by interpreting each to the other (Das 1982). The arts both interpret existing cultural symbols and create new ones by contributing to and indeed creating the enrichment of the imaginative repertoire of a society.

In this belief, and practice as a critic of Indian literature, Das followed the philosophy of the distinguished Sri Lankan (the Ceylonese) art historian and cultural critic Ananda Coomaraswamy who argued in the 1940s for the concept of the 'creative critic', whose role is not the deconstruction of the creative writer or painter's work, but rather to assist in drawing out and explicating the original vision that moved the artist to create in the first place (Coomaraswamy 1948: 69). To achieve this in both his creative writing and literary criticism, Das drew on sources familiar to him as an Indian – local history, Oriya literature, the oral literature, songs and poems of rural Indians (often of excluded castes and groups) and the incredibly rich mythology of Hinduism. He not only drew on them but attempted to show in fiction and non-fiction, that these forms of indigenous cultural expression are not only interesting in their own right, but also embody ecological wisdom, social knowledge and complex ways of interpreting and managing the external world and its inevitable problems. In this sense, while certainly not minor in either volume or quality, Das's writing perhaps constitutes an example of what the French cultural theorists Gilles Deleuze and Felix Guattari have called "Minor Literature" (Deleuze and Guattari 1986). "Minor" here refers not to quality (they include the major European writer

Franz Kafka in this category) but to literature with several distinct qualities: it is from the 'margins' rather than the 'centre' as defined by the current arbiters of taste (and so much vernacular literature falls into this category), and which rather than engage directly with the two more obvious literary strategies of ideological/political critique or alternatively retreat into purely personal symbolism, take a significantly different path of radical practice, notably that of transforming 'limitations' – lack of economic resources, invisibility or marginality in society, lack of access to the current literary or intellectual metropolitan centres – into its strength.

In Das's case this has meant on the one hand exploring imaginatively his local resources (although he also knew world literature well) drawn from myth, sociology, folk tales and the works of other vernacular writers to create a body of writing independent of any explicit ideology, embodying a distinctive local and Indian aesthetics, and creating a form of social critique by way of art quite different from normal political analysis. We have in the work of this largely unknown, outside of India, writer, a potential model of a new literature, and one quite difficult to contain within the (mostly Western) categories of 'post-colonial literature'. Certainly Das is in temporal terms a post-colonial writer, but his work is not of the 'subaltern' type at all. Rather it represents a mode of engagement with the world that both crosses out of the boundaries of a narrowly defined literature to encompass sociology, criticism, local literary history, philosophy, religion and folklore, and which is affirmative in nature, drawing on the rich imaginative resources of Indian vernacular literature and folkways.

In practice this involved a number of steps: recovering local literatures, written and oral, and their associated cultural histories, the promotion of an aesthetic education in his readers and in particular young people, the deconstruction and critique of dehumanizing traditions, however much sanctified by time and custom, dialogue with other indigenous intellectuals, writers and artists, and a value commitment: that literature, certainly in its Indian context, cannot mean art for art's sake, but must take the form of a means for the transformation of life, culture and society.

Chitta Ranjan Das's work shows in practice the creation or operation of what Frederic Jameson has called the "third space", an idea elaborated by Homi Bhabha as a hybrid location in which counter-authority can be opened up and minority or subordinated knowledge reinstated (Bhabha 1993, Childs and Williams 1997: 142). A rather different 'take' on things can be found in the magisterial Palestinian novel *On the Hills of God* by Ibrahim Fawal which deals with the establishment of Israel from the perspective of a young Palestinian who experiences the loss of ancestral land, violent displacement, confusion of identity, what amounts of a civil war, or at least war between the Palestinian indigenes and the Zionist settlers, issues of gender, family and marriage in a situation of sudden and extreme change in which all the old cultural markers are suddenly falling away and the long term traumas of such massive upheavals. Although the novel deals with one particular situation and actual historical reality, it raises many of the key issues of Third World literature: change at many levels in ways that are so fast and multiple that they cannot be assimilated into either traditional categories or even simply everyday experience, loss of land, upsetting of social and familial hierarchies, the sudden need to rethink radically identity, political positions and future expectations. Since the future for many Palestinians was in fact refugee camps, or a marginal life in neighbouring Jordan (where Fawal's novel was originally published in Arabic) or in Lebanon, soon itself to be wracked by civil war and then Israeli invasion, the novel encapsulates many of the issues of displacement, being colonized, loss and trauma that accompany both imperialism and many forms of development. The novel can indeed be seen as an example of what some call the 'literature of trauma' – a literature produced by those who have experienced war, profound up-rooting, exile, loss of status and identity crises as a result. Such a literature emerged for example from the trenches of the First World War, and more recently from veterans of the American war in Vietnam (Tal 1996), and a great deal of Third World literature represents another form of such literature: not only exposure to war, but also to displacements at many levels: physical, cultural and sociological, that accompany 'development' and globalization in so many of their manifestations.

Commentaries on Palestinian literature, poetry (of which there is a major tradition in Arabic), novels and also autobiography of writers, many of whom are in exile or living under Israeli occupation, take up many of these points: that such literature is a cry, a protest, a way of representing exile, a struggle to find an identity and a therapy in so far as it provides a medium to express these very sentiments, and a way to organize and reorganize memories, which become extremely important in situations of both external displacement (exile or refugee status), or internal (becoming a minority in what was one's own country in which the landmarks are now all changed or inaccessible). Literature then becomes very much a means of resistance, cultural continuity, publicity about the situation and a way of re-creating a new identity or sense of self (Rooke 1996). In such conditions, even imaginary homelands are vital to both psychic health and political strategies.

In many Western countries, poetry, while formally admired, is not actually much read. The major exceptions to this are probably Russia and parts of Eastern Europe, and Ireland and parts of Wales, where the Bardic tradition still exists. But this is not true of Latin America, where poetry continues to be a major literary form, and as such is one of the primary written and spoken mediums through which social issues are addressed. In a continent of many poets it is hard to pick on one example (if one includes the Caribbean, it has in the fairly recent past produced three Nobel laureates in literature who are primarily poets: Pablo Neruda, Octavio Paz and Derek Walcott). But from the point of view of social critique, one exemplary figure certainly stands out: the Chilean poet Pablo Neruda. Neruda (1904–1973) was perhaps the paradigm case of a committed writer. A lifelong Communist, he was also a lover of wine, women and song; a humanist in the true sense of the word; a politician (serving as a Senator in the Chilean parliament, and standing on one occasion as presidential candidate, only to stand down in favour of the ill-fated Salvador Allende); a diplomat; a friend of Picasso, the leading Spanish poet Lorca (murdered by the Franco regime), Aragon and other major French poets; and certainly Chile's greatest modern poet himself and a towering figure amongst Latin

American literary figures. As his biographer Adam Feinstein aptly summarizes his life: "Neruda felt that man – and writers, above all – had a duty to embrace life and commit to seeking social justice" (Feinstein 2005: 2). Despite his intense public life, including periods in exile in Argentina and Europe, he produced a prodigious amount of first-class poetry, including his monumental *Canto general,* and his collected works (including speeches and letters) runs to five substantial volumes (Loyola 1999–2001). Although occasionally (but rarely) Neruda did write didactic poems (in praise of Communism, or of Stalin, or against some obvious social evil), the body of his extensive work weaves together social, existential and political themes in a seamless way, making his work both highly readable, good literature and embodying social comment all at the same time. This is a rare talent, and a large part of Neruda's reputation derives from this skill in striking at several levels of human interest simultaneously.

Neruda himself of course needs to be placed in the context of Latin American literature, and specifically poetry, in a continent that has experienced the extremes of uneven development, brutal military dictatorships, revolutions and counter-revolutions, and is immense and diverse in its geography, ecology and local cultures, its complex relationships with both North America and Europe, and its place in the world system of modernization and globalization. As suggested above, poetry in Latin America has a privileged status. Even those writers who turned primarily to other forms of expression such as the distinguished Columbian writer Gabriel Garcia Marquez approvingly quotes his countryman, the poet Eduardo Carrenza who says that

> If poetry does not make my blood run faster, open sudden windows for me into the mysterious, help me discover the world, accompany this desolate heart in solitude and in love, in joy and in enmity, what good is poetry to me.
>
> *(Marquez 2004: 252)*

Part of our problem in the West is that we tend to separate culture from social action. In Latin America this distinction is much weaker: cultural action *is* social action, so poetry can be as much a tool of struggle as strikes, marches or guns, a point of view as we have seen, shared by many of Latin America's leading visual artists as well as its writers. There are interesting parallels here with Eastern Europe where the most recent phase of 'development' has involved the move from Communism to a market economy, from socialism with its many virtues (guaranteed housing, medical care, full employment, universal education, high levels of support for the arts) directly into the arms of capitalism, which of course guarantees none of those things. This wrenching transition experienced in Poland, East Germany, Hungary, and throughout the rest of the former Soviet satellite states, has also been reflected in its literatures, and significantly in its poetry.

The Nobel Prize–winning Polish poet Czeslaw Milosz has written at some length about this in the published version of his Charles Eliot Norton Lectures *The Witness of Poetry* (Milosz 1983). There he argues that poetry, far from being a marginal cultural activity (where socially speaking it clearly is not in Russia, Latin America, Japan and Eastern Europe, and in societies that still have a strong oral tradition), is implicated in the rebirth of the miraculous (perhaps identical to what the art critic Suzi Gablik called the "re-enchantment of the world"), in a tempering of the technological hubris of our allegedly scientific civilization, in re-shaping the relationship between humans and nature and the struggle for the planet, and as a servant of Eros. The poet is also responsible for the shaping of language, a not insignificant task in a world where the very tools of communication have become corrupt and degenerated into the devices whereby advertising men and politicians manipulate our lives. Poetry then is potentially, and at its best really is, a source of hope, re-enchantment, a reservoir of beauty, a zone of imagination, a defender of pure language. While seeing clearly (and having experienced) that development brings disintegration, he suggests that this hope is not simply a chimera, but a psychic means of advancing into a future that transcends one-dimensional man and points to a far richer and humane conception of civilization. The poetry of the West is certainly not unaware of these issues and in particular the environmental crisis has been addressed by many poets working in the developed world. Good examples would be the North American poets Gary Snyder, Denise Levertov, and the beat poet Allen Ginsberg and the Japanese poet Nanao Sakaki (whose work is available in English: Sakaki 2013), and the very many Western poets who have made nature their theme over many generations.

Finally, let us mention again contemporary African writing. The stories and essays collected in the special edition of *Granta* mentioned above, represent a cross-section of many of the issues that preoccupy many mainly younger-generation African writers today. For the older generation the issue was colonialism. With the demise of at least formal colonialism a whole new agenda of challenges have arisen, both those brought about by global processes – economic globalization, climate change, AIDS and aid – and those brought about by processes within African societies themselves – dictatorships, civil war, corruption, crime, hyper-urbanization, refugees and religious conflict, to name only some of the most prominent ones. In that edition a number of prominent African writers have published short stories dealing with class (Chimamanda Ngozi Adichie), civil war (Moses Isegawa), migration and exile in cold northern climates (Segun Afolabi), the violence and crime in South African cities (Ivan Vladislavic), the rediscovery of traditional spirituality (Helon Habila) and race (Nadine Gordimer). Other non-fiction essays in the same collection discuss stereotypes in writing about Africa (Binyavanga Wainaina), historical photographs of Black South Africans (Santu Mofokeng), returning to Africa on the part of people who had migrated to the West (Adewale Maja-Pearce), and the emerging role of China in Africa (Lindsey Hilsum), amongst others. It is evident from even such a small selection that the issues of development loom large. Migration, post-colonial violence, new aid donors (and buyers up of extensive tracts of land) such as China and continuing problems of race and ethnic and religious conflict, war lords and the arms trade, are very real issues, and despite independence and decades of 'development', continue to plague the continent, and to provide major themes for its writers. The major Nigerian novelist Chinua Achebe (well known for his novels *Things Fall Apart* and *No Longer at Ease*) for example has recently turned from fiction to autobiography in his book on his experiences of growing up in the last days of colonialism and the first days of independence, experiencing an elite English language education in a prominent government college, going on to read English Literature at University College, Ibadan, experiencing the Nigerian civil war and emerging as one of the country's best known authors. The book in question is his *There Was a Country* (2012), and is interesting not only for what it says, but for its silences about why Achebe continued to write in the colonial language rather than Igbo, his native tongue, and his own ambiguous relationship to the colonial powers, deriving his education from their influence, but also seeing them as deeply implicated in the tragedies of the Biafran war. But in a way, his personal experience reflects the situation of many other African writers: to reject or selectively embrace the legacy of colonialism? To write in the vernacular or in English or French? To rejoice in the independence of their countries or to criticize the corruption, uneven development and despotisms that have subsequently emerged? These are almost universal problems, and not only in Africa, for the same issues to varying degrees are the context in which writers in Southeast Asia and India also produce. What they reveal is the complexity of any 'post-colonial' writing, embedded as it now is in another paradigm of globalization, modernization, and development. The problems facing writers in societies such as South Africa which have been colonized from without, and then subject to a particularly vicious form of internal colonialism (apartheid) are even deeper. Not only those of language, but also of the many 'levels' of interpretation and representation that such complex and multi-layered societies contain and which set major challenges for the writer of fiction who would embody them in a meaningful form (Ndebele 1994).

We suggested above that many of these issues are found today not only in the developing world, but also in the world of transition in Eastern Europe and Central Asia. Writers from those regions have consequently turned to similar themes. The Czech novelist Milan Kundera whose novels (such as *The Joke, The Unbearable Lightness of Being, Life is Elsewhere*) are now easily available in English and French, has devoted two works of non-fiction to discussing the problems of writing under Communism and in the transitional society (Kundera 1990, 1996) and about the art of the novel generally in a 'post-modern' world, and where he raises questions of the novel in relation to history, particularly when that history has been a dark one, and affirming the continuing relevance of this form of literature in a rapidly changing and conflict-ridden global society, "Because therein lies the power of culture: it redeems horror by transforming it into existential wisdom" (Kundera 1996: 234).

We see then Third World literatures changing as the global context also shifts, not simply in response to it as many local issues continue to be the themes of vernacular writing, but as the context in which that literature occurs. Issues of nationalism, colonialism, revolution and new technologies and social mores preoccupied an earlier generation of writers – in Southeast Asia for example where thirty or forty years ago the issues were still ones of identity as countries like Singapore and Malaysia emerged from colonialism, where Vietnam was still coming to terms with its war of liberation, and where questions of ethnicity and religious pluralism were at the forefront, and in some cases prevented from spilling over into conflict by the shared goal of modernization which gave local governments a kind of unifying ideology (Tham 1981). Some of those issues still exist, but in many cases have been supplanted by newer questions: urbanization, the impact of new technologies, new geo-political alignments, new forms of globalization, cultural as well as economic, and new global challenges such as climate change. It is in response to these issues, along with the lingering heritage, both good and bad, of colonialism, and with the political and social problems of the now fully independent countries of the 'developing' world (corruption, ethnic and religious divisions and so forth), that the creative writers of the Third World will now have to contend, and the signs are very positive: they are doing so, and are doing so in ways that transform and enrich world literature immensely. Indeed, in a sense, in a globalized world, all literature is world literature.

The oral and the aural

In the context of literature and development, it is important to note that not all literatures are written: oral traditions still persist throughout much of the world, including the 'developed' world, where poetry is often read aloud or recited, or turned into song. These oral literatures are of many kinds, and some have been recognized by UNESCO as constituting what has become called "The Oral and Intangible Heritage of Humanity" (UNESCO 2003). These include the Al-Sirah Al-Hilaliyya epic poem form of Egypt, the Akyns or epic storytelling tradition of Kyrgysztan, the Meddahlik public storytelling of Turkey and many other forms which often cross the boundaries between storytelling, poetry, theatre, song and epic chanting (UNESCO 2003). While some of these forms of oral literature restrict themselves mainly to traditional themes, others improvise constantly and introduce comments on contemporary social and political issues, gender questions, the environment, and many other topical themes. The poetry and song of village women in Karnataka in South India for example, sung and chanted while working collectively in the fields, are songs of protest, satire, commentaries on caste and other inequalities, and make fun of their husbands and men in general. Many of these women are illiterate, but literacy alone does not make a literature. India still has a tradition (under pressure from television, Bollywood and modernization in general) of oral epics, usually recounting stories of overcoming injustice, opposing caste inequalities and achieving health and well-being. The western Indian state of Rajasthan still has its local *bhopas,* who are both bards and healers, and who can recount from memory epic tales that can last literally for days, against the backdrop of a *phad* or picture scroll illustrating the events in the story (Dalrymple 2009: 78–111). In hunting and gathering cultures language itself reflects landscape and deep local knowledge. In his beautiful book *The Spell of the Sensuous* David Abram points this out:

If we listen, first, to the sounds of an oral language – to the rhythms, tones, and inflections that play through the speech of an oral culture – we will likely find that these elements are attuned, in multiple and subtle ways, to the contour and scale of the local landscape, to the depth of its valleys or the open stretch of its distances, to the visual rhythms of the local topography. But the human speaking is necessarily tuned, as well, to the various nonhuman calls and cries that animate the local terrain. Such attunement is imperative for any culture still dependent upon foraging for its subsistence. Minute alterations in the weather, changes in the migratory patterns of prey animals, a subtle shift in the focus of a predator – sensitivity to such subtleties is a necessary element of all oral, subsistence cultures, and this sensitivity is inevitably reflected not just in the content, but in the very shapes and patterns of human discourse.

(Abram 1997: 140)

Amongst such discourse is of course oral literature – traditions of storytelling, recounting of myths and origin tales, and forms of song. This is not entirely restricted to non-literate cultures: in highly literate ones storytelling continues and much of the cultural memory of such societies is embedded in its fairy tales, children's stories, the cycle of religious celebrations, and of course is increasingly embodied in film – in the fantasy movies that we referred to in the previous chapter (Bettelheim 1976). In terms of globalization I find it significant too that the 'World Music' section of CD stores has now hugely expanded in the last decade from a tiny corner to now an often substantial proportion of the store. In that section it is possible to find African, Middle Eastern, Indian, Tibetan, Caribbean, Sephardic Jewish and many other musical cultures represented. Groups such as the Refugee All Stars – a group that quite literally began as refugees and have now attained world level visibility, and whose songs comment on the refugee experience, displacement, loss of home and friends – are a poignant reminder that music too can very much speak to the issues of development and its negative sides. A good contemporary example of this is the singer Angélique Kidjo, originally from Benin, whose songs are about African village life, solidarity with women, African rhythms and African languages. Kidjo does not read music, but like a traditional singer memorizes by ear, and writes songs in the West African languages that she grew up with, mainly Fon and Yoruba. She spends time as a UNICEF goodwill ambassador, has set up her own Batonga Foundation to help bring education to deprived African girls, has sung against apartheid in South Africa, collected traditional songs and music from West Africa and has said that "An artist's role is not to ignite violence. You ignite peace" (Parales 2014: 17). Beginning her career as an expatriate in Paris at the CIM jazz school she moved on into recovering and incorporating her own African background into her own music. Jazz, as is well known, began as a music of protest and has continued to be closely connected to identity politics (Kofsky 1970). Both music and 'folk literature' are very live traditions and in societies where an oral tradition is still strong are keys to expressivity, identity and modes of protest and commentary on the world (Iteanu and Schwimmer 1996).

The humanities in development

Possibility, hope, critique, analysis, enchantment, entertainment, protest and many other necessary forms of giving voice are expressed in literature. The humanities are certainly not irrelevant to development. As Martha Nussbaum has persuasively argued, they are in fact essential to the creation and maintaining of democracy (Nussbaum 2010). True development requires the development of culture, and despite the inroads of electronic communication, there is little sign that reading and writing are disappearing. Essentially they cannot, as expressivity in many forms is inherent in human cultures, and literature, whether written or oral, will always remain a very significant part of that total cultural complex and of the constellation of the arts as a whole. The need to speak, to tell one's story is not only an inner need, but also a political one. As the novelist Italo Calvino has put it:

> Literature is necessary to politics above all when it gives a voice to whatever is without a voice, when it gives a name to what as yet has no name, especially to what the language of politics excludes or attempts to exclude. I mean aspects, situations, and languages both of the outer and of the inner world, the tendencies repressed both in individuals and in society. Literature is like an ear that can hear things beyond the understanding of the language of politics; it is like an eye that can see beyond the color spectrum perceived by politics. Simply because of the solitary individualism of his work, the writer may happen to explore areas that no one has explored before, within himself or outside, and to make discoveries that sooner or later turn out to be vital areas of collective awareness.
>
> *(Calvino 1986: 98)*

As was noted before, David Korten has spoken about the need to create 'new stories' if our civilization is to survive. These new stories – narratives of possibility – rarely arise from the work of politicians, political scientists or economists, but almost always from the pens of writers. The whole genre of utopian literature is an example of this, but so are the hints and intimations of a new world found in many literary forms. Literature is like a kind of linguistic water filter, constantly purifying language of the pollutants and distortions introduced into it by the advertisers and politicians. It helps to reset the issues by asking the questions not being addressed in so much of the public sphere. The poet and essayist Alison Hawthorne Deming has rightly said:

> I think of these tasks as cultural activism – nurturing lives devoted to creating meaning rather than to amassing things – because the crisis between our culture and its natural foundations is a crisis of beliefs and values at least as much as it is a crisis of policy and governance.
>
> *(Deming 2001: 58–9)*

Such activism is based on an appreciation of the vast evolutionary role of culture, which is now the most powerful element intervening in the development of the world. Culture based on false values then becomes the most powerful agent of destruction, of the natural environment and of peoples and ways of life that stand in the way of its view of things:

> Art can serve activism by teaching an attentiveness to existence and by enriching the culture in which our roots are set down. Culture is both the crop we grow and the soil in which we grow it. And human culture is the most powerful evolutionary force on Earth these days. The grief we feel at abuses of human power is the first positive step toward transforming that power for the good. Legislation, information, and instruction cannot effect change at this emotional level – though they play a significant role. Art is necessary because it gives us a new way of thinking and speaking, shows us what we are and what we have been blind to, and gives us new language and forms in which to see ourselves. To effect profound cultural change requires that we educate ourselves about our own interior wildness that has led us into such a hostile relationship with the forces that sustain us. Work on the self is work on the culture.
>
> *(Deming 2001: 68)*

This is true, and particularly so when literature confronts both the local problems of development and change, and the injustices that so frequently accompany them, and situates itself in relation to the bigger forces that shape the entire context in which literature is produced – and particularly globalization. The cultural economy and political economy cannot be easily separated, and it is one of the key roles of literature in the context of development to interrogate that political economy and to demand from it the gifts that it promises if the sacrifices required to produce them are really worthwhile, and to ensure that those gifts are equably distributed. But even when this is done, the underlying and universal existential issues remain, and these above all, while concretized in local situations, will always remain the province of literature. Perhaps we can give the last word to the Mexican Nobel Prize–winning poet Octavio Paz:

> Although the problems of the 'underdeveloped' societies are exactly the contrary [to those of the industrialized ones], they likewise require the exercise of imagination, both political and poetic. We have to invent models of development that are less costly than those constructed by Western 'experts'. More viable ones, and above all, ones more in keeping with each country's national character and its history. I mentioned above the need for an Indonesian Swift or an Arab Voltaire; the presence of an active imagination, rooted in native mental soil, is also indispensable: dreaming and working in terms of one's own reality.
>
> *(Paz 1990: 197)*

The examples and cases adduced above would suggest that he is right, but also that those Swifts and Voltaires do already exist. Their problem is being recognized on the world stage and being regarded as prophets in their own countries.

Key readings

The essential place to start would be by reading Edward Said's two major books, which between them originally defined the problems of colonial and post-colonial writing: Edward W. Said: *Orientalism*, London: Penguin Books, 1985, and *Culture and Imperialism*, London: Chatto and Windus, 1993. For the view from the developing world itself read Ngugi wa Thiongo's *Decolonizing the Mind: The Politics of Language in African Literature*, (London: James Curry, 1986). For a good survey of post-colonial studies and in particular literature, a good guide is Peter Childs and Patrick Williams (1997) *An Introduction to Post-Colonial Theory*, Hemel Hempstead: Prentice Hall Europe. For an Eastern- and Central-European perspective look at Czeslaw Milosz's *The Witness of Poetry* (Harvard University Press, 1983) and for a trenchant view on the essential role of the Humanities read Martha C. Nussbaum (2010) *Not For Profit: Why Democracy Needs the Humanities* (Princeton University Press).

Resources

Literary writing about/from development has so far generated rather little in the way of online and similar resources. The books themselves are the thing! But certainly look at the Botnetwork of committed writers in South Africa (www.botsotso.org.za). On the relation between ecology and literature there now exists a dedicated organization based in India – the Organization for Studies in Literature and Environment. There is also a poetry magazine devoted to ecology and literature: *Green Fuse*, which describes itself as "a poetry journal devoted to the preservation of the planet" and which is well worth reading. More universities and colleges are beginning to create centres or programmes relating the humanities and the environment. These include the Center for Environmental Arts and Humanities at the University of Nevada, Reno; 'nature writing' retreats and seminars at the North Cascades Institute (www. ncascades.org); degree courses in "Transformative Language Arts" at Goddard College in Vermont (www.goddard.edu) and short courses at Schumacher College in Devon, England (www.schumachercollege.org.uk), Hawkwood College in the English Cotswolds (www.hawkwoodcollege.co.uk) and at Navdanya (an "international school for sustainable living") at Dehra Dun in North India.

DISCUSSION QUESTIONS

1. What is 'Post-Colonial Theory' and how does it incorporate the study of literature into its paradigms?
2. Give examples, citing particular authors, of the ways in which literature from the developing world has contributed to the critique and reformulation of the development process (including colonialism and globalization).
3. Poetry has played an important role in the literature engaging development and social justice in the 'Third World'. Why do you think this is so? Discuss with examples.

References

Abram, David (1997) *The Spell of the Sensuous*. New York: Vintage Books.

Achebe, Chinua (2012) *There Was a Country*. London: Allen Lane.

Asad, Talal (ed.) (1975) *Anthropology and the Colonial Encounter*. London: Ithaca Press and New York: Humanities Press.

Ashcroft, Bill, Gareth Griffiths and Helen Tiffin (eds.) (1989) *The Empire Strikes Back: Theory and Practice in Post-Colonial Literatures*. London and New York: Routledge.

Atkins, E. Taylor (2010) *Primitive Selves: Koreana in the Japanese Colonial Gaze, 1910–1945*. Berkeley and London: University of California Press.

Benitez-Rojo, Antonio (1998) *A View from the Mangrove*. Trans. James Maraniss. London and Boston: Faber and Faber.

Bettelheim, Bruno (1976) *The Uses of Enchantment: The Meaning and Importance of Fairy Tales*. New York: Alfred A. Knopf.

Bhabha, Homi K. (1993) "How Newness Enters the World: Postmodern Space, Postcolonial Times and the Trials of Cultural Translation". In his *The Location of Culture*. London and New York: Routledge, pp. 217–230.

Calvino, Italo (1986) *The Uses of Literature*. Trans. Patrick Creagh. New York: Harcourt Brace Jovanovich.

Carpentier, Alejo (1971) *Explosion in a Cathedral*. Harmondsworth: Penguin Books.

Childs, Peter and Patrick Williams (1997) *An Introduction to Post-Colonial Theory*. Hemel Hempstead: Prentice Hall Europe.

Clammer, John (1975) "Colonialism and the Perception of Tradition in Fiji". In Asad 1975, pp. 199–222.

Coomaraswamy, Ananda (1948) *The Dance of Shiva*. Bombay: Asia Publishing House.

Dalrymple, William (2009) *Nine Lives: In Search of the Sacred in Modern India*. London: Bloomsbury.

Das, Chitta Ranjan (1982) *A Glimpse into Oriya Literature*. Bhubaneswar: Sikshasandham.

Das, Chitta Ranjan (2011) *On the Side of Life In Spite Of*. Bhubaneswar: Sikshasandham.

Davis, Carole Boyce (1994) *Black Women, Writing and Identity*. London and New York: Routledge.

Deleuze, Gilles and Felix Guattari (1986) *Kafka: Towards a Minor Literature*. Trans. Dana Polan. Minneapolis: University of Minnesota Press.

Deming, Alison Hawthorne (2001) *Writing the Sacred Into the Real*. Minneapolis: Milkweed Editions.

Fawal, Ibrahim (2002) *On the Hills of God*. Montgomery, AL: NewSouth Books.

Feinstein, Adam (2005) *Pablo Neruda: A Passion for Life*. London: Bloomsbury.

Giddens, Anthony (1991) *Modernity and Self-Identity: Self and Society in the Late Modern Age*. Stanford: Stanford University Press.

Giri, Ananta Kumar (ed.) (2012) *A New Morning with Chitta Ranjan Das: Adventures in Co-Realization and World Transformation*. Bhubaneswar: Sikshasandham.

Glissant, Edouard (1989) *Caribbean Discourse: Selected Essays*. Trans. J. Michael Dash. Charlottesville: University of Virginia Press.

Granta 92 (2005) *The View from Africa*. London and New York: Granta Publications.

hooks, bell (1992) *Black Looks: Race and Representation*. Boston: South End.

Infante, G. Cabrera (1990) *A View of Dawn in the Tropics*. Trans. Suzanne Jill Levine. London and Boston: Faber and Faber.

Irele, Abiola (1981) *The African Experience in Literature and Ideology*. London: Heinemann.

Iteanu, André and Eric Schwimmer (1996) *Parle, et je t'écouterai: Récits et traditions des Orokaiva de Papouasie-Nouvelle-Guinée*. Paris: Gallimard.

Kofsky, Frank (1970) *Black Nationalism and the Revolution in Music*. New York: Pathfinder Press.

Kundera, Milan (1990) *The Art of the Novel*. London: Faber and Faber.

Kundera, Milan (1996) *Testaments Betrayed.* London: Faber and Faber.

Lemaire, Gerard-Georges (2008) *The Orient in Western Art.* Berlin: h.f.ullmann.

Lewis, Martin W. and Karen E. Wigen (1997) *The Myth of Continents: A Critique of Metageography.* Berkeley and London: University of California Press.

Loyola, Hernán (ed.) (1999–2001) *Pablo Neruda: Obras Completas.* Barcelona: Galaxia.

Marquez, Gabriel Garcia (2004) *Living to Tell the Tale.* London: Penguin Books.

Milosz, Czeslaw (1983) *The Witness of Poetry.* Harvard: Harvard University Press.

Ndebele, Njabulo S. (1994) "Defining South African Literature for a New Nation". In Carol Becker (ed.) *The Subversive Imagination: Artists, Society, and Social Responsibility.* New York: Routledge, pp. 148–153.

Nussbaum, Martha C. (2010) *Not For Profit: Why Democracy Needs the Humanities.* Princeton and Oxford: Princeton University Press.

Parales, Jon (2014) "Angélique Kidjo puts a continent on her musical map". *International New York Times,* January 18–19, p. 17.

Paz, Octavio (1990) *Alternating Current.* Trans. Helen Lane. New York: Arcade Publishing.

Ratan, Jai (ed.) (2003) *Modern Hindi Short Stories.* New Delhi: Srishti.

Rooke, Tetz (1996) "The Most Important Thing is What Happens Inside Us: Personal Identity in Palestinian Autobiography". In Lisbeth Littrup (ed.) *Identity in Asian Literature.* Richmond: Curzon Press for the Nordic Institute of Asian Studies, pp. 231–153.

Said, Edward W. (1985) *Orientalism.* London: Penguin Books.

Said, Edward W. (1993) *Culture and Imperialism.* London: Chatto and Windus.

Sakaki, Nanao (2013) *How to Live on the Planet Earth: Collected Poems.* Nobleboro, ME: Blackberry Books.

Tal, Kali (1996) *Worlds of Hurt: Reading the Literatures of Trauma.* Cambridge: Cambridge University Press.

Tham, Seong Chee (ed.) (1981) *Literature and Society in Southeast Asia: Political and Sociological Perspectives.* Singapore: Singapore University Press.

Thiong'o wa Ngugi (1986) *Decolonizing the Mind: The Politics of Language in African Literature.* London: James Curry.

Thiong'o wa Ngugi (1993) *Moving the Centre: The Struggle for Cultural Freedom.* London: James Curry.

Toer, Pramoedya Ananta (1981) *This Earth of Mankind.* Trans. Max Lane. Harmondsworth: Penguin Books.

UNESCO (2003) *Second Proclamation of Masterpieces of Oral and Intangible Heritage of Humanity.* Paris: UNESCO.

Wickramasinghe, Martin (n.d.) *Ape Gama: Lay Bare the Roots.* Trans. Lakshmi de Silva. Dehiwala: Tisara Prakasakayo.

Winichakul, Thongchai (1994) *Siam Mapped: The History of the Geo-Body of a Nation.* Honolulu: University of Hawai'i Press.

7

ARTS EDUCATION FOR DEVELOPMENT AND SOCIAL JUSTICE

The impact of the arts on development, and on the pursuit of social justice in general, is much enhanced if the ways in which the arts are taught are specifically linked to those questions. This can be understood in a number of ways – as orienting art education towards social issues rather than as pure 'creativity'; incorporating an awareness of issues such as poverty, human rights, ecological degradation and so forth into the curriculum of art schools, whether in the visual arts, performing arts or film (almost all art colleges have some form of 'complementary studies', which sometimes includes subjects such as sociology or literature as well as art history and aesthetics as supplements to studio based training); or as actually using art as a means in itself to raise awareness about and to address social justice questions. In this chapter we will explore all three of these approaches, and suggest ways in which art education for development (and in developing situations) can be created where it does not yet exist, and enhanced and deepened where it does.

Let us start with the issue of arts education for social justice. A movement has arisen, primarily in the United States of what is being called CRAE: Culturally Relevant Arts Education for Social Justice (Hanley, Noblit, Sheppard and Barone 2013), that is exploring the nexus between the arts, education and social justice, with a view to forming methodologies, sharing strategies and exploring ways in which the arts can address such questions (equally implicit in development) as racism, social exclusion, gender based inequalities, the justice system, the role of the museum and violence. The Hanley *et al* volume just cited stands as a landmark in this respect, as the first systematic attempt to address these issues, cite and draw attention to the scattered literature and promote dialogue and sharing between individuals and organizations working at the interface of art and social justice, but who do not yet form a community of scholarship and practice. Mary Stone Hanley, the lead editor, quite rightly points out three important things in her introduction to the book: that deprivation of *cultural* resources is as much an issue of social justice as is deprivation of material ones; that creativity and imagination represent our

> hardwired capacity to change the world into what we imagine, whether for good or ill, and even to establish the moral compass that will determine our direction. . . . Thus, creativity is empowering: you take risks, test the world, shape media and meaning, and thereby change the world.
>
> *(Hanley 2013: 3)*

And that this empowerment leads to the

> clarification of the internal voice through works of expression. Through the arts we can study the known and the ubiquitous unknown on conscious, and unconscious, intellectual, intuitive and emotional levels; we can inform, empathize, envision possibilities and raise critical consciousness. No matter how deep the oppressive conditions, artists can reclaim humanity for themselves and their communities through their creative agency, and they model possibilities for others who search for meaning and a way to empowerment.
>
> *(Hanley 2013: 5)*

The ensuing chapters develop these ideas through two main means: the development of methodologies whereby the arts can be made relevant and through different media. The latter include many of the forms that we have been discussing in this book: storytelling, theatre, photography, music, documentary film and dance. But even more importantly the authors discuss in detail methodologies for linking the arts and social justice issues, and these are important, since they provide the actual tools with which an arts-based development education might be created. Let us note some of these that have direct relevance to development education as they are potential models for a transformative pedagogy.

1. Storytelling for social justice: through supporting young people to "identify, talk back to, and imagine alternatives to stock stories about them and their communities that rationalize their subjugated position in society" (Bell, Desai and Irani 2013: 15). This is done through a participatory approach that helps young people think critically about inequalities by means of developing counter narratives that challenge the normalizing or hegemonic stories of the dominant communities, deconstruct the self-interested assumptions of those majority discourses, and allow the experiences of minorities to emerge as the valid stuff of stories. Here there are three levels of methodology: analysis, resistance stories and emerging and transforming stories. This latter category is very important as it takes the whole process beyond simply critique into creating change, and produces the emotional and intellectual capacities for transformation. There, in other words, real alternatives are imagined and expressed.

2. Theatre: by building on the model of the theatre of the oppressed with two intentions in mind: to assist communities in using theatre as a method for pursuing social justice, and in helping individuals learn new tools for potential transformation. This is done through using theatre and workshops based on acting techniques to awaken imagination, invite experimentation, to model potential transformative communities and to actually create such communities by bringing people, often of very diverse backgrounds and possibly (as in the Northern Ireland example) conflictual positions together and having them work cooperatively and collectively in the process of the workshops and in some cases in the final production of an actual public theatrical event (Harlap and Aristzábal 2013). These techniques are of course derived from Boal's pioneering work discussed in chapter four, and have been developed in quite radical directions by performance artists such as Guillermo Gómez-Peña, Roberto Sifuentes and Coco Fusco (Gómez-Peña and Sifuentes 2011) who have developed detailed pedagogies for addressing issues of cross-cultural communication and deconstructing hegemonic attitudes to race, gender and colonialism. Others have developed such techniques to raise awareness of and to promote positive identity amongst migrants and migrant-origin communities, and to do so in ways that remain entertaining and avoiding didactic and preachy approaches to social change (Modirzadeh 2013).

3. Hip hop, music and dance: such expressive forms are not only deeply rooted in specific minority cultures, but are also highly attractive, especially to younger people, as forms of entertainment and expression. Utilizing such forms has been found to enhance communal knowledge, a sense of identity and place, as well as promoting sensory and motor skills, and problem solving, as well as providing a means of resistance to the oppressive qualities of dominant cultural forms that tend to disempower those not 'literate' in their particular symbolic language, and hence to take on a political form: culture as a means of protest and affirmation. This it seems is particularly true of hip hop (Clemons and Clemons 2013), but also of dance forms rooted in particular cultures through which the displaced can recover a sense of dignity, identity and the beauty and expressiveness of their own particular body types, shapes and colours (Woodley 2013).

4. Film and photography: In the media-saturated culture in which so many of us live, attraction to and awareness of film is built into almost everybody's lives in both the over-developed world and the developing world, where film and TV are highly important media (in India for example). Give almost any child a camera and she/he will immediately begin to produce an often quite remarkable visual record of what is seen (and with sound, also what is heard). In the context of social justice education, film and still photography have proved to be highly creative teaching and learning tools, teaching the power of representation, personal agency and responsibility, providing an exciting new means of documentation of lives and circumstances, promoting civic participation, encouraging the viewing of reality from multiple perspectives, creating a huge sense of achievement when a successful shoot is completed, and helping participants to articulate alternatives while investigating social justice issues (Anderson 2013).

In all of these cases, and others documented in the Hanley volume, approaching social justice issues through the arts proves highly effective, in part because it engages the emotions and sensory skills that are hardly utilized or encouraged in academic, textually based education. Such an approach also encourages a sense of place, new modes of perception and the enhancement of older and taken-for-granted modes, teaches new skills and promotes often high-impact but non-verbal means of communication and consciousness raising.

All this suggests that an arts-based approach to development education is highly important and a fresh and creative way of addressing development problems. The difficulty is an institutional one: that very little education *about* development (in universities and institutes of Development Studies) incorporates any such approach, and that art schools are rarely connected in any way with development issues. A child exposed to some of the arts-based pedagogies in school of the kind described in the Hanley volume faces a problem on graduation from high school – notably where to continue to pursue such a direction in any coherent form of higher education. At the moment, the main possibility is to combine them by taking courses in both development-related issues and in an art, although in many universities such combinations are simply not possible or do not exist and credit sharing arrangements between universities and art schools hardly exist. And if this is a problem in the developed world, where many such institutions of both kinds exist, it is an even bigger problem in the developing world where in many cases an arts-based education hardly exists at all, at any level. This is not only a huge absence institutionally, but pedagogically too, as studies have shown clearly that the arts are not simply marginal to other forms of development – intellectual, cognitive and emotional, but are deeply implicated (or should be) in the production of rounded personalities and fully functional people (Eisner 2002). A major challenge then is to encourage forms of development education that address the big issues in fresh ways. The failure of so many development projects can often be traced to the neglect of the cultural dimensions on the one hand (of the communities being subjected to development), and to the lack of a rounded development education on the part of the practitioners, who have not been taught to see the subtle aesthetic, religious, emotional and expressive qualities of the communities and peoples that they are no doubt genuinely attempting to help. If Paolo Freire was able to revolutionize the teaching of literacy through linking it intimately with the culture and analysis of the oppressive life conditions of Brazilian peasants, much the same needs to be done for culture in general in relation to development thinking and practice, a process that entails taking expressive culture in all its many forms very seriously indeed.

Education for transformation

Arts education for development and social justice can be seen as part of a wider movement that some call Transformative Learning (O'Sullivan 1999). A great deal of conventional education is apparently designed to fill people with equally conventional knowledge, much of which will be immediately forgotten, and with skills for the 'marketplace' – i.e. work in the business institutions of the capitalist society. Very little education, despite the vague promises in the glossy brochures of schools and colleges, especially the ones that claim to be 'international' in nature, to provide a world-changing education, is not in fact directed towards deep social or personal transformation, but rather for making a successful career in the status quo situation. Transformative learning on the other hand is directed at nurturing fundamental change: first in the individual learner and then as a result in the wider society. According to Edmund O'Sullivan such an education should have a number of key elements, including dealing with the sense of despair and loss that arises as we face the fact that the promises of universal 'development' have failed, and we are left with a complex mess of ecological, social, economic and political problems that few of us know where to begin to effectively address or even comprehend these problems; learning deeply rooted in a cosmological vision in which ecological literacy is the foundation; that it should be transformative in intent, and not simply devoted to maintaining what is and just making more of it (the fallacy of the everlasting growth paradigm). The pedagogical result is that history should be taught as what is now being called "Big History", i.e. the universe story rather than the small history of kings, emperors and nations that still seems to make up much of conventional school history syllabi; that educational strategies should be grouped around the three main themes of peace, social justice and diversity (both social and biological); that children (and adult learners) should be given a planetary vision as well as a local one in this globalized world and that the nurturing of creativity rather than stuffing with 'facts' (themselves often selected on a highly ideological basis) should be the goal. Such an education should in O'Sullivan's view promote a feeling not much encouraged in business schools – notably a sense of awe in the face of the incredible nature of the universe and the finely balanced factors of heat, light, atmosphere, gravity and photosynthesis that make life as we know and experience it possible at all.

This kind of vision is shared by a number of other progressive educators and writers on the contemporary global crisis and what might be done about it. In the former camp I would place the work of Brian K. Murphy, (Murphy 1999) whose work I will refer to in more detail in a moment, and in the latter I would urge readers to consult David Korten's book *The Great Turning: From Empire to Earth Community* (Korten 2006), Sara Parkin's *The Positive Deviant: Sustainability Leadership in a Perverse World* (Parkin 2010), David Gershon's *Social Change 2.0: A Blueprint for Reinventing Our World* (Gershon 2009) and Robert Theobald's *We DO Have Future Choices: Strategies for Fundamentally Changing the 21st Century* (Theobald 1999). All of them stress the need for major changes in the direction and content of education if any real progress is to be made in the direction of creating a genuinely sustainable society. Let us return for a moment to the work of Brian Murphy, a book which he introduces by saying that "the global situation will improve: not by chance, but by the active, critical choice of millions of individuals to transform their lives, and their societies to ensure global interdependence and justice, and the free expression of human potential" (Murphy 1999: 9). Culture is critical in this process, but the problem is in Murphy's view that culture itself has become fragmented, superficial and commoditized. A central question then is how to recover culture: to restore to it integrity, quality and life-enhancing properties.

One of the key elements in this recovery is art, and its essential role in transformative action and thinking:

> A final aspect of humankind that conditions our capacity for transformative action is closely related to the technological aspect: the *artistic* character of human experience and creation. Just as technology is the extension of the human soma and rationality, so art is the extension of the human psyche, and the combined power of intellect and emotion. Art is the expression of the emotional integration of perception, of aesthetic and moral values, of enduring beauty and knowledge. Art is the expression of human vision. Art personalizes life and reality, infusing existence with passion and significance. Art is the *avant-garde* of the human psyche, continually breaking ground on the frontiers of the possible, creating new modes of perception and human expression, reinterpreting the past, redefining the present, recreating the future before its time. The artistic character of human-kind is the most mysterious of capacities: subjective, emotional, intuitive, unruly and brash, yet refined and penetrating; radically individual, yet profoundly universal. If our technology and our use of it tells us *what* we are, art tells us *who* we are, and could be.
>
> *(Murphy 1999: 48)*

The practical consequence of this is that education should respect this artistic character of human nature and experience, and so once again imagination becomes the energizing force that should be cultivated and encouraged:

> Imagination and vision are the cutting edge of knowledge. Knowledge is derived from the process of forming reality in the mind, the questioning this 'reality' by re-forming it in the world. Knowledge is merely the present answers to the questions of the imagination.
>
> *(Murphy 1999: 90–1)*

This viewpoint in Murphy's view (and mine) has profound consequences for development education. These can be summarized as follows: that both education *for* development and education *about* development needs to move away from the conception of development as primarily an economic phenomenon, to understanding it as a socio-cultural one "to be measured in terms of quality of life, self-reliance, cultural viability and vitality, human freedom, civil and social justice and equality of opportunity for health, growth and creativity" (Murphy 1999: 126–7); that development is a global phenomenon, and so education itself and its issues need to be re-directed in a planetary direction and that if this is effectively done, development education comes to be the means through which the vital issues of the day are addressed – it is an education that "promotes a transformation of paradigm, and the corollary transformation of social, cultural, economic and political practice necessary for authentic development of all persons and peoples on the planet" (Murphy 1999: 127). In other words, far from development being just one specialized and rather depressing field amongst many others, it becomes the defining field, the one that encompasses the other disciplines because (as philosophy was supposed to have done in the past) it integrates them into a single global vision, names the crucial issues and begins to suggest courses of action to address them. But this can only be done if the conception of development that we are working with is broad and capacious enough: it must include the cultural, the existential, the psychological and the aesthetic as well as the economic, which itself then finds its true place, not as the leader of human progress, but as its servant (Clammer 2012). Or as Murphy once again puts it very nicely:

> In this context, development education can be defined as the development of peoples with attitudes, knowledge, vision and skills which allow them to participate actively in the development of humankind and a world characterized by global quality-in-life; self-reliance *and* mutuality – that is, interdependence; cultural viability and vitality; civil and social justice and equality; and individual freedom, health, growth and creativity.
>
> *(Murphy 1999: 127)*

The notion of development then becomes the big frame which sets the intellectual and educational agenda globally and locally, and within that frame the promotion of creativity and imagination – the arts – becomes an essential element, and perhaps one in the long run more significant than the technical knowledge dished out in business schools and institutes of (conventional) development studies.

Such a vision places a large onus of responsibility not only on educators (in general as well as development educators), but also of course on artists. The social irrelevance, narcissism and commercialization of so much modern art, especially in the visual arts, certainly suggests that not all artists are attuned to their social responsibilities or to arts activism of any kind. This is in part because of the nature of art education, which while rightly stressing skills development, overlooks the social and environmental context in which those skills will be deployed. Art schools consequently have the responsibility to rethink their mission, and to encourage awareness of the social dimensions of the work and careers of their students, as well as rightly fostering creativity and imagination which are at the heart of good artistic production that is at the heart of the artistic enterprise. No one wants to encourage bad art (there is already enough of it around), or to return to the stodgy themes and stereotyped poses of Socialist Realism (even though that has its charms), or to turn art into propaganda. Great skill and sensitivity will be needed to walk the fine line between work excellent in its own right, and work which does address the pressing issues of global crisis, but in a way which maintains a high level of artistic quality. And obviously this has been done, and the examples cited in previous chapters prove this. A practical question becomes that of promoting such a dimension in art education, especially in the developing world itself.

Arts education in the developing world

There is a strong correlation between the presence of high quality arts schools and the vibrancy of the arts environment in developing countries. This is true of the visual arts, the performing arts and film. Certain other art forms – pottery in particular – are still often learnt through a master-apprentice style of training. Many self-taught artists also exist, but the availability of arts education has a number of usually positive effects: it creates venues for learning and skill enhancement, legitimizes the production of art and art as a career, in part by certifying the graduates in ways parallel to that of other professions, makes available spaces for showing art, creates a sense of community amongst graduates and between teachers and students and often creates a parallel community of patrons, buyers and art lovers who attend shows, buy art and encourage in the wider society an appreciation of art. A major problem for artists in many developing countries is that there is not yet a developed art market or community of art lovers to acquire and appreciate their output. All too often it is recognition abroad that confers reputation and status on a local artist, recognition not forthcoming at home. A good art school performs many functions (including of course generating employment for artists as teachers, workshop supervisors and arts administrators). Think for example of the German Bauhaus, a school that in its original incarnation lasted less than twenty years, yet changed the course of European art, architecture and design, was a home to some of Europe's most distinguished contemporary artists, and through the dispersal of its faculty and students after the rise of Nazism spread its influence to North America, Mexico and as far afield as India and Japan (Hochman 1997, Clammer 2011).

In countries where art colleges were founded early, usually by the colonial authorities, high levels of art output of great quality have continued into the post-colonial period, and art has become a respected profession for many. Conspicuous examples are India, where colleges were established from the late nineteenth century, the first in Calcutta, which still exists as the Government College of Arts and Crafts, and later in Bombay, Madras (now Chennai) and Lahore (now in Pakistan). Many private art colleges were also established and when the writer, poet and later painter (and Nobel Prize laureate in literature) Rabindranath Tagore established his new experimental university at Santineketan in Bengal, one of the first departments to be founded was the Kala Bhavan, or faculty of art, which became a major centre of art training and produced some of late colonial India's most prominent painters such as Nandalal Bose, and many more since as the department still exists and is one of western India's most distinguished art schools even though the university itself has been nationalized. Other private art schools were established in Bombay, Baroda, Delhi, Calcutta and in other smaller cities (Mitter 2007). The result has been a vibrant art community, much of it with government support in the national colleges and universities, a widening network of private art galleries, and of government-supported museums such as the Museum of Modern Art with its main branch in New Delhi and with secondary branches in Bangalore and other cities, and the teaching of art in schools, together with a very extensive culture of traditional musical forms, and of both classical and modern dance. Much the same can be said of Indonesia where early art education took place through the medium of expatriate Dutch artists in Java and Bali, and where after independence the government developed these early academies into national institutions – at the Institut Teknologi Bandung as a faculty of art and design, creating an art education institute; the Institut Keguruan Ilmu Pendidikan, for teacher training; establishing an academy in the traditional cultural capital of Yogyakarta (the Akademi Seni Rupa Indonesia) to promote indigenous art forms and the Institut Kesenian Jakarta in the capital, with programmes in visual arts, performing arts and film studies, and with close connections to the nearby Taman Ismail Marzuki national cultural centre, and another institute for arts education, the Jakarta Institute of Arts Education, or Lembaga Pendidikan Kesenian Jakarta in Indonesian, in the same complex (Soemantri 1999: 60–67). Thailand has taken a parallel course, which has long had a government Fine Arts Department, responsible for the oversight of antiquities and which sometimes employed foreign sculptors and artists, which saw the foundation of a school of arts and crafts as early as 1913, which evolved into the School of Fine Arts and later, in 1943 into an art university – Silpakorn – which still flourishes and which was expanded in 1978 with the addition of a department of Thai arts to help conserve and promote traditional cultural expressions in painting, sculpture and mural creation in particular, as well as to train students in the conservation of temples and other distinctively Thai structures (Clark 1998: 161–164).

In Africa the situation has been rather different, with few national-level art schools, but rather private schools or workshops mainly initiated by expatriates, and many of the older academies and vocational schools have been badly disrupted or discontinued by civil war, the displacement of their teachers and students into refugee camps or neighbouring countries, or economic difficulties. Traditionally the route to an artistic education in much of Africa was through apprenticeships, and this system still exists. Other forms of training have been provided by the workshops established by outsiders, although some of these have had considerable influence. Examples include the workshops and museum of popular art founded by Ulli and Georgina Beier in Oshogbo, Nigeria; by Frank McEwen in what was then Rhodesia; Pierre Romain-Desfossés in Elisabethville (now Lubumbashi) in the Belgian Congo; Father Kevin Carroll of the Society of African Missions in Nigeria; the Polly Street Centre in Johannesburg and the Swedish Evangelical Lutheran Art and Craft Centre at Rorke's Drift in KwaZulu-Natal in South Africa. These were designed to foster indigenous talent (although sometimes against a rather mystical background of belief in an inherent artistic quality in the African character). All were designed to help artists develop their techniques, creativity and ultimately market as a way to make a livelihood. Others began with a directly 'development' goal, such as the Khwe Cultural Project in South Africa and the Kuru Development Trust in Botswana designed from the outset to provide a means of artistic livelihood for displaced and marginalized and traditionally semi-nomadic peoples on the edge of the cash economy. The result has been a highly successful project incorporating weaving, woodcarving, leatherwork, painting and printmaking, and work from the project has been exhibited in galleries in Europe, the USA, South Africa and Botswana (Kasfir 1999: 50–1, 57–61, 78–81). New models are beginning to appear, as with the Ivuka Arts Kigali centre in Rwanda, discussed in chapter two, a model for the use of the arts in healing a traumatized and divided society. The workshop model has been popular in Africa in part because it is closer to the traditional master-apprentice system than the formal art school, and partly because of the common belief of many of the founders that too much academic training would stifle the inherent and indigenous creativity of the local artists, and that formal art school education tends to lead the students to mimic Western or other currently popular forms of art, quite outside of their local traditions. This is of course not the only pattern: South Africa, the largest economy in Africa if one excludes the oil riches of Nigeria, also has a very developed arts infrastructure of galleries, dealers, artists associations, museums and publications. Cape Town in particular has a very rich artistic culture and a very visible arts community, showing of course that economic development does also correlate with the expansion of the arts world, making more possible funding, the emergence of patrons, an art market and purchasers of art and attenders of concerts, plays and shows.

All this points to a number of practical and policy ideas: the encouragement of arts-based education in developing countries as a way to encourage local talent, build livelihoods, encourage cultural tourism, export cultural artefacts as important economic products, promote cultural self-esteem and sustain indigenous cultures threatened by the homogenizing effects of globalization. We have stressed a number of times in this book that the *development of culture* should for multiple reasons be a major plank of any integrated development policy. One important way to do this is to encourage art education at all levels, and to see art schools as being ultimately as important as universities, business schools and colleges of technology. Part of the resistance to this comes from patterns of socialization: most of us made art in elementary school and perhaps beyond, but then for many it drops out of the conventional educational curriculum in favour of purely academic subjects (oddly the one major exception to this is compulsory physical education) and art, if it continues at all, is relegated to the category of hobby or pastime except for those few who continue to make a career in art or design or who cross over into the one profession that does bring together the interests of the dominant culture and the arts – notably architecture. To resist this hegemony of technocratic and managerial thinking and practice is important in both the developing and developed world. It is harder in the developing world where scarcity of resources, lack of career opportunities, and simply unawareness of the potential role of the arts in development is common, but yet where, paradoxically, the arts are part of everyday life – in the textiles worn, in forms of entertainment, in interior and exterior decoration, in daily utensils. The task is to turn this into a development resource, not only an economic one, although that is what people often think of first, but a realization that it constitutes what we might call 'deep development', by analogy with the familiar notion of deep (as opposed to shallow) ecology. Indeed some have begun to refer to such cultural resources as the 'true economy' or as 'deep economy' – that which lasts and is fundamental to long term human well-being and flourishing (e.g. McKibben 2007).

One way to encourage this is through the expansion of the idea of 'arts management'. One idea spreading through the Western academy is that the management of art institutions (galleries, museums, opera houses, orchestras, ballet companies) is somewhat different from the management of more conventional forms of business. While these institutions do also of course have to be economically viable (unless heavily subsidized by the state or private patrons), they operate on a very different basis from retailing, manufacturing or transportation businesses. Their personnel, patrons, markets, modes of advertising and many other features make them rather more like NGOs than conventional businesses. This fact has now begun to be realized and a small but increasing number of business schools and universities are now offering arts management as a specific subject. It is related to although also different from curatorial training, the latter being more concerned not with the management of the institution, but with the management and development of the collections, particularly in the case of visual art institutions such as galleries and museums. Many people entering degree programmes in arts administration and management are not surprisingly from an arts background (often art history) rather than business, since a detailed knowledge of the art form in question and its peculiarities and specific requirements is a necessary qualification. Unfortunately, however, as yet there have been few attempts to develop programmes in arts management for development, or in developing countries, where the conditions of art production and the art market may be very different from places with a long established arts infrastructure. New York and Bombay, Paris and Accra, London and Bandung or Tokyo and Bogota, have very different art histories, institutions, infrastructures, schools, publications (including art magazines and art publishers), galleries and museums. The management and promotion of the arts in these different settings requires a different approach, considerable cultural sensitivity, and a different knowledge of local networks, patrons and politics. This then is a big and exciting challenge for arts-based development: to develop programmes of arts management appropriate to local conditions, and which will both enhance creativity amongst the local artistic communities and will tie that creativity to larger social, justice and development goals.

While we are talking about infrastructure and education we should mention two other very important institutions: museums and libraries. To take the latter first: almost no indicator of development known to me (the World Bank annual reports or the UNDP annual Human Development Report) lists libraries as an important indicator. Schools, hospital beds per capita, roads and other conventional factors are always listed, but never libraries. This is an important omission and if anyone should write a history of the library as a key institution of development and social transformation, they would find a lot to say. Many of the most transformative ideas in history have been thought up, researched, documented and refined in libraries (one always thinks of Marx reading and note-taking in the library of the British Museum in London, and producing the books that for good or ill have changed both thinking and the world in myriad ways). Many of us have judged the universities we were privileged to go to by the quality of their libraries. It is often forgotten that for artists of all media, visual inspirations are not the only source of their own creativity. Reading, the history of costume or of architecture, history (think of Shakespeare), political and social ideas, other literatures, the history and scriptures of religions and many other sources constantly fuel artistic creativity, be it in painting, dance, theatre, film, fashion, cuisine, design or architecture. Libraries are often the source of these ideas and inspirations. They are of course the basis for other forms of intellectual and expressive activity as well, including business, technology and all other forms of contemporary knowledge and investigation. So libraries should not be thought of as separate from art education: they are the basis of all forms of education and the maintaining of knowledge and skills throughout life. Acquiring literacy in any field is not much good if it is not then sustained by the resources that will allow that skill to be expanded and enriched, and the library, even a small one, is a principle means through which this can be done. There are many ways through which this can be done, as with the mobile libraries that used to tour English villages stocked with books of all kinds from the central libraries in the towns, or similar attempts by NGOs to create travelling libraries in South India utilizing converted buses and likewise stocked with books in the local vernacular languages as well as in English and Hindi.

The role of the museum in relation to development is perhaps more controversial and less obvious. Most of us have been in museums that either glorify a mythical past, or distort in ideological ways, a real one. What they show or do not show shapes perceptions in important ways. In the past colonial expositions and world fairs were often the ways in which the art and dance of colonized cultures were shown to the world (and such world fairs still continue to this day as 'showcasing' different cultures, and as a result almost always essentializing and idealizing them), and as such were very biased forms of representation – presenting the colonized as seen by the colonizers (Lagae 2002). Such displays, in some cases virtually human zoos, did sometimes have their creative effect: there are many recorded instances of Western artists, choreographers and playwrights visiting such exhibitions and having their conventional artistic worlds revolutionized once having seen Balinese dancing, the Japanese *Noh* plays, Chinese opera, or other performative forms entirely outside of their cultural experience up to that moment (Bertolt Brecht being a famous example). Museums are ambiguous creatures. As Rustom Bharucha points out in a trenchant critique of what he calls the "New Asian Museum" (Bharucha 2002), museums by 'freezing' a dynamic reality can produce very strange representations of the history or culture that they are enshrining. For this reason, not only do they enter cultural politics by making decisions about what to show and how to show it and label it, they are often, quite frankly, boring. The 'living traditions' displayed are often anything but: they are often a hodgepodge of the classical art of the past, cases of stuffed animals, fossils and all sorts of eclectic junk. Ethnographic museums are often as bad, and perpetrate an image of 'primitive' cultures through badly (and often wrongly) labelled artefacts with no social or cultural context provided whatsoever.

But this does not have to be the case: through awareness of the potentially static and misleading character of museums, what might be termed 'museum activists' have in some very interesting cases turned to creating museums that are educational, participatory, consciousness raising and promote pride in local cultural identity. A very good example of this is the Museo AJA de Culturas y Artes Populares para la Ciudadania Global y Planetaria (the AHA Museum of Folk Arts and Cultures for Global and Planetary Citizenship) in El Salvador (described in Desmond and Benavides 2013). As readers may know, El Salvador experienced a vicious civil war lasting for twelve years until terminated by the 1992 peace accords. The result was a deeply scarred and traumatized society and the Twenty-Third-Century movement began as a social movement devoted to the creation of a culture of peace. One of its projects was the establishment of a people's museum, with free admittance and participatory activities linking the arts, environment and social justice. This was finally successfully done and the museum has rooms devoted to crafts, planetary citizenship with exhibits relating to sustainability, the Millennium Development Goals, water, recycling, permaculture and the local ecology, global citizenship with arts and crafts from around the world and an active educational programme devoted to social transformation through encouraging a culture of peace, in which the arts play a central role. While the Museo AJA is a local project, it is framed not in terms of globalization, but of *planetary* awareness: to cultivate a sense of global citizenship quite at variance with the tendencies of neo-liberal globalization. But in this context, others have pointed out that, notwithstanding the warnings darkly uttered by Bharucha, museums and art galleries can have a very positive role in the global context, by creating a kind of international public culture, by allowing access to the art and artefacts of other cultures and by creating a sense of the oneness of the planet. They have important educational roles and may promote a sense of civil society and democracy by giving access to forms of culture that were previously the preserve of the elite (Karp, Kreamer and Lavine 1992, Sylvester 2009). The obvious ideal here is to keep a sense of critical and appreciative balance: recognizing the conservative, reactionary and distorting uses to which museums can be put, while recognizing equally the profound educational role that they can play when well planned, and arranged in an open and participatory way, with clear progressive social intentions. Examples other than the AJA that might be cited include the architecturally spectacular Tjibaou Cultural Centre by the architect Renzo Piano built for the indigenous Kanak people of New Caledonia; the Museum of Struggle and the Gold Reef Apartheid Museum, both in South Africa; the Holocaust Museum in Washington, DC (Findley 2005) or the Jewish Museum in Jerusalem, to cite a few significant examples. These all reflect the idea that museums should be community centres, not just repositories of objects, that they have potentially a highly educative function, and can even be places of healing, both personal and collective. It might be noted too, that public art can have similar functions, and memorials, while they are often devoted to the cause of nationalism or the glorification of political or military figures, can also be potent educational and consciousness raising tools, as perhaps with the Vietnam War memorial in Washington.

Beyond the gallery

This discussion points beyond education to a much more socially transformative vision of art. To begin with it takes art out of the gallery and situates it in the life of people engaged in the everyday struggles for survival, identity and dignity in much of the Third World. It suggests ways in which while art is intimately linked with struggles for social justice, one important aspect of that justice is economic: art as creating sustainable livelihoods, maintaining and re-vitalizing craft traditions and traditional performance, linking art with ecological and development literacy, and very much linking arts to creating cultures of peace (Lederach 2005). Folk art, by its very communal nature is part of or potentially part of the solidarity economy – economy based not just on the individual pursuit of profit, but equally on social ends designed to promote communal solidarity, sustainability and just economic practices (while in this case also producing beautiful and functional artefacts). It is also important to note the connection that many artists make between art and spirituality – linking their work to larger and often ecologically informed perceptions and representations of the world, contemporary social issues and utopian rethinking of the nature of society, culture, relationships and artistic modes of interacting with the world (Wuthnow 2001). Much contemporary social theory has been concerned with deconstruction. We have now reached a civilizational point at which we now need to return to the creative and reconstructive imagination, and where we need to seek for fresh sources of *social imagination* – images of possible societies and their cultures and of the new stories that we need to write and tell to get us there. This has always been in principle if not always in practice the role of both art and education. When the two are put together and focused on the crucial issues of development and social justice, the potential creative and political synergy is enormous.

Key readings

The essential book (which itself contains extensive bibliographies to the various chapters which collectively cover the main literature on arts education for social justice) is the volume edited by Mary Stone Hanley, George W. Noblit, Gilda L. Sheppard and Tom Barone, *Culturally Relevant Arts Education for Social Justice: A Way Out of No Way*, London and New York: Routledge, 2013. Other key readings are Edmund O'Sullivan, 1999, *Transformative Learning: Educational Vision for the 21st Century*, London and New York: Zed Books, and Brian K. Murphy (1999) *Transforming Ourselves: Transforming the World: An Open Conspiracy for Social Change*, London and New York: Zed Books.

Resources

The Museo AJA website can be found at http://museo-aja.blogspot.com. The *Storytelling Project Curriculum* can be accessed at www.barnard.edu/education. A very useful survey by the International Centre for Art and Social Change is available at www.icasc. ca/research. The work of the Educational Video Center can be viewed at www. evc.org. Amongst colleges addressing these issues are Naropa University and Goddard College, the latter offering a master's degree in Transformative Language Arts (www.goddard.edu). In the UK courses are offered at Schumacher College which touch on some of these issues (www.schumachercollege.org.uk) and many of the resources listed in the previous chapter also apply here.

DISCUSSION QUESTIONS

1. Follow up and explore in detail an example of arts education for social justice discussed in this chapter. In what ways could you develop and expand on it, and apply it to a development situation with which you are familiar?
2. How might you conceive of an arts education for development curriculum if you were planning an art college (in any of the creative arts) in a developing society of your choice?
3. Is culture missing from the Millennium Goals? If so, is this a major reason why they are still far from being fulfilled in much of the world?

References

Anderson, Stephanie M. (2013) "Editing Lives: The Justice of Recognition Through Documentary Film Production". In Mary Stone Hanley, George W. Noblit, Gilda L. Sheppard and Tom Barone (eds.) *Culturally Relevant Arts Education for Social Justice: A Way Out of No Way.* London and New York: Routledge, pp. 108–118.

Bell, Lee Ann, Dipti Desai and Kayhan Irani (2013) "Storytelling for Social Justice: Creating Arts-based Counterstories to Resist Racism". In Mary Stone Hanley, George W. Noblit, Gilda L. Sheppard and Tom Barone (eds.) *Culturally Relevant Arts Education for Social Justice: A Way Out of No Way.* London and New York: Routledge, pp. 15–24.

Bharucha, Rustom (2002) "The 'New Asian Museum' in the Age of Globalization". In Rasheed Araeen, Sean Cubitt and Ziauddin Sardar (eds.) *The Third Text Reader on Art, Culture and Theory.* London and New York: Continuum, pp. 290–300.

Clammer, John (2011) "Bauhaus in Asia: Future Model or Modernist Past?" In Laura Colini and Frank Eckardt (eds.) *Bauhaus and the City: A Contested Heritage for a Challenging Future.* Würzburg: Verlag Königshausen und Neuman, pp. 113–28.

Clammer, John (2012) *Culture, Development and Social Theory: Towards an Integrated Social Development.* London and New York: Zed Books.

Clark, John (1998) *Modern Asian Art.* Honolulu: University of Hawai'i Press.

Clemons, Kawachi A. and Kristal Moore Clemons (2013) "What the Music Said: Hip Hop as a Transformative Educational Tool". In Mary Stone Hanley, George W. Noblit, Gilda L. Sheppard and Tom Barone (eds.) *Culturally Relevant Arts Education for Social Justice: A Way Out of No Way.* London and New York: Routledge, pp. 58–70.

Desmond, Cheryl T. and Marta Benavides (2013) "Kindling the Imagination: The Twenty-Third-Century Movement (Movimento Siglo XXIII) and the AHA Museum of Folk Arts and Cultures for Planetary and Global Citizenship (Museo AJA de Culturas y Artes populares para la Ciudadania Global y Planetaria)". In Mary Stone Hanley, George W. Noblit, Gilda L. Sheppard and Tom Barone (eds.) *Culturally Relevant Arts Education for Social Justice: A Way Out of No Way.* London and New York: Routledge, pp. 36–46.

Eisner, Elliot, W. (2002) *The Arts and the Creation of Mind.* New Haven and London: Yale University Press.

Findley Lisa (2005) *Building Change: Architecture, Politics and Cultural Agency.* London and New York: Routledge.

Gershon, David (2009) *Social Change 2.0: A Blueprint for Reinventing Our World.* West Hurley, NY: High Point/Chelsea Green.

Gómez-Peña, Guillermo and Roberto Sifuentes (2011) *Exercises for Rebel Artists: Radical Performance Pedagogy.* London and New York: Routledge.

Hanley, Mary Stone (2013) "Introduction: Culturally Relevant Arts Education for Social Justice". In Mary Stone Hanley, George W. Noblit, Gilda L. Sheppard and Tom Barone (eds.) *Culturally Relevant Arts Education for Social Justice: A Way Out of No Way.* London and New York: Routledge, pp. 1–14.

Hanley, Mary Stone, George W. Noblit, Gilda L. Sheppard and Tom Barone (eds.) (2013) *Culturally Relevant Arts Education for Social Justice: A Way Out of No Way.* London and New York: Routledge.

Harlap, Yael and Hector Aristzabal (2013) "Using Theatre to Promote Social Justice in Communities: Pedagogical Approaches to Community and Individual Learning". In Mary Stone Hanley, George W. Noblit, Gilda L. Sheppard and Tom Barone (eds.) *Culturally Relevant Arts Education for Social Justice: A Way Out of No Way.* London and New York: Routledge, pp. 25–35.

Hochman, Elaine (1997) *Bauhaus: Crucible of Modernism.* New York: Fromm International.

Karp, Ivan, Christine Mullen Kreamer and Steven D. Lavine (eds.) (1992) *Museums and Communities: The Politics of Public Culture.* Washington, DC and London: Smithsonian Institution Press.

Kasfir, Sidney Littlefield (1999) *Contemporary African Art.* London and New York: Thames and Hudson.

Korten, David C. (2006) *The Great Turning: From Empire to Earth Community.* San Francisco: Berrett-Koehler Publishers and Bloomington, CT: Kumarian Press.

Lagae, Johan (2002) "Displaying *Authenticity* and *Progress*". In Rasheed Araeen, Sean Cubitt and Ziauddin Sardar (eds.) *The Third Text Reader on Art, Culture and Theory.* London and New York: Continuum, pp. 47–61.

Lederach, John Paul (2005) *The Moral Imagination: The Art and Soul of Building Peace.* New York: Oxford University Press.

McKibben, Bill (2007) *Deep Economy: The Wealth of Communities and the Durable Future.* New York: Holt Paperbacks.

Mitter, Partha (2007) *The Triumph of Modernism: Indian Arts and the Avante-garde, 1922–1947.* New Delhi: Oxford University Press.

Modirzadeh, Leyla (2013) "Documentary Theatre in Education: Empathy Building as a Tool for Social Change". In Mary Stone Hanley, George W. Noblit, Gilda L. Sheppard and Tom Barone (eds.) *Culturally Relevant Arts Education for Social Justice: A Way Out of No Way.* London and New York: Routledge, pp. 47–57.

Murphy, Brian K. (1999) *Transforming Ourselves, Transforming the World: An Open Conspiracy for Social Change.* London and New York: Zed Books.

O'Sullivan, Edmund (1999) *Transformative Learning: Educational Vision for the 21st Century.* London and New York: Zed Books and Toronto: University of Toronto Press.

Parkin, Sara (2010) *The Positive Deviant: Sustainability Leadership in a Perverse World.* London and Washington, DC: Earthscan.

Soemantri, Hilda (ed.) (1999) *Visual Art.* Indonesian Heritage Series. Singapore: Archipelago Press.

Sylvester, Christine (2009) *Art/Museum: International Relations Where We Least Expect It.* New York: Routledge.

Theobald, Robert (1999) *We DO Have Future Choices: Strategies for Fundamentally Changing the 21st Century*. Lismore, NSW: Southern Cross University Press.

Woodley, Heather Homonoff (2013) "Embrace the Dance: Embrace the Body". In Mary Stone Hanley, George W. Noblit, Gilda L. Sheppard and Tom Barone (eds.) *Culturally Relevant Arts Education for Social Justice: A Way Out of No Way*. London and New York: Routledge, pp. 216–227.

Wuthnow, Robert (2001) *Creative Spirituality: The Way of the Artist*. Berkeley and London: University of California Press.

8

ART, CULTURE AND INTEGRAL DEVELOPMENT

The very notion of 'development' has been hotly disputed. There are those who argue that it is just a polite name for a kind of neo-colonialism: some people imposing on others specific and historically dominant forms of 'progress' and planned change, with little regard as to whether in the long run those changes are either necessary or desirable (or will even work), and with little sensitivity to the diversity and autonomy of local cultures. The perilous state of our planet today suggests that there is a good deal of sense in this argument. In the name of development, our species-greed has been given full rein to pollute, destroy and over-utilize natural capital, make the beautiful ugly, engage in endless conflicts over dwindling resources, exploit each other, neglect the rights of animals and even to change the climate on which our agriculture, health and well-being ultimately depends. But at the same time we have to recognize that, whatever the short-comings of the word and concept behind it, 'development' also names the major social problems of our times: poverty, social injustice, conflict, ecological degradation, urbanization, the ambiguous role of technology, militarization and over-consumption. A large part of the problem with the idea of development is that, as actually practiced, it is very unbalanced, with, despite frequent disclaimers from many of its practitioners, mostly to do with economics and the belief that 'growth' will bring happiness, health and prosperity to everybody. This is despite the historical evidence, now so clear as to be un-ignorable, that this is just not empirically true. The whole argument of this book has been that for any notion of 'development' to be viable conceptually, practically or morally, it must be holistic. This is what is meant by 'integral development': forms of intervention in the human condition in the realization that that condition is fully embedded in nature, that seek to enhance the fullness of being. This implies not only increase in material resources and security (economics), but also in a sense of dignity, opportunities for expression, meaning generation, enjoyment and conviviality (culture), safety, security and human rights (politics), happiness (psychology) and a benevolent and reciprocal relationship with nature (ecology). Only by seeing these as an integral package can real and lasting development be said to happen.

This is of course a goal towards which societies strive and from which many regress at points in their history, some to the point that they never recover – hence the collapse of civilizations. The argument here has been for such a holism that must contain at its core a transformative notion of culture, and that the arts, in their various manifestations, are a vital component of this total package. It is not so difficult to establish that culture in a broad sense is necessary to an adequate understanding of what development should be even if this is only expressed in pragmatic terms – culture as a *means* to development (or as was much discussed in development thinking in the 1970s and 1980s, as a barrier or impediment to development, then usually described under the rubric of 'modernization'). But to establish the role of the arts might at first seem harder, seen both by 'hard-core' developmentalists and by the broader public as something of a luxury, the icing on the cake when the cake has grown to certain fairly large proportions. This entire book is designed to show that this is not the case: that not only is the concept of culture totally inadequate without understanding the role of the arts in constituting that culture, but far beyond that to the position that the arts are the primary means (along perhaps with religion) that senses of expression, performance, identity creation, ideology, meaning and creative intervention in the world are made possible. If this is true, then it has huge social effects: imagination is the faculty through which new social possibilities are engendered, changes and evolution in the arts (i.e. cultural change) creates large areas of social change (in fashions, foods, leisure, morals and more), and shifts in artistic vision translate into new ways of seeing the world that spill over into almost every area of social life: just think of architecture and its impact as styles of buildings both public and private have changed, and how these intersect with our ideas of happiness, themselves often built on our perception of or desire for 'ideal' spaces (De Botton 2006).

Yet even 'alternative' thinking about development has largely failed to take culture seriously or to incorporate any role for the arts into its conception of the future to which we are supposed to be working – for example the absence of any perspective of this kind in the otherwise excellent *The Post-Development Reader* (Rahnema and Bawtree 2003). Hopefully the previous chapters have established that the arts and holistic development are intimately connected. In this final chapter we will deepen and extend this link, and suggest some of the ways in which it might impact on policy and practice. Before we set out to do this, let us remind ourselves that while linking culture and development in a pragmatic sense is often important (helping a particular development plan or intervention to be successful through cultural sensitivity to local conditions), that does not exhaust the subject. What is equally important is the *development of culture:* the deliberate enhancing of cultural resources, capabilities, education and career opportunities that give meaning, depth, dignity and a sense of cultural rootedness, while safeguarding cultural diversity, and accepting that artistic creativity can spill over into many other areas of social, cultural, political and economic life. In the face of our current planetary crisis, it is also important that encouragement be given to artists of all media to link their work to human and environmental needs and to the enhancement of life in all its forms, for it is from such endeavours that a post-crisis, post-oil and maybe post-capitalist culture will emerge. After all, who is doing the creative thinking if not the artists, writers, theatre producers and film-makers? Placing culture back at the centre of development, and the arts at the core of our conception of culture, has many consequences in the practice, policy and theory of development, and creates new visions of how future society might be. For this one does not need science fiction, or even revolutionary theory, but a grasp of the transformative actuality and potential of the arts as social agents and inspirers of the imagination, and imagination by its very nature, knows no bounds. What starts out as an idea in the arts may well prove to be the seed of major future transformations.

Promoting cultural diversity

Biologists and ecologists have long been aware that biodiversity is a key, if not *the* key to the health of the total life world (which includes us). Biodiversity does not just guarantee variety in nature – of plant, animal, bird and fish species – which is attractive in itself (imagine a world with only one colour flower or only one kind of animal), at least to humans, but also creates strength in the whole and total ecosystem. One of the principle dangers of species loss is that we do not know in anything like enough detail the role that any particular species plays in that totality. Our usual and selfish short-term interest is whether it is useful to *us* – as a food source or medicine for example – without necessarily considering what role it might have in maintaining the integrity of the total ecosystem. Humble creatures turn out to have very important roles: the honey bee for example, which not only miraculously produces that wonderful and nutritious sweetener, but even more significantly, pollinates. The decline in the bee population, occurring all over the developed world, probably because of overuse of chemical pesticides, has potentially huge consequences for human agriculture and horticulture. Would it not be a tragicomedy if our immense and technologically sophisticated civilization collapses because we have not nurtured the bee? Complexity then is a quality of strong systems in which the many elements contribute, often in indirect and unseen ways, to the beauty and resilience of the whole. Nature in fact is the ultimate example of a holistic system, and we forget to our peril that we are part of that system. But what of culture? A similar case can be made for the role of cultural diversity in sustaining the totality of human life on the planet. This can be understood in a number of ways. One is that different cultures have worked out over time both different systems of social organization and different relationships to the environment, in terms of what is eaten or not, how to dress, shelter, artefacts and so on. This is why anthropology is important: as the comparative study of human cultures it reveals through ethnography the actual immense variety of human adaptations and creative responses to our common situation. From these cultures we can learn an immense amount about how to live lightly and successfully for millennia on our planet (for example Haverkort, van 't Hooft and Hiemstra 2003). Another is that these cultures are as worthy of preservation as any others if they provide satisfactory and sustainable social and ecological lifestyles for their members. But the third is the parallel with biodiversity: the probability that these varieties of culture rather than fragmenting or diminishing the whole, contribute to its overall strength.

Again, a number of arguments can be made for that position, including that different cultures represent different ways of being-in-the-world developed often over long periods of time and are often highly adaptive (indeed, if they last, they must be). They are also, it should not be forgotten, expressions of human social creativity (their social arrangements including kinship, economic, religious and political systems) and artistic creativity (their music, dance, literature written or oral, dramas, myths, visual arts, textiles, pottery, architecture and body decoration). The history of the arts shows clearly how much cultures borrow from one another in advancing their own modes of artistic expression: Picasso from African art, Indian artists from the West, Western and Indian artists from Japan, the Japanese from China and Korea, and so on in endless permutations, now speeded up by the rapid circulation of mass media and popular cultures. It may well be that the strength and even survival of civilization depends on the ideas and cultural forms being produced in one of the 'minor' cultures: this may be the seed bed of future civilization if we continue so systematically destroying the one we have (Kötke 1993, Hartmann 2004). It is not surprising that the United Nations Educational, Scientific and Cultural Organization (UNESCO), as a body in principle representing almost all nations on the globe, has turned its attention to this issue in an attempt to encourage cultural diversity as a basis for a "globalization with a human face" (UNESCO 2004). This it has done through the 2005 UNESCO Convention on Cultural Diversity, a document designed to remind its member states that cultural diversity is essential to a healthy and peaceful world society, and that, as with biology, monocultures are almost always boring and sterile. While UNESCO and similar UN bodies like to use high-sounding notions such as "Dialogues of Civilization", the definition of culture that the Convention uses is formal and abstract. What is important to note, which the drafters seem to have missed, is that culture is dynamic, is a site of struggle, and needs to be located in relation to the economic and social changes that influence it and which it reciprocally influences.

Nevertheless, the UNESCO Convention does draw international attention to the role of culture in development and the necessity to protect cultural diversity. If its implications are unpacked it actually goes beyond this and a critical but sympathetic reader might find that it stirs up a number of positive ideas. One of these is the link between culture and a number of other key areas, including development, social justice and political economy. The first two have of course been central to this book; the third needs stressing because cultural processes are deeply entwined with economic developments which impact funding, tastes and consumer trends, and create (or do not create) physical spaces for cultural performances or displays (concert halls, galleries, museums) and are closely related to educational opportunities and subsequent career paths. But beyond these are yet other levels. The very idea of diversity obviously implies differences, and differences that should not only be 'tolerated' but actively appreciated and cultivated. In the context of the arts, this should have several concrete outcomes, including the major expansion of the currently very weak field of comparative aesthetics, hardly mentioned in the philosophy departments where aesthetics is usually and perhaps wrongly taught and studied, and the great expansion of non-Western art history. A glance at most of the standard 'Histories of Art' makes it quite clear that the main paradigm is Western art, and other forms are somehow peripheral to that hegemonic story. Non-Western art, where it is taught at all, is relegated to area studies departments. When I was a student the history of art was Western and taught in the Art History department; Chinese, Japanese and Indian art were taught in the Faculty of Oriental Studies and usually only to students who were studying the appropriate languages and everybody else's art was either ignored or, if considered at all, studied in the Anthropology department and in the ethnographic museum. In fact, as we have seen, the non-Western 'developing' world has an enormous and rich tradition in all the arts, and these are as much a part of world heritage as the arts of the West. Valuable for appreciation in their own right, they are also intimately connected with social development at the many levels which have been the subjects of the preceding chapters.

Art, development and social theory

While throughout this book we have been concerned mostly with the practice of development and the role of the arts in that practice, it is also the case that our discussion has many major implications for development theory, and such theory is important because it frames and directs discussion about development, and as such in the end has profound effects on actual practices. In one previous book (Clammer 2012) I have argued at length for the inclusion of culture in development, attempted to demonstrate how this might be done by broadening development discourse to include such previously ignored issues as the emotions, aesthetics, social movements, solidarity economics and cultural conceptions of climate and shown how these issues can be related to interesting debates in the rapidly expanding field of cultural studies. In another (Clammer 2014) I have explored in detail the connections between art and society and the implications for this of our whole conception of those 'societies' and have shown how the constitution of society goes far beyond the old sociological categories of 'social structure' to include the expressive, performative, emotional, artistic and meaning-generating activities that actually make up the reality of 'culture', which is really a set of practices, not a 'concept' in an abstract sense at all. Our whole notion of 'development' is hugely refined and expanded if we can see it in this broader context of social and cultural theory.

Let us try and map what some of these implications for development of an arts-based approach might be. The first, I would suggest, is to see that there can be processes of deep social and cultural change that are not 'political' in the narrow sense of that word, while recognizing on the other hand that seemingly non-political activities, such as music, painting or dancing, can indeed have profound but subterranean political implications and effects. Contemporary social theory, or much of it, has been obsessed with power to the exclusion of other possible constituents of social order and social change. It has also assumed a very limited range of theoretical or ideological possibilities, in many cases the choice being between either Marxism or neo-liberalism and social democracy. Alternatives to these major paradigms have been largely marginalized or thought of as 'utopian' without serious further examination. An important exception to this has been the neglected Brazilian social theorist Roberto Mangabeira Unger, whose work of what he calls "constructive social theory" is embodied in a series of literally weighty volumes of the writing project *Politics*, a trilogy consisting of the themes "False Necessity", "Social Theory", and "Plasticity into Power". Here is not the place to embark on a detailed examination of Unger's thought: rather what I will briefly do is draw out some of the implications of his ideas for the relationship between art and development, a theme that he himself does not specifically touch on.

The volume of his project that will concern us here is entitled *False Necessity: Anti-Necessitarian Social Theory in the Service of Radical Democracy* (Unger 2001). The title of the book clearly signals the theme: that contradicting Margaret Thatcher's infamous claim that "there are no alternatives", it is indeed very possible with some hard thought to find alternatives to the ruling political and economic orthodoxies and their commitment to a particular and destructive form of globalization. Rich in ideas, many have a direct connection to the theme of this book, and I will try to draw out the most significant of these. The project of his book is set out in the opening words of the introduction:

> This book is an attempt to understand why contemporary societies are organized as they are, and to imagine how we can reform them to empower humanity – all of humanity. How can we make ourselves greater, individually and collectively, we who live in a restless peace, after the slaughters and the crusades, the catastrophes and the posturings, the illusions and the disillusionments, that filled the twentieth century? How can we make ourselves greater, when an unforgiving skepticism has shaken or destroyed our inherited faiths?
>
> *(Unger 2001: xvii)*

Unger's answer to this is basically twofold: to move beyond "false necessity" – the idea that while we recognize the shaping effects of social structures, they are not iron-clad laws and can be changed; and the promotion of empowering democracy. 'Society' is not a given, it is also something that we can constantly make and re-make:

> The developed conception of an alternative, promising a way to realize more fully our interests and ideals, puts the will on the side of the imagination. The illusions of false necessity arise because we surrender to the social world, and then begin to mistake present society for possible humanity, giving in to the ideas and attitudes that make the established order seem natural, necessary or authoritative.
>
> *(Unger 2001: xx)*

If we re-orient our thinking and our practices, much 'necessity' can be ceded to choice.

As a species, we don't seem to change until we are confronted with disaster, but at this present and critical juncture, while this may well be (disastrously) true once again, it need not be: perhaps for the first time in history we have both the knowledge (for example, of climate change) and the imaginative resources to confront the challenges. The question is of course, will we put these together? A new type of politics is necessary to accomplish this that goes way beyond the "normal" politics to which we are familiar, and the occasional exciting, disruptive but in the long run not necessarily creative revolutionary politics. This new politics – what Unger calls "transformative politics" works differently: "Transformative politics changes, part by part and step by step, the context of institutional arrangements and enacted belief that shapes the practical and discursive routines of social life" (Unger 2001: xxv). It has many parallels in fact with what other thinkers such as Michael Lerner have called "The Politics of Meaning" (Lerner 1996). Its key idea is that we must begin to do transformative politics in the mind and in culture before it begins to emerge as a major alternative in society as a whole. We make cultural futures within the given social present, by imagining the possible as well as the actual. This is the role of the arts, and within the context of a model such as Unger's, a profoundly important and transformative one, for as Unger argues, the core of transformative ideas must be the imagination (Unger 2001: xlix), and the imagination understood as having prophetic qualities:

> Thus, prophecy must join calculation. The votaries of the progressive alternative must speak not in tongues, but in two tongues. They must continue to appeal to people's present understanding of their identities, interests, and ideals. However, they must also invoke a changed world, in which ordinary humanity, raised in its powers and roused in its ambitions, can discover that it is not so ordinary after all. The content of the prophecy, not its many and surprising forms, is what matters most. It is a vision of the energizing of the ordinary lives of ordinary men and women; the raising up of our powers, making possible the magnanimity that depends on the strength of self-possession; the overcoming of the contrast between the sleep-walking in which we pass much of our lives and the exceptional moments of full alertness and engagement. It promises intensity without war and zeal without illusion. It cannot be the creation of politics alone; it requires a change of heart. Before lifting our powers, such a change must raise our expectations.
>
> *(Unger 2001: ciii)*

What this book has been about are the means, or one of the main means, with which to accomplish this 'prophecy'. Indeed art, politics and religion come together here in an interesting way: scholars of the Old Testament have come to a similar conclusion about the nature of prophecy. Walter Brueggemann has suggested that the role of the Biblical prophet had several dimensions, including the major task to "bring to public expression those very hopes and yearnings that have been denied so long and suppressed so deeply that we no longer know they are there", and to 'offer symbols':

> In offering symbols the prophet has two tasks. One is to mine the memory of this people and educate them to use the tools of hope. The other is to recognize how singularly words, speech, language, and phrase shape consciousness and define reality. The prophet is the one who, by use of these tools of hope, contradicts the presumed world of the kings, showing both that that presumed world does not square with the facts and that we have been taught a lie and have believed it because the people with the hardware and the printing press told us it was that way.
>
> *(Brueggemann 1988: 66–79)*

These offerings do not necessarily have to be practical in nature:

> The prophet engages in futuring fantasy. The prophet does not ask if the vision can be implemented, for questions of implementation are of no consequence until the vision can be imagined. The *imagination* must come before *implementation*. Our culture is competent to implement almost anything and to imagine almost nothing.
>
> *(Brueggemann 1988: 45)*

The poet does not necessarily change external politics, but reclaims the imagination.

If we return for a moment to Unger, we see much the same ideas expressed in the idiom of social theory, and particularly in his key idea of "anti-necessity": that which we have been taught to think of as the real, may well not be anything of the kind, but rather ideology masked, as it usually is, in the language of everyday experience. The major task for the critical social theorist and for the artist is to formulate what Unger calls a "Visionary Language":

> Success in executing all the tasks of transformative practice previously discussed will not ensure the availability of a language in which to discuss practices and programs. The forms of discourse now available to radical transformative movements are largely unsuited to the program of empowered democracy. Some represent the sloganlike versions of deep-structure social theory. Others merely appeal to established conceptions of group interest. Some have a utopian content almost devoid of institutional specificity. Others describe institutional reforms without making explicit their connection to any general program of human empowerment or emancipation. In a very real sense the movement must talk itself into power, and its talk, like its more worldly stratagems, must be both a tool of persuasion and a device of discovery.
>
> *(Unger 2001: 430)*

And we might add, not only its 'talk' (including its literature), but also its painting, its films, its public art, its theatre and its dance. Indeed, without mentioning these expressive forms, Unger goes on to argue that there must be what he calls a "cultural revolutionary counterpart" to any political/institutional programme of reform or development: that in other words any fundamental change is ultimately cultural in nature (Unger 2001: 556–570).

The basis for this must be the creation of the "new stories" of which David Korten speaks as the path along which civilization might turn from what he calls "Empire" – human relations of exploitation, hierarchy and domination – to "Earth Community" – a civilization based on networks of partnership, sharing, social justice and a creative and sensitive relationship to nature. There are political and economic dimensions to the turning towards these life-affirming values and practices, but also cultural ones which provide their basis (economics after all is the expression of a set of values):

> The Great Turning begins with a cultural and spiritual awakening. Economic and political turning can only follow a turning in cultural values from money and material excess to life and spiritual fulfilment, from relationships of domination to relationships of partnership, from a belief in our limitations to a belief in our possibilities, and from fearing our differences to rejoicing in our diversity
>
> *(Korten 2006: 22)*

If this be true, then culture has and always has had a very significant historical role. Far from being peripheral or epiphenomenal in the Marxist sense – secondary to and derived from primarily economic forces – it turns out to be one of the motors of history, and the content of that history, a view obscured by the concentration of politics as if that constituted the whole story. For this reason utopian thinking is still important, for it is one area in which *social imagination* can be given full play, and it is no accident that in many utopias, arts and crafts play a major role, not only as highly valued activities, but even as defining what makes that society a utopian one (for the theory see Jacoby 2005, and for a contemporary example of utopian writing, in this case heavily embedded in environmentalist discourse, see Callenbach 2004). One of the most important thinkers about utopias as serious political projects in the twentieth century, Ernst Bloch, saw art and culture in general (including religion and conceptions of nature) as fundamental to history, and to his famous theory of "hope" – of what might be, and how we might envision it, and move in practical ways towards it (Geoghegan 1996). Bloch was also a major analyst of both Marxism and fascism, and like others, he was convinced of the intimate connections between art and revolution, an insight borne out both by the actual experience of 'real' revolutions (the Soviet, Chinese or Cuban ones for example) and which has continued down to the present day, where resistance through art to globalization and to attempts to create new forms of community persist in many forms (Raunig 2007).

New perspectives on art and sustainability: bringing art and development together

Sustainability is usually thought of in terms of environment, but it can also apply equally to social institutions. But here a problem can arise with what is termed 'arts activism', since much of that activism can and is directed at social disruption. As the art scholar Shannon Jackson puts it on her book on this subject

> While some social art practice seeks to forge social bonds, many others define their artistic radicality by the degree to which they disrupt the social. This book questions models of social engagement that measure artistic radicality by its degree of anti-institutionality. While the activist orientation of some social practice displays the importance of an anti-institutional stance in political art, I am equally interested in art forms that help us to imagine sustainable social institutions. In the projects that I consider, time and collectivity serve as medium and material for exploring forms of interdependent support – social systems of labor, sanitation, welfare, and urban planning that coordinate humans in groups over time.
>
> *(Jackson 2011: 14)*

Although her examples are drawn primarily from US and First World situations, the thrust of her work has equal applicability to art in developing situations. It is particularly significant that Jackson focuses on examples of *performance*:

> For me, this is also where a performance perspective offers the discourse of social practice a certain kind of critical traction. Performance's historic place as a cross-disciplinary, time-based, group art form also means that it requires a degree of systematic coordination, a brand of stage management that must think deliberately but also speculatively about what it means to sustain human collaboration spatially and temporally. When a political art discourse too often celebrates social disruption at the expense of social coordination, we lose a more complex sense of how art practices contribute to inter-dependent social imagining. Whether cast in aesthetic or social terms, freedom and expression are not opposed to obligation and care, but in fact depend upon each other; this is the daily lesson of any theatrical ensemble.
>
> *(Jackson 2011: 14)*

Agency, as we have seen throughout this book does not have to be only subversive (although this too is an important function in many situations). Art can be constructive as well as destructive: the issue is one of balance between these functions, as it is between the aesthetic autonomy of art and its need to engage with social issues. The position which Jackson takes towards First World art applies equally well to art in relation to development (and indeed, many of the social problems now being encountered by the metropolitan countries – poverty, social exclusion, homelessness,

AIDS, domestic violence, urban decay, labour issues and unemployment – are not so different from those being experienced by the developing countries). Globalization has in a sense ironed out or democratized such problems: now we all experience them regardless of our spatial location.

Humanizing development

It is significant that one of the discourses that has emerged in this 'reconstructive' context has been that of "Re-enchanting the World/Re-enchanting art" (Gablik 2002, Faria and Garcia, n.d.). In an increasingly mechanized and technological world, the sense of mystery, of there being something beyond or behind the banality of so much of everyday existence, can easily weaken. It is one of the important roles of the arts to keep alive that sense of mystery, not as mystification, but as a sense of wonder, which is not just an aesthetic response, but a social one too. As John Berger puts it

> yet we do not live in the first chapter of Genesis. We live – if one follows the biblical sequence of events – after the Fall. In any case, we live in a world of suffering in which evil is rampant, a world whose events do not confirm to our Being, a world that has to be resisted. It is in this situation that the aesthetic moment offers hope. That we find a crystal or a poppy beautiful means we are less alone, that we are more deeply inserted into existence than the course of a single life would lead us to believe.
>
> *(Berger 1993: 8–9)*

Development, like any form of induced or forced social change, while it brings benefits to some, indeed in many cases to many, is also a form of violence, especially as it impacts culture. Traditional forms of expression are uprooted, communities destroyed, migration becomes a way of life for millions, old sites of memory and significance are built over and transformed beyond recognition. The homogenizing effects of mass media deepen and hasten this process. The result in many cases is something akin to the "iron cage" of which Max Weber wrote a century ago: we have created a new civilization, but now we have it we don't like it: it is in so many respects ugly, alienating, inhuman and socially cold: the mass society has little space for compassion, reflection or aesthetic values beyond those expressed in advertising. The result of development has proved to be in so many cases a technologically sophisticated society with high levels of unhappiness and stress, and which through its practices of consumption, pollution and resource extraction, is undermining the very physical basis on which it ultimately depends. If the rest of the world takes the path that the so-called developed world has taken, this clearly spells disaster for the planet as a whole: it simply is not sustainable either physically or psychically.

While much of the literature and research on development, quite rightly up to a point, concentrates on the physical aspects (economics, poverty, infrastructure), experience has shown that this is clearly not enough. Integral development requires the development of the whole person and the whole society, its cultural base as well as its economic base. Re-enchanting the world means going beyond the cultural wasteland that is often the outcome of conventional development, and making available the cultural resources that enable and stimulate a sensitive and appreciative relationship to nature. I have argued throughout this book that it is precisely the arts that make this possible: they are, collectively, the cultural resource for humanizing development, both in the sense of mitigating some of the worst negative effects of so much of that development, and in the even more important sense of suggesting alternatives. Constantly I have stressed the role of the imagination: in the search for social justice, and seeking a sense of larger meaning and a wise and respectful relationship to nature, we turn to the cultural resources that address in apparently indirect, yet highly effective ways, exactly these deep existential issues. Many have argued that art does not change society, but merely (important as that is) prepares for such change. Here I have expounded a much stronger argument: that it is the arts that in a sense make life worth living, and that accumulatively they have huge impact, in the form of cultural change, on society and processes of social change.

It was one of the most important aspects of the work of the theorists of the Frankfurt School of critical social theory, that they treated culture as a substantive part of society, not as a mere epiphenomenon, and resisted focusing simply on its content (as for example art historians tend to do) without linking that content to wider process of social and economic structure, as is seen in the work of some of its leading members such as Theodor Adorno and Walter Benjamin (Jay 1996). Art is of course socially double-edged – it can both confirm existing values and critique them: the 'culture industry' is a major part of contemporary productivity, churning out films, television programmes, magazines, pulp fiction, video games and any number of other quasi-artistic products, mainly to entertain and stupefy rather than to liberate. Both cultural critique and many forms of arts activism must necessarily contest this normalizing function of cultural products, precisely by subjecting them to constant analysis to disallow popular culture in particular from becoming simply an ideological tool to create passivity and conformity in large sectors of the population (Dant 2003, 108–130; Thompson 2012).

Integral development is that form of social change initiated with the intention of bringing positive and humanly and ecologically responsible progress (if one may still use that rather nineteenth-century term) to the largest number of people possible, while avoiding as far as is possible the psychically, culturally and sociologically negative effects of change. Change as is often pointed out, is inevitable. We now know enough about it to be more sensible about the ways in which it is conceived, planned and managed. Seen from this perspective, development is a moral rather than a technical field. The practical questions become those of how to bring together development in its more material aspects with art (creativity, expression, imagination) and ecology, to strive to find a synthesis of social justice, environmental justice and visual justice in such a way that holistic human development can take place in ways that are emotionally, spiritually, expressively and psychically satisfying and meaningful. This is no doubt a tall order: what we have argued in this book is the essential role of the arts in integral development and the inadequacy of any model of development that ignores, suppresses or marginalizes the cultural aspects of human life. Culture is the site upon which identities are forged, defended and extended. The arts are not alternatives to reality, but means of analysis of it, and of the consequent re-conceptualizing of it in such ways that it can in many cases be changed. Society after all is not a physical artefact, but the outcome of multiple interactions and images, and as such is itself an imaginative work. While Benedict Anderson has spoken of nations as "imagined communities" (Anderson 1991), it can also be said that societies and cultures are equally "imagined communities" (and it is significant that the print media form the basis for much of Anderson's argument about the formation of these strange and artificial political groupings). The imaginary looms large in the construction of any human entity – nation, society, tribe, religion, commune, regiment, club – but in much social analysis the actual nature and content of this imagination is not explored, but somehow just assumed. But if indeed we do take the trouble to explore it, we see that the expressions and performative forms examined in this book form the very substance of that imagination.

The imaginary is not simply fantasy, although fantasy plays a very important part in our emotional and psychic lives as attested by many cultural forms from fairy tales and myths or utopias and science fiction, it is also the means by which we try out ideas before imposing them on the world, in which we explore alternatives, express our deepest longings for the kind of societies and relationships in which we think we would like to live, and through which we constantly surprise ourselves with fresh ideas, symbols and images that seem to arise from some unknown depth (as indeed they do). The arts are the channelling of these processes in such a way that they become public, and as such potential tools for the transformation of society in ways that we consider desirable. As the Mexican poet, diplomat and Nobel Prize–winner Octavio Paz has succinctly put it "Imagination: a faculty of our nature to change itself" (Paz 1990: 78), or as the French sociologist of art Jean Duvignaud phrases it

> The imagination, therefore, is much more than the imaginary. It embraces the entire existence of man. For we do not only respond with feeling and admiration, but participate, through the symbols offered by a work of the imagination, in a potential society that lies beyond our grasp.
>
> *(Duvignaud 1972: 209)*

With this I agree, except to say that such a society may not lie far beyond our grasp: its imaginative conception is the first step to its realization. The imagination then is deeply political. The ethics of development thus needs to be integrated with the aesthetics of development, and both seen as an integral part of a properly cultural approach to development in general. The insight of the old 'basic needs' theory that beauty is essential to a full human life was a very valid insight, one lost sight of in much subsequent development thinking. The time has now come to reaffirm it.

The bottom line is really the definition of the 'good life'. If our civilization is the 'problem' in relation not only to its ecological destructiveness, but also to its constant generation of exclusion, conflict, violence, unfairness in access to many opportunities, unhappiness and stress, then it is clearly to the nature of that civilization that we need to give primary attention. The root of a civilization is its culture: this is where its values, sense of identity and cosmology are found, and its basic sense of ontology – of its way of being in the world in relation to both nature and other people within and without its boundaries. If development is seen as the constant growth and export of the model with which we are currently familiar, it has become totally apparent to all but the absolutely socially blind, that it is the route to environmental destruction and to increasing human misery rather than higher levels of human fulfilment. If this is the case then we must look urgently for alternatives. In a nutshell the argument of this book is threefold: that culture is essential to any viable or sustainable notion of development, a notion that must take us way beyond simply economic and political conceptions of development; that the arts are the inevitable core of culture and have huge relevance to development not only as a means but also as an end; and that as a consequence fresh methodologies of the kinds sketched here are necessary to rethink what we mean by development, and to conceive of ways to reach the goals for our planetary society, human and non-human, that we really desire. It is through art, itself transformed into a social as well as purely aesthetic enterprise, that such goals might be approached in ways that truly humanize development and provide the meaning-filled, convivial and beautiful world in which most of us of goodwill would like to live and see our children inherit.

These factors apply at many levels – the individual, the local community and international society and in the formulation of development policy as it pertains to all of these. Govert Buijs (2004: 102) has coined the term "the disenchanted methodologies of development cooperation", thinking specifically of the ways in which long before contemporary globalization and development were even conceived of, the leading German sociologist Max Weber (1966) advanced the idea that having created a highly rationalized, managerial and bureaucratic society in the pursuit of efficiency and 'progress' we have trapped ourselves in an 'iron cage' of our own making: the world has become in fact disenchanted. In Weber's view one of the roles of religion is to help us reassert that lost enchantment. But in a secularized society, religion may play that role for only a minority, but art, not being linked to any particular ideology or ethnic identity, has the potential to be a major element in overcoming the disenchanted and often shallow and existentially unsatisfying analyses of development policies, the blind spots often accounting for the "misfit that occurs so often between developmental intentions and development results" (Buijs 2004: 102). This book is an extended analysis of the missing element of culture, and within culture, the arts, and how these address the 'misfits' that lead to so many development failures and wrongly conceived development policies.

A generation ago the German-American political philosopher Hannah Arendt raised the question of whether what she called "storytelling" (the arts) can contribute to the creation of positive and humane social change, and she answered in the affirmative:

> Compared with the reality which comes from being seen and heard, even the greatest forces of intimate life – the passions of the heart, the thoughts of the mind, the delights of the senses – lead an uncertain, shadowy kind of existence unless and until they are transformed, deprivatized and deindividualized, as it were, into a shape to fit them for public appearance. The most current of such transformations occurs in storytelling . . . Each time we talk about things that can be experienced only in privacy or intimacy, we bring them out into a sphere where they will assume a kind of reality which, their intensity notwithstanding, they never could have had before.
>
> *(Arendt 1958: 179–80)*

The arts have the power to take us beyond the abstract by their creation of images and juxtapositions that provide new insights into reality and relationships. It is for this reason that 'cultural work' can be as significant as any other form of intervention (through politics, activism in social movements and so forth). Speaking of struggles for social justice, the Indian social philosopher Lata Mani sums this up as follows:

> The intent is to enable individuals and groups to freely exercise and enjoy all the rights and privileges accorded to them as equal constituents of society. This objective requires not merely the transformation of institutions, but also of the consciousness of each person in society and of the culture as a whole. Cultural work is thus integral to social activism.
>
> *(Mani 2009: 144)*

This is different from the rational and managerial order (just think of such horrible terms as 'environmental management'!) that has actually brought us to our current impasse. "The post-development era is in dire need of a commitment from all good men and women to the creation of an aesthetic world order in which new forms of friendship and solidarity will be able to interact" (Rahnema 2003: 400). Cultural work, of which the arts form the core, is thus essential to humane development and social transformation. This book demonstrates in a modest way some of the ways in which this might be done, and of the many ways in which the arts themselves, often also in a transformed and responsible form can contribute to this task. Cultural workers of the world unite!

Key readings

The reader is invited to select a number of key texts from the references below. Strongly recommended are Majid Rahnema, with Victoria Bawtree (eds.) (2003) *The Post-Development Reader*, London and New Jersey: Zed Books, for a range of essays on aspects of 'post-development', a concept very close to that of integral development. For deep theoretical reading go to Roberto Unger's (2001) dense but rewarding text *False Necessity: Anti-Necessitarian Social Theory in the Service of Radical Democracy*, London and New York: Verso. For a more accessible guide to similar issues see Michael Lerner's (1996) *The Politics of Meaning: Restoring Hope and Possibility in an Age of Cynicism*, Reading, MA Addison-Wesley. Specifically on art, good sources are Shannon Jackson's (2011) *Social Works: Performing Art, Supporting Publics*, London and New York: Routledge; and the collection of essays in Nato Thompson's (2012) *Living as Form: Socially Engaged Art from 1991–2011*. Cambridge, MA: MIT Press. For an integral approach to development, see John Clammer's (2012) *Culture, Development and Social Theory: Towards an Integrated Social Development*, London and New York: Zed Books.

DISCUSSION QUESTIONS

1. This chapter proffers the idea of 'integral development'. What do you understand by this and how do the arts fit into it?
2. How might the arts as creative enterprises translate into promoting the 'social imagination' – alternative ways of conceiving of society?
3. Can the artist be seen as a kind of secular prophet? Explore why many utopian societies include the practice of the arts as a core activity of all their members.

References

Anderson, Benedict (1991) *Imagined Communities: Reflections on the Origin and Spread of Nationalism*. London and New York: Verso.

Arendt, Hannah (1958) *The Human Condition*. Chicago: Chicago University Press.

Berger, John (1993) *The Sense of Sight*. New York: Vintage International.

Brueggemann, Walter (1988) *The Prophetic Imagination*. Philadelphia: Fortress Press.

Buijs, Govert J. (2004) "Religion and Development". In Oscar Salemink, Anton Van Harskamp and Ananta Kumar Giri (eds.) *The Development of Religion and the Religion of Development*. Delft: Eburon, pp. 101–108.

Callenbach, Ernest (2004) *Ecotopia*. Berkeley: Banyan Tree Books.

Clammer, John (2012) *Culture, Development and Social Theory: Towards an Integrated Social Development*. London and New York: Zed Books.

Clammer, John (2014) *Vision and Society: Towards a Sociology and Anthropology from Art*. London and New York: Routledge.

Dant, Tim (2003) *Critical Social Theory: Culture, Society and Critique*. London and Thousand Oaks, CA: Sage.

De Botton, Alain (2006) *The Architecture of Happiness*. London: Hamish Hamilton.

Duvignaud, Jean (1972) *The Sociology of Art*. Trans. Timothy Wilson. London: Paladin.

Faria, Hamilton and Pedro Garcia (n.d.) *Re-enchanting the World*. Bangalore: Pipal Tree.

Gablik, Suzi (2002) *The Reenchantment of Art*. London and New York: Thames and Hudson.

Geoghegan, Vincent (1996) *Ernst Bloch.* London and New York: Routledge.

Hartmann, Thom (2004) *The Last Hours of Ancient Sunlight: The Fate of the World and What We Can Do Before It's Too Late.* New York: Three Rivers Press.

Haverkort, Bertus, Katrien van 't Hooft and Wim Hiemstra (eds.) (2003) *Ancient Roots, New Shoots: Endogenous Development in Practice.* Leusden, The Netherlands: ETC/Compas and London: Zed Books.

Jackson, Shannon (2011) *Social Works: Performing Art, Supporting Publics.* London and New York: Routledge.

Jacoby, Russell (2005) *Picture Imperfect: Utopian Thought for an Anti-Utopian Age.* New York: Columbia University Press.

Jay, Martin (1996) *The Dialectical Imagination: A History of the Frankfurt School and the Institute of Social Research, 1923–1950.* Berkeley: University of California Press.

Korten, David C. (2006) *The Great Turning: From Empire to Earth Community.* San Francisco: Berrett-Koehler Publishers and New York: Kumarian Press.

Kötke, William H. (1993) *The Final Empire: The Collapse of Civilization and the Seed of the Future.* Portland, OR: Arrow Point Press.

Lerner, Michael (1996) *The Politics of Meaning: Restoring Hope and Possibility in an Age of Cynicism.* Reading, MA: Addison-Wesley Publishing Company.

Mani, Lata (2009) *Sacred Secular: Contemplative Cultural Critique.* New Delhi: Routledge.

Paz, Octavio (1990) *Alternating Current.* Trans. Helen Lane. New York: Arcade Publishing.

Rahnema, Majid (2003) "Towards Post-Development: Searching for Signposts, a New Language and New Paradigms". In Rahnema and Bawtree 2003, pp. 377–403.

Rahnema, Majid with Victoria Bawtree (eds.) (2003) *The Post-Development Reader.* London and New Jersey: Zed Books.

Raunig, Gerald (2007) *Art and Revolution: Transversal Activism in the Long Twentieth Century.* Trans. Aileen Derieg. Los Angeles: Semiotext(e).

Thompson, Nato (ed.) (2012) *Living as Form: Socially Engaged Art from 1991–2011.* Cambridge, MA: MIT Press.

UNESCO (2004) *Globalization With a Human Face: Benefitting All.* Paris: UNESCO and Tokyo: United Nations University.

Unger, Roberto Mangabeira (2001) *False Necessity: Anti-Necessitarian Social Theory in the Service of Radical Democracy.* London and New York: Verso.

Weber, Max (1966) *The Theory of Social and Economic Organization.* Trans. A.M. Henderson and Talcott Parsons. New York: The Free Press.

INDEX